Cosworth and Ford
THE ROAD CARS

The Insiders' View

Cosworth and Ford
THE ROAD CARS

The Insiders' View

Graham Robson

THE CROWOOD PRESS

First published in 2006 by
The Crowood Press Ltd
Ramsbury, Marlborough
Wiltshire SN8 2HR

www.crowood.com

British Library Cataloguing-in-Publication Data
A catalogue record for this book is available from the British Library.

ISBN 1 86126 838 6
EAN 978 1 86126 838 9

Designed an typeset by Focus Publishing, 11a St Botolph's Road, Sevenoaks, Kent TN13 3AJ

Printed and bound in Great Britain by CPI Bath

Contents

Acknowledgements

As I have been in regular touch with many helpful people at Ford and Cosworth for at least forty years, this could be a very long list. Having owned my first Cosworth-influenced Ford in 1965, I have always consulted experts and knowledgeable managers for their opinions many times since then. Without their help, originally, later and (in some cases) over a very long period indeed, this book could never have been completed.

Over such a long period I have been regularly helped by such luminaries as Keith Duckworth and Mike Costin (the founders of Cosworth), by Walter Hayes of Ford, and by Peter Ashcroft, Colin Dobinson, Mike Moreton, Henry Taylor and Stuart Turner of Ford Motorsport. They, in any case, are truly the star names behind the Cosworth-Ford link.

Others who regularly put me straight on historical and technical matters included Chris Costin, John Dickens, Bernard Ferguson, Paul Fricker, Mike Hall, Dave Lee and Mike Richards of Cosworth. Many people at Ford, including Terry Bradley, John Bull, Bill Camplisson, Philip Dunabin, John Griffiths, Bob Howe, Rod Mansfield, Bill Meade, Gordon Prout, John Taylor, John Wheeler and Martin Whitaker have provided facts, figures and invaluable insight too.

Ruedi Eggenberger, Dick Johnson and Andy Rouse told me more than I ever expected to learn about their motor racing activities, while Malcolm Wilson provided invaluable information about the Escort World Rally Car programme. Restorer and peerless Lotus guru Miles Wilkins topped up my knowledge of Lotus-Cortina engines, and Brian Hart has often told me much about his work with Ford, and Cosworth, which contributed so much to this story.

Two people at Ford, in particular, helped with the fact-finding and illustration of this book. I owe a lot to Tom Malcolm, the keeper of Ford's Heritage collection, and especially to Dave Hill, whose Photographic Archive is an inspiration to all historians like myself.

My grateful thanks to them all.

Graham Robson, 2005

Introduction

Cosworth and Ford! That's a link that has been around for a long time. In fact, millions of motoring enthusiasts can't remember a time when there was no Cosworth company, and no Cosworth-engined Fords. Was it a marriage made in heaven? Maybe not, but there have been so many successful joint projects that it now seems difficult to consider one company without the other being involved.

I suppose it was inevitable that I would eventually begin to write this book. Quite by chance, it seems, I have been close to this often turbulent marriage for more than forty years, and absorbed all the ups and downs. Along the way I have driven every Cosworth-engined Ford, owned several of them, and lusted after every single example.

Yet when I drove my first Cosworth-influenced Ford – the original Cortina GT – in 1963, I didn't even know of the connection. Even when I then drove one of the first Lotus-Cortinas, which had the twin-cam engine Cosworth had rescued from oblivion, that name was never mentioned.

After that my experience became ever more personal. In the 1980s my son's godfather ran an RS500 Cosworth for a time (he it was who confirmed that one could not see the 'POLICE' sign in the rear window because of the big spoiler!), and I managed to grab the loan of more than one three-door 'whale-tail' car.

Having driven BDA-engined cars, most memorably the mid-engined, turbocharged RS200s for four years, I then came to know the actual Cosworth-badged Fords quite intimately. To follow the RS200s, I ran two successive Sierra Cosworth 4 × 4s for a total of two years

and 40,000 miles, a Scorpio 24V for another year, and finally topped it all off during 1993 and 1994 by running not one, but two, Escort RS Cosworths for another 50,000 miles in total.

Predictably (we are talking about Cosworth-engined cars here) none of those cars ever gave a smidgen of mechanical trouble, and all of them exhilarated me with their capable combination of high performance, reliability and sheer ability. When the last of the Escort RS Cosworths left me, I was devastated.

It's because of the length of the Cosworth-Ford link that I had to limit the scope of this book, for covering a forty-year partnership would have filled more than one volume. In the end, and not without a great deal of debate, we decided that we could only do justice to the fast Fords whose cars carried the 'Cosworth' name – either on the cars themselves, or proudly emblazoned on the camshaft covers themselves. Although Cosworth had already designed the engines that powered the Escort RS1600, Escort RS1800 and RS200 models, I decided that this story should really begin with the evolution of the Sierra RS Cosworth – the first Ford to carry the 'Cosworth' name in its title.

Describing back to back, and in logical sequence, the careers of the various Sierra RS Cosworths, the Escort RS Cosworths and the Scorpio 24V, this is a fascinating story of engineering endeavour, marketing bravery and motor sport success. To be close to this story throughout the years has been a real privilege, and I hope that today's thousands of 'classic' owners will enjoy relearning all about their cars.

Sierra RS Cosworth Family Evolution

Date	Event
1982/83	Cosworth started work on a 16-valve 'Pinto' engine conversion.
Summer 1983	On a visit to Cosworth, Ford top bosses chanced to see the 16-valve conversion. Within weeks, the Sierra RS Cosworth project took shape.
Spring 1984	The first Cosworth YAB (turbocharged version of the 16-valve 'Pinto' engine) began test running.
March 1985	Official preview of the Sierra RS Cosworth came at the Geneva Motor Show.
April 1986	First few Sierra RS Cosworth production cars assembled at Genk, in Belgium: series production began in June 1986.
13–21 November	Building of 500 Sierra RS Cosworths at Genk, immediately sidelined for later 1986 conversion into RS500 Cosworths at Tickford in Bedworth.
3 December 1986	5,000th Sierra RS Cosworth three-door built at Genk.
1 January 1987	Sierra RS Cosworth homologated for use in Group A motor sport.
20 June 1977	Completion of first RS500 Cosworth production cars at Aston Martin Tickford Ltd, Bedworth, Coventry.
30 July 1987	Completion of 500th (and last) RS500 Cosworth production car at Bedworth.
January 1988	Introduction of four-door saloon 'Sapphire' Sierra RS Cosworth.
February 1990	Introduction of new four-wheel-drive Sierra Cosworth 4 × 4, a four-door saloon, which was a direct replacement for the rear-drive 'Sapphire' model.
December 1992	Official end of Sierra Cosworth 4 × 4 assembly at Genk.

Escort RS Cosworth

April 1988   Concept of new 'ACE14' – Escort RS Cosworth, at Boreham. Months later
                    the only 'mule', with Escort RS Turbo body shell, completed.

September 1990 Prototype Escort RS Cosworth shown, and won Talavera rally in Spain.
                    Road cars promised for 1992.

April 1992   Escort RS Cosworth road car assembly began at Karmann, near Osnabruck
                    Germany.

1 January 1993 Escort RS Cosworth homologated for use in Group A motor sport. First
                    major rally win (Hanki, Finland) followed in February.

May 1994   Technical changes to Escort RS Cosworth include smaller turbocharger
                    and EEC IV engine management system.

January 1996   Escort RS Cosworth assembly closed down.

1997 and 1998   Limited-production/special-build Escort World Rally Car models used in
                    World and later European rally events.

Scorpio 24V

1986   Brian Hart Ltd designed a four-valve/twin-overhead-camshaft conversion
                    of the Ford 'Cologne' V6 engine. This design was absorbed by Cosworth
                    following the takeover of BHL, and much changed for use in a production
                    car.

December 1990 Official preview of Ford Scorpio 24V model, with new Cosworth FB-type
                    V6 engine.

March 1991   Sales of Scorpio 24V began. Four-door saloon and five-door hatchback at
                    first, estate car added from late 1993.

October 1994   Revamped Scorpio range (new front and rear ends, new interior) included
                    uprated Scorpio 24V models.

Mid-1998   Assembly of all Scorpio models ended.

DEDICATION

Keith Duckworth, the founder of Cosworth and the genius behind all the engines which are central to this story, died in 2005. In memory of a great man, I dedicate this book.

1 Cosworth and Ford – the Beginning

Although the first Cosworth-badged Ford didn't actually go on sale until mid-1986, Cosworth had already been working on Ford engines for many years. Not only was Cosworth's founder, Keith Duckworth, the first engineer to develop a race-tuned Formula Junior version of the Anglia 105E engine in 1959, but within three years he was also closely linked to the Lotus-Ford twin-cam engine, and to the Cortina GT/Capri GT engines that followed in 1963.

Before 1959, and the launch of the all-new Anglia 105E, Ford didn't have any performance cars to boast about, nor did they have any outstanding engines. Although Jeff Uren had just won the British Saloon Car Championship in a Ford Zephyr, this was a privately financed car with a highly modified engine by Raymond Mays: at that time Uren and Mays,

for sure, knew more about performance tuning than the whole of the Ford Motor Company's engine design staff.

Nor, indeed, was Ford very interested in motor sport. Unlike BMC, where 'works' cars – MGs, Austin-Healeys, Austins and Morris models – were all regularly entered in rallies and races, Ford merely dabbled in selected rallies with motley fleets of lightly modified Anglias and Zephyrs driven by Ford dealers and their chums. There didn't seem to be any coherent development, marketing or sporting strategy.

The arrival of the Anglia 105E engine made all the difference. Not only was this Ford's first overhead-valve small engine, with a sturdy, three-bearing crankshaft layout, but experience soon showed that it was almost bomb-proof, no matter how much one abused it.

The very first Cosworth-Ford connection came in 1959, when Keith Duckworth began work on race-tuning the new 105E engine. Jim Clark's Lotus 18 was the first to win a race with Cosworth power – at Goodwood during Easter 1960.

In the meantime Keith Duckworth and Mike Costin got together to found Cosworth Engineering (COStin and DuckWORTH provided the roots of the company's name), which started trading on 30 September 1958, initially with Imperial College-educated Duckworth as its only active employee. Having started by building the jigs for a Vanwall F1 cockpit bubble canopy, and on preparing a Coventry-Climax-engined F2 car for Dennis Taylor, Keith then turned his attention to working on the currently popular overhead-camshaft Coventry-Climax 4-cylinder engines.

Like other engine-tuners, Keith Duckworth's first approach to Formula Junior preparation had been to investigate the Fiat 1100 power unit, but Keith changed his mind after an ex-college friend, Howard Panton, who had gone on to work with Ford, told him about the imminent arrival of the new 105E engine:

> To me, the 105E sounded like a reasonable proposition because of its design, so as soon as possible I got hold of a couple of engines, and started work on them …

At the same time Keith cultivated his relationship with Mike Costin at Lotus, and landed the order for providing tuned 105E engines for the first mid-engined Lotus 18 Formula Junior cars. Jim Clark recorded the first victory for a Cosworth-Ford-powered Lotus at Easter Goodwood in 1960 – after which Cosworth rarely needed to look back.

Even so Duckworth's relationship with Lotus's founder, Colin Chapman, continued to be turbulent:

> Colin was a stranger to the truth in many ways – he used to lie for no reason! I think he did that to make life complicated, to keep his mind agile. He always needed a lot of things to consider. If he told different things to different people, he was going to have some explaining to do, so he kept his mind sharp in digging himself out of the holes that he had himself created …

King of Formula Junior

From 1960, no question, Cosworth-prepared Fords became the dominant power units in Formula Junior. Keith Duckworth became a self-taught genius in the black arts of cylinder head air-flow development, and in camshaft design. Not only that, but the 105E engine, and the enlarged versions that were to follow, were an ideal base for Cosworth to squeeze improbable power outputs out of them. By that time Duckworth had relocated Cosworth to Friern Barnet in North London (and taken on its first employees); by the end of 1960 not only had Cosworth delivered well over 100 FJ engines to Lotus, but development continued. The first enlarged power units were also being developed.

Once Cosworth had shown that it could extract up to 90bhp from a 1-litre 105E engine, and 105bhp from the longer-stroke 109E engine of the Ford Classic, Ford's own engineers sat up and began to take notice. No sooner had that dynamic PR genius, Walter Hayes, joined Ford, charged with revitalizing

Ford's dynamic public relations chief, Walter Hayes, was the marriage broker who brought Cosworth and Ford closer in the early 1960s.

Keith Duckworth (1933–2005)

Although the Cosworth name has appeared, proudly, on several famous Ford road cars, the founder, Keith Duckworth, probably didn't design any part of their engines. Even by the 1970s, when Cosworth's BDA transformed the original Escort, Keith had become the ringmaster who controlled his brilliant team of engineers. While stalwarts like Mike Hall developed new road car engines, Keith kept on designing the best F1 engines that money could buy.

Lancashire-born Duckworth read Mechanical Engineering at Imperial College in London, rejected the idea of working with Rolls-Royce on aircraft engines, or Napier, and then joined Lotus in 1957 as a development engineer working on the sequential change 'Queerbox', which was used in the contemporary F2 and F1 cars.

After befriending Mike Costin at Lotus, and after quarrelling with Lotus founder Colin Chapman, Keith got together with Costin to set up Cosworth Engineering, which started up in business on 30 September 1958. Owing to Mike's contractural ties to Lotus, he had to be a Cosworth 'sleeping partner' until 1962,

so Keith ran the fledgling business by himself until then.

According to Keith, the new company's philosophy was no more complicated than:

> It must be possible to make an interesting living, messing about with racing cars and engines.

Before long that came to mean concentrating on the super-tuning of existing engines, and from 1963 on the design of entirely new engines.

Although Keith was not only the founder, but the controlling shareholder of Cosworth, he liked to be known only as 'Chief Engineer'. It was Keith, and Keith alone, who conceived the Ford-based FVA F2 engine of 1966, and the DFV F1 V8 of 1967, but once Cosworth turned to designing road car engines like the BDA, he entrusted Mike Hall with such work.

Keith was the guiding light behind every Cosworth development until he retired from the business in 1989, although he kept a fatherly eye on what was being done 'in his name' for many years after that.

its image, than he met up with Keith, got on famously with him, and made sure that he was not being tempted to work with any other concern. It was not until 1972 that Cosworth was to be associated with any other company – that being on the design of the twin-cam/16-valve cylinder headed conversion of the North American Chevrolet Vega power unit.

Hayes, given a free hand by Ford's dynamic chairman, Sir Patrick Hennessy, saw success in motor sport as a great way to transform Ford's image. Totally enthused by the way that Duckworth's 105E-based Formula Junior engines performed, he often told people just how unburstable these little engines actually were, and that their ability to rev up to 9,000rpm and beyond in race-tuned form meant just how bomb-proof they were in a family road car.

Because he loved the way that Colin Chapman's Lotus chassis could use all that power, and was impressed by Chapman's inventive designs, he made haste to bring the two towering (and very different) personalities –

Chapman and Duckworth – closer together. At the same time he made sure that Ford's still-small engineering team knew all about the extrovert Mr Duckworth's talents, for he felt sure that the road car engines could be improved by using some of Cosworth's less extreme tricks.

Lotus-Ford Twin-Cam Engine

Everyone surely knows that the first truly 'fast Fords' of the 1960s were powered by an 8-valve twin-cam Lotus engine, which not only figured in the Lotus-Cortina and the Escort Twin-Cam, but was also used in a series of fast and agile Lotus sports cars, including the Elan and the Europa.

Everyone, too, will have read the Lotus-fuelled legend of this engine's design – but how many people realize that it was Keith Duckworth and Cosworth who finally turned it into a viable proposition? Lotus and Colin Chapman, for sure, would rather this information did not leak out (nor did it do so for many

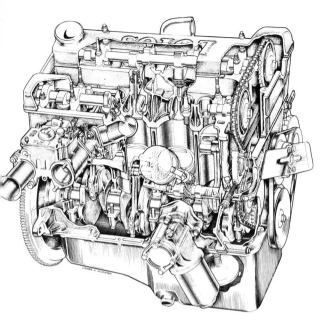

Keith Duckworth was not at all impressed by the original prototype Lotus-Ford twin-cam engine, and spent months in 1962 turning it into a viable, reliable proposition. Such engines were used in Ford Lotus-Cortinas and Escort Twin-Cams, and in Lotus Elans and Plus Twos.

years) – but without Cosworth's help that engine might have been a failure.

The development story went something like this:

In 1960 Harry Mundy, one-time chief designer of the BRM V16 Grand Prix engine, and later of the Coventry-Climax FPF power unit, was then *Autocar*'s Technical Editor. At this time he took on a freelance commission to design a new twin-cam cylinder head for the French Facel Vega Facellia sports car project. When financial difficulties meant that this project stalled without any metal being cut, Harry's good friend Colin Chapman asked him to do a similar job for Lotus. Harry was given no choice of basic engine – for Chapman had decided that, although the cylinder head itself was to be in the latest 8-valve/twin-overhead-camshaft (Coventry-Climax, really) tradition, and cast in aluminium alloy, the bottom end of the engine was to be the latest, five-main-bearing version of the 105E/109E/

116E Ford 4-cylinder unit, which had a good, solid cylinder block.

Mundy's reward for what was effectively only a scheme and a set of drawings was apparently a mere £200. Harry accepted this, instead of the alternative of a royalty of £1 per engine built that he was originally offered (If he had accepted that he would have earned more than £25,000!) All the further detail design work was carried out by Richard Ansdale, another of Chapman's associates, who at that time was a transmission designer at Thorneycroft. Ansdale's job was over once the paper design was completed, and Lotus's Steve Sanville took up the development task.

To get the show on the road, the very first engine to be built was a three-main-bearing 1340cc unit, but by May 1962 the new head had been mated to the brand new five-bearing 1498cc 116E block (as scheduled for use in Cortina and Classic 1.5-litre cars). Even so, although it was very promising this was, after all, Lotus's very first road car engine, and was

Keith Duckworth's contribution to the Capri GT/Cortina GT engine was to design the inlet manifold/carburettor layout and to provide a new camshaft profile.

The very first Ford road car to feature a Cosworth-developed engine was the Classic Capri GT of 1963.

by no means ready for production. Not to put too fine a point on it, in the opinion of Lotus engine specialist Miles Wilkins:

> …the whole project was in a bugger's muddle.

With the launch of his new Elan sports car only a few months away, with no viable engines likely to be ready, and with financial disaster staring him in the face, Colin Chapman swallowed his considerable pride – and invited Keith Duckworth to look it over. He was wise to do so. As Keith recalls:

> Colin approached us, not only to make a racing version of the engine, but to sort it out to go in a production car. It wasn't all bad [Keith, at this point, was being typically sarcastic …] but at the time the head joint wasn't sound, the head structure wasn't any good, and its ports didn't look like ports ought to look.

Thus it was that in mid-1962 the TA project – the very first of Cosworth's legendary two-letter project codes, in this case meaning 'Twin-Cam Series A' – came into existence:

> By that time we thought we knew a lot about ports – we tended to bore them as far as possible, to keep them straight, to make sure there were no valve guide bosses to get in the way …
>
> I didn't think the ports were as free-flowing, or as straight, as they should be. We did think we had a fair idea of how you should get air, at high velocity, through ports, and to work properly. So we straightened up the ports – we just arbitrarily redesigned them – then we added a bit of structure into the head too.

As Miles Wilkins wrote in his book *Lotus – the Twin-Cam Engine*:

> Therefore, the final shape of the head, including the oil breather arrangement, was produced by Keith Duckworth.

15

Cosworth's second home was at Edmonton in North London, where work was done on the original Lotus-Ford twin-cam engine, and on the Cortina GT power unit. High tech? Certainly not!

Although this sounds simple and straightforward – and was completed in less than six months – it was really only feasible due to the amazing competence and ever-increasing expertise of Keith Duckworth and Cosworth. Early 1558cc production Lotus-Ford engines produced 105bhp, the initial 1598cc Cosworth-prepared race engines produced 140bhp, and within five years the best fuel-injected versions were producing more than 180bhp.

Cosworth achieved all this, please note, with the very minimum of time and facilities (even though the company had moved yet again, this time into an ex-Lotus factory at Edmonton, it was still very crudely and sparsely equipped), although as Keith Duckworth once told me:

When we started making good profits, I would always spend the money on new machine tools, rather than on myself.

Within three or four years, in any case, Keith had decided that engines like the Lotus-Ford twin were technically obsolete. The Twin-Cam, after all, only had two valves per cylinder opposed at no less than 54 degrees, which was not the way that his deep thinking considered future engines ought to look like. His famous

4-valve racing engines, and the original Ford BDA road car 16-valver, showed why this should be.

Even so, everyone at Lotus (and, of course, at Ford) was always highly impressed by what had been achieved. When the time came for Ford to tap into more high-performance engine expertise, they knew exactly which way to turn.

Capri GT and Cortina GT

In the meantime, Duckworth had already made his first breakthrough into a Ford production-car project. Even before the new Cortina saloon was ready for launch (it was due to be sold from late 1962 in 1198cc and 1498cc guise, both engines having the latest five-main-bearing crankshaft), Walter Hayes had urged the chief engineer, Fred Hart, to produce a more powerful version of the larger engine:

There was some discussion about what we should do. I remember talking to Fred Hart, and he was going on about having a 'secret weapon'. I'm not sure about the final idea, but Fred's team already had a 105E engine with twin carburettors.

Cosworth Engineering

Founded in September 1958 by Keith Duckworth and Mike Costin, Cosworth was originally run on the basis that: 'It must be possible to make an interesting living, messing about with racing cars and engines'. Duckworth was always the design genius and Costin the development engineer.

The first Cosworth 'factory' was in the stable of the Railway Tavern in Friern Barnet, in north London, and the first Ford-based tuning project was to develop the 105E Formula Junior power unit.

Cosworth's first own-design cylinder head was on the SCA Formula 2 engine of 1966, its first twin-cam head being for the 1.6-litre FVA engine of 1967, and its first road car engine being the original BDA of 1969 (for which Mike Hall did most of the actual design work).

By this time, of course, Duckworth had also conceived the legendary V8 DFV F1 engine, a power unit that sealed Cosworth's (and his own) reputation for all time.

Cosworth's BDA was their first road car deal with Ford. This relationship becoming ever closer as the years passed, notably with the turbocharged YB (Sierra RS Cosworth/Escort RS Cosworth) and 24-valve Scorpio power units.

To follow the DFV, Cosworth also developed the turbocharged DFX engine for Indycar use, following this with a series of new F1 and Indycar engines that brought major championships for Nigel Mansell (Indycars 1993) and Michael Schumacher (F1 1994). V10 F1 engines followed for Sauber, Stewart, Minardi, Jaguar, Jordan and Red Bull.

Cosworth lost its independence in 1980, then had several different parents before being split into two businesses in 1998. The motor sport section, Cosworth Racing, was acquired by Ford in September 1998, although Ford sold it off to independent North American interests in September 2004.

Hart's engineers, in fact, had already been in touch with Keith, who says:

Ford obviously took notice of our winnings with the 105E engine. Quite early on, we were sent a Classic Capri engine in 1.3-litre form, to try to do something about it.

We produced the camshaft profile for that, and an inlet manifold – the two-ring type of manifold which had a Weber carburettor sitting on top of it.

Ford's original Cortina GT of 1963–66 (this is a late 1964 model) was a bestseller, helped along by the Cosworth-designed engine modifications.

Ford's Lotus-Cortina of 1963–66 used the Lotus-Ford twin-cam engine, which had two valves per cylinder, this being an engine finalized by Keith Duckworth of Cosworth in 1962.

This is why we were always so popular with Webers, because we introduced Ford to Weber carbs for the Classic Capri, and for the Cortina GTs. Ford used Webers on other engines after that, too.

By the way, the surge problem was still there with the GT camshaft. I was very surprised that Ford cleared our cam to run up to 6,000rpm, for I could hear it surging, quite clearly, at about 5,800rpm.

In the end, I sold the design of the GT camshaft to Ford for £750, but I had to have a great argument with one of the buyers about that.

When fully developed the Lotus-Ford twin-cam could produce up to 160bhp with rally-long reliability. Roger Clark on the way to winning the Scottish rally of 1967.

In what was to be a typically understated way, by providing a different carburettor, camshaft profile and set of manifolds, Cosworth had managed to push up the power of the 1498cc engine from 60bhp @ 4,600rpm, to 78bhp @ 5,200rpm – a 30 per cent boost, with no loss of flexibility or operating economy.

This was an engine that turned ordinary Cortinas, in particular, into fast and enjoyable road cars. In the mid-1960s the author owned two Cortina GTs, running them for two years,

both being early examples of the 76,947 Cortina GT Mk Is that were produced within three years. A further 177,217 Cortina GT Mk II types would follow, all at premium prices.

The accountants rubbed their hands with glee since this was, without question, the start of a beautiful friendship. Having captured this amazingly resourceful high-performance engine specialist, which had no ties to any other car-making concern, Ford brought Cosworth closer and ever closer into its engineering plans.

The next step was to unleash Cosworth on an altogether more ambitious project – the BDA.

Opposite *Cosworth's big move, from North London to Northampton, was completed in 1964. Keith Duckworth saw this as a major step at the time but in the 2000s this was just one corner of a much-expanded site.*

2 BDA – Ford's First Cosworth-designed 16-valve Engine

New engines are usually influenced by what has gone before. This certainly happened with the 'Sierra' YB. It might have been drawn up by Mario Illien in 1982, but its direct ancestor was the legendary Cosworth-Ford BDA family of the 1970s, and *that* engine was a direct relative of the earlier FVA F2 engine – not using the same components, of course, but the same generic layout.

Historically, therefore, the original characteristics (the DNA, if you like) of the famous YB engine were established as early as 1965, when for £100,000 Ford asked Keith Duckworth to design a pair of brand new racing engines. It was Keith, and no-one else, who conceived, schemed up and laid down the architecture of these engines: it was not until 1966, when time was pressing, that some of the detail work regarding pumps, ancillaries and installation work was farmed out to Mike Hall, who became a very important personality in the story that follows.

The deal, which had been very informally negotiated, went public in October 1965. Even then it looked like an astonishingly good bargain for Ford, and Keith later admitted that he may have underestimated his worth! We now know that the first of the engines had been designed, and had started test-bed running in the spring of 1966, before Cosworth (that is, Keith Duckworth) actually got round to signing a contract to do so.

Surely everyone knows that the amazing DFV V8 F1 engine was one of those two power units, but many have forgotten that it was the 4-cylinder FVA F2 engine that came first and effectively kick-started the entire

Keith Duckworth's reaction to old-type 2-valve heads was typically trenchant: 'Well, hemispherical heads, they should have been turfed out yonks ago: they're wrong, and those angles are all wrong …' This inspired him to evolve the narrow-angle/4-valve layouts for which Cosworth became famous.

process: by the original deal, Cosworth gained only £25,000 for designing that FVA power unit but, as Keith later pointed out, he needed the FVA to prove that his first-ever F1 engine, the DFV, would be likely to work.

Not only was the FVA (Four Valve, Series A) the very first 4-valve/twin-overhead-camshaft engine to be designed by Cosworth, but it was based on the sturdy five-main-bearing, iron cylinder block of the 1498cc Cortina GT power unit. By that time Keith had already decided to tackle the design of his first 4-valve twin-cam cylinder head. His aim was to get better combustion and increased gas flow from a 4-cylinder engine, since with his 1-litre SCA single-cam 8-valve F2 engine of 1964 he dis-

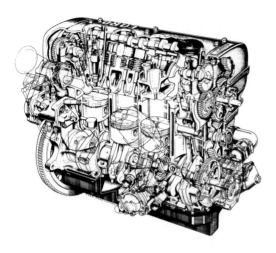

Cosworth's original 4-valve/twin-cam engine was the FVA F2 power unit of 1966, which was based on the 1.6-litre Cortina GT cylinder block. Its concept and layout, if not its detail, inspired the legendary DFV V8 F1 engine, and later the 1.6-litre BDA road car engine.

covered that 11,000rpm was the absolute limit:

> … so we obviously needed more valve area. That's what really started me thinking about 4-valve heads.

Because it was so fundamental to Cosworth's future design philosophy, Keith's reasoning bears repeating. Referring indirectly to engines like the Lotus-Ford Twin-Cam (which he had not designed, but had rescued), he once told me:

> The hemispherical head was correct many years ago, when engine strokes were very long. And the compression ratio you could get on available fuels was fairly low. Therefore, with a flat-topped piston, and two large valves fitting nicely into the chamber, and a spark plug fairly near the centre, you got rather a nice chamber … Once bores started getting bigger, and the usable or sensible compression ratio went up, then people started adding lumps to the top of pistons. The chambers became orange-peel shaped, with valve pockets in the side of the

pistons … Even the first 4-valve engines of the 1960s, which were for motorcycles (and Honda did an F2 engine to compete with our SCA), still had 80- or 90-degree included valve angles …

> When I came to design my first 4-valve head, I looked around and said: 'Well, hemispherical heads, they should have been turfed out yonks ago, they're wrong, and those angles are all wrong. My criteria were that I didn't want any surplus combustion chamber area, I wanted to use a pent-roof combustion chamber with the valve angles adjusted to make a flat-top piston reasonable, with a compression ratio of about 10.0:1.

> It means that I am responsible, by a completely original piece of thinking, for the modern narrow-angle 4-valve head.

At that time other concerns – Coventry-Climax and BRM in the vanguard – were already working towards those goals (in later years Weslake was another vocal counter-claimant), but the fact is that Keith was right. Not only did he personally think through this theory, but he then went on to design, build and triumphantly demonstrate a magnificent pair of power units to prove his point.

This, then, was the seminal moment at which the design principles, and the general layout, of many later Cosworth engines were established. But we were still many years away from the birth of the famous YB, the 'Sierra' engine, as it became known at Cosworth. In 4-cylinder terms, first of all there was the FVA of 1965, a pure racing engine, followed by the BDA road car engine of 1968, which just happened to be very tuneable for motor sport purposes – yet the YA/YB Series did not appear until 1982/83.

Laying the Foundations

When Duckworth settled down to design the original FVA, he established certain Cosworth principles that would soon be familiar to the rest of the motor industry. In many ways, what he established in those solitary hours spent hunched over a drawing board at his own

The 16-valve FVA was a F2 engine, seen here in a Brabham single-seater of 1966.

Ford component was squat and well-buttressed, yet remarkably light.

To remind the reader, this engine family had first appeared in 1959, as a very 'over-square' (large bore, short stroke) 997cc power unit with three main bearings (for the Anglia 105E), had soon been enlarged. For use in the Cortina 1500, the block was then modified, not only to have a five-main-bearing bottom end, but to be 0.66in (16.8mm) deeper so that a longer stroke could be accommodated.

It was this 1.5-litre block on which the original (non-Cosworth, of course) Lotus-Ford twin-cam engine was based. Purely for interest, the bore and stroke dimensions of the three related engines may be found in the accompanying table (see right).

Aeroplane & Motor Aluminium Castings made the FVA cylinder head castings for Cosworth, naturally from high-quality aluminium. It was Cosworth's very first four-valves-per-cylinder layout (two inlet, two exhaust) with what was to become that characteristic narrow opposed angle between the line of valves, and with a single sparking plug in the very centre of the combustion chamber.

Even so, in later years Keith Duckworth acknowledged errors made due to his lack of experience:

home (not at the Cosworth factory, please note) would be replicated in later years on the YB family.

First of all, for the FVA he used the rock-solid cast iron cylinder block of a mass-production Ford engine. Although he had no choice on this occasion (one of the regulations of engines to be used in the new 1.6-litre F2 was that the block had to be a mass-production unit), this was no handicap, as the modern

Proof, if any were needed, that the FVA was based on a Ford Cortina cylinder block – this very neat installation was in one of Alan Mann Racing's red-and-gold Lotus-Cortina Mk IIs of 1968.

Bore and Stroke Dimensions			
Engine	*Valve Layout*	*Bore × Stroke*	*Capacity (mm) (cc)*
Cortina 1500	Pushrod ohv	80.96 × 72.8	1498
Lotus-Ford	Twin-cam, two valves/cylinder	82.55 × 72.8	1558
FVA	Twin-cam, four valves/cylinder	85.7 × 69.3	1599

But I still got it wrong in one way. I had set the valve angle at 40 degrees, but that left me with a combustion chamber which was too big. We found we could run with even higher compression ratios, and ended up with a piston growing up into the head. That's one reason the DFV angle came down even further, to 32 degrees.

On this (a pure racing engine, don't forget), camshaft drive was by a series of gears mounted at the front of the engine, but this could never have been practical for road cars, as BDA designer Mike Hall later confirmed:

It was fairly obvious that we couldn't use the gear drive from the FVA engine [on the BDA], because apart from the expense it was very noisy.

Keith Duckworth emphasized that noise problem, by once telling me that:

at odd periods you get gear crash occurring, and it makes a noise enough to wake the dead.

At this point it is worth noting that although the four-valve layout, completed with its inverted bucket-type tappets, looked conventional enough, it was detailed for motor racing only – to be as light as possible, and without any thought to cheap or speedy maintenance.

The result was a 1.6-litre engine that produced 200bhp on its very early test runs, and which was later certified at 220bhp. By 1967 this, a 137.5bhp/ltr rating, was astonishing,

especially as it came with a great deal of useable mid-range torque. It is a matter of record that the FVA went on to become *the* F2 engine of this 1.6-litre formula period, for it notched up innumerable successes between 1967 and 1971.

BDA – the First Belt-driven Cosworth

At this point a tall, modest and totally unassuming engineer called Mike Hall enters the story. His arrival shortly led to work starting on Cosworth's first road car engine for Ford, the now-celebrated BDA [Belt Drive, Series A]

Cosworth's Ford V8 DFV F1 engine first appeared in 1967, and was still winning World Championship races fifteen years later. Hundreds were built, and the concept, if not the detail, of the 4-valve/twin-cam heads evolved into engines like the YB 'Sierra' engine in later years.

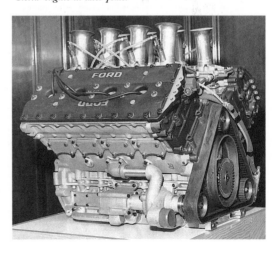

The public's first sight of the Cosworth-Ford DFV came in 1967, with the launch of the Lotus 49 F1 car. Graham Hill is at the wheel in this shot.

power unit. Without one (Hall) there might not have been the other (BDA), for at this time Keith Duckworth was totally bound up in the design, finalization and early racing career of the DFV F1 engine.

Having joined Cosworth (from BRM) in 1966, Mike Hall immediately took on much detail work on the FVA and, later, the DFV F1 V8 engines, but it wasn't long before he became, *de facto*, Cosworth's 'road car engines' engineer. Not only would Mike Hall create the BDA engine but, before he retired from Cosworth in the 1990s after a quarter-of-a-century's service, he led an ever-expanding road car engines operation that produced, among other projects, the YB Sierra engine and the FB V6 for the Scorpio. In the context of this book, Mike Hall is probably the single most significant character behind the appropriate power units.

The timing of what happened in the next few years is important:

1966: The FVA started its career. Mike Hall joined Cosworth.

1967: The FVA started winning in F2. Mike Hall began work on the BDA engine.

1968: Prototype BDAs ran for the first time.

1969: Ford showed prototype BDA-engined Capris. Keith Duckworth and Ford's Stuart Turner decided to re-engine the Escort Twin-Cam by inserting the BDA power unit.

1970: Ford announced the Escort RS1600. BDA production began. RS1600 victories began.

By the spring of 1967 Mike Hall was coming to the end of his original work on the DFV F1 V8 (it would race – and win – for the first time in June 1967). Unknown to him, he was about to take on the entire responsibility for designing the new BDA engine, and once told me:

It all started in May 1967, very much as a 'handshake job'. Harley Copp, who was [Ford's] director of engineering, Walter Hayes and Henry Taylor, who was competitions manager, were in on it. For a time, very few people knew about it. I only dealt with Henry Taylor. It was all rather informal.

I don't think there was a written contract, but Ford gave us some money … [Keith Duckworth later confirmed that the fee was £40,000, and a £1 royalty on every engine subsequently made] … and asked us to build about ten complete engines.

There was no specific performance target, though naturally it had to be better than the Lotus-Ford Twin-Cam. We aimed for about 120bhp for the road car's engine, which it achieved quite comfortably. At the time we even found that it would run on 2-star petrol.

There was never any intention, though, that Cosworth would build the engines in quantity. Ford was going to look after that – we were just the design and development contractors. We started in May 1967. I designed the whole thing, with the help of three or four detailers, and the first engine must have run in June 1968.

Basically the requirement was for a 4-valve, 2-cylinder engine, the productionized version of the FVA F2 engine, for use in a road car. It was to replace the Lotus-Ford Twin-Cam, and it had to be suitable for racing, for rallying, and for use in a road car. All the work we did here, initially, was for the engine to go into the Lotus-Cortina. In fact the first road work we carried out was in two Lotus-Cortinas – I ran one of them for around 40,000 miles.

At this juncture I ought to pick up on Mike Hall's remark that the BDA was meant to be a 'productionized version of the FVA'. In fact the two engines were almost completely different, as can be seen from the accompanying comparison. Just to rub in the differences, Mike Hall stated:

> the head casting was new, the exhaust ports curled over, the water flow was utterly different, the cam carrier design was simplified, the valve actuation was changed, the oil flow along the head was different, there were carburettors instead of fuel injection …

It was in effect a brand new engine, still Ford-based, of course, but one that used a whole variety of race-proven principles. Were there any common components? Except, perhaps, for a few nuts, bolts and washers, I think not.

For the next twenty years BD-based engines did great things for Cosworth, and for Ford. At this stage it is worth pointing out that, although thousands of BDA road car engines were eventually built – even in 2005/6, as their website confirmed, Cosworth was still able to provide almost every component, including major castings – Cosworth never built the engine in series themselves. At one point or

Comparing the FVA Engine with the BDA Engine		
Feature	*FVA Engine*	*BDA Engine*
Intended use	F2 motor racing	Road cars, racing and rallying
Capacity	1599cc	1599cc (sometimes quoted at 1601cc)
Bore and stroke	85.7 × 69.3mm	80.96 × 77.62mm
Cylinder block	Based on Cortina 118E	Based on Cortina 3036E, this 3036E having a 1.13in/28.7mm deeper casting
Lubrication	Dry sump	Conventional 'wet' oil sump
Camshaft drive	Chain of gears	Internally cogged belt
Angle between line of valves	40 degrees	40 degrees
Fuelling	Lucas fuel injection	Two twin-choke Weber carburettors

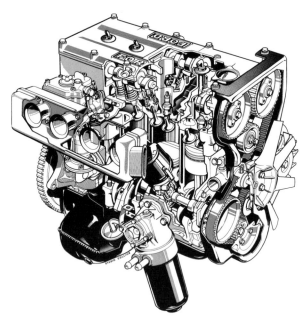

The Ford-Cosworth BDA 16-valve engine was designed in 1967–68, and was a direct ancestor of the YB 'Sierra' engine of the 1980s. This famous engine featured belt-drive to the twin overhead camshafts.

From 1972 the Ford-Cosworth BDA engine featured an aluminium cylinder block – an indulgence never granted to the 'Sierra' YB engines that followed.

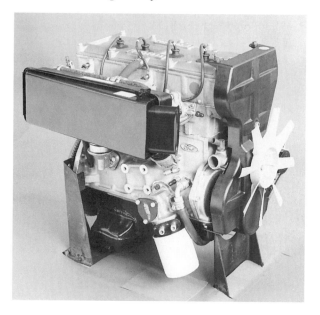

another, BDAs and their evolutions were produced by Harpers of Letchworth, by Weslake Engineering, by Brian Hart Ltd or by JQF.

In a phenomenally glamorous life, BDs were produced in sizes as small as 1.3 litres (for use by Escort 'RS1300s' in British Saloon Car Championship) or as large as 2.1 litres (the final BDT-E engine as used in RS200 'Evolution' cars), and in Ford road cars such as the Escort RS1600, the Escort RS1800 and in the RS200. For the RS1600 road car, a BDA produced 120bhp, while for a rallycross-tuned RS200E a BDT-E produced 650bhp.

Brian Hart Ltd developed a light–alloy cylinder block in 1972, which Ford later adopted for road car use. The BDA powered any number of Escorts to major international race and rally victories, and the turbocharged BDT (later, in 2.1-litre form, the BDT-E) was the engine used in all successful RS200s, both in rallying and in rallycross.

Lessons for the Future

Across the 1970s and 1980s both Ford and Cosworth learned many important lessons from the BDA project, each and every one of

Like all modern high-performance engines, the BDA was almost as wide as it was long, for the Weber carburettors were bulky and the exhaust manifolding flamboyantly curved. The turbocharged YB that followed would be even wider.

4-valve Heads

Let's be quite clear about this – Cosworth wasn't the first company to use 4-valve cylinder heads, On the other hand, it was probably the first to produce an integrated 4-valve/cylinder head/ignition/breathing layout that was suitable for road car power units.

The very first successful 4-valve/twin-cam heads were found in Peugeot GP engines in 1912, while W.O. Bentley's 'vintage' sports cars of the 1920s were the first to use 4-valve heads (with a single overhead camshaft) in a road car chassis. Two decades later, the remarkable Rolls-Royce Merlin aero engine always used 4-valve heads – and we know how vital that engine was to Britain's supremacy of the air during the Second World War.

During the 1950s and 1960s all high-output road car engines (Ferrari V12s, Mercedes-Benz 300s, and similar engines all spring to mind) had two valves per cylinder. In the early 1960s racing engine makers such as Coventry-Climax, Ferrari and Gurney-Weslake (for the Eagle) all turned to 4-valve/twin-cam heads. Cosworth's engineering genius, Keith Duckworth, then refined the installation and thinking behind the layout, by gradually evolving the narrow-opposed-angle philosophy. His first such design was the Ford-based four-cylinder FVA of 1966 (a formidable F2 engine), then came the legendary DFV F1 engine, while the BDA, first seen in 1969, was the first such Cosworth road car 4-valver.

After that the flood gates opened, and the world's motor industry rushed to copy what Duckworth had already perfected.

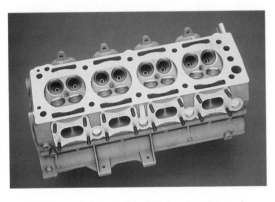

The cylinder heads layout of the BDA engine of the early 1970s laid down a marker for future Cosworth 4-valves-per-cylinder power units. For Cosworth, no other truly logical top end layout really existed.

them being filed away to help eliminate similar problems in future projects.

Cosworth, for sure, came to wish that they had been able to manufacture BDA production engines themselves, for the sheer number built was far higher than they could ever have expected. Keith Duckworth, with that well-honed Northerner's worship of a good financial profit, never hid the fact that other companies were making money from Cosworth's own design, which somehow didn't seem fair.

Cosworth also regretted that the Ford cylinder block, on which the BDA engine was based, could not be stretched reliably by as much as the customers wanted. Designed as a 1.6-litre unit,

The BDA engine family had an astonishingly successful career, which culminated in use in the mid-engined four-wheel-drive Ford RS200 of the mid-1980s. In 2.1-litre 'rallycross' form it could produce up to 650bhp!

Two important Cosworth personalities of the 1970s – Mike Hall (left, who designed the BDA engine) and Bill Brown (production boss) – with the Ford-Cosworth GA power unit, a 3.4-litre monster that developed up to 450bhp when used in Ford Capri RS3100 race cars.

it soon grew to BDB (1.7 litres) and to BDE (1.8 litres), but further increases could only follow if the cylinder block was either butchered, internally, or the casting changed considerably. It was only when Brian Hart's light-alloy casting did just that that the BDG (2.0 litres for race and rally applications) came along.

When the time came to develop the YA/YB family, Cosworth always made it clear that their new engine was a dedicated 2.0-litre power unit, and that they, not others, would be delighted to make every single power unit!

In the 1970s Ford soon realized just how resourceful the Cosworth company had become, and how it would be lunacy to allow them to drift away into the hands of any rival. As Cosworth's ownership drifted through several stages of ownership in the 1980s, they often worried about this, but did not make any concrete moves to buying the business until 1998.

Having thought about it, thought about it again, and analysed all the possibilities in their own inimitable way, Ford concluded that they could never justify setting up their own facilities to manufacture small numbers of engines. If they were ever again to encourage the limited production of very high-output engines for use in their cars, they would have to award the contract to the same company that designed them, make sure that company made the engines itself, and monitor the whole process in a much more businesslike manner.

Even though it had not been considered at the time, does all this sound as if Ford was mentally writing a specification for the concept, and production, of the YB family? Maybe, and maybe not, but I have no doubt that without the BDA, and all its ramifications, the YB might never have been produced.

3 Sierra RS Cosworth – the First Cosworth-badged Ford Car

I ought to make one thing quite clear at this stage – until the Sierra RS Cosworth was virtually 'invented' in the course of a bucolic lunch in a pub garden near Northampton in 1983, no-one at Ford had seriously thought about making such a car. I will go even further. If the Escort RS1700T rally car and C100 sports-racing car projects had not failed in 1983, and if Stuart Turner had not returned to Motorsport from a seven-year sojourn in Public Affairs, the opportunity to develop a truly hot Sierra may never have arisen.

Ford needed the Sierra to be a race car winner, but the V6-engined XR4i was not powerful enough.

When the Sierra was introduced in September 1982 there were 4-cylinder engines from 1.3 litres to 2.0 litres (60bhp to 105bhp), V6 versions (90bhp and 114bhp) for sale only in Europe, and the promise of a 150bhp/V6 XR4i to follow during 1983. No-one, it seems, had given a thought to the idea of adding super high-performance Sierras to that range.

The 'RS' brand, too, was in recess at the time, too. Escort RS and Capri RS models had sold well in the 1970s, but in the early 1980s it was the newly invented 'XR' brand that was taking most of Ford's 'prestige/performance' attention. The only RS model on the market

When the time came to develop an ultra high-performance Sierra, the unique XR4i style – this car – was considered, but rejected in favour of the conventional three-door layout.

by 1982 was the limited-production front-wheel-drive Escort RS1600i.

Motorsport? With a new supremo at the helm, Karl Ludvigsen, who was far more interested in circuit racing than his predecessors, the emphasis in those days was divided between a new-type Escort (RS1700T) for rallying and a new Cosworth DFL V8-engined C100 for sports car racing. Neither car was yet oven-ready, nor yet winning events. As for saloon car racing, where Ford Escorts and Capris had been successful for so long, Ford no longer seemed to have any interest.

All Change at Motorsport

Gradually, but insidiously, though, everything started to go wrong at Ford. In 1981 the prospects for both new projects had been good, but in 1982 neither had the opportunity to win, or even appear regularly, in major events. For 1983, not only did it look as if the C100 project was still not likely to beat the dominant Porsche 956s, but the rear-drive Escort RS1700T was not yet homologated, and would eventually have to face up to Audi's already-dominant four-wheel-drive Quattros. Ford was not accustomed to being an underdog: what on earth could be done?

Even though he was currently moving in high corporate places at Ford-USA in Detroit,

Walter Hayes picked up the murmurs of discontent, called his old Motorsport colleague Stuart Turner in the UK, and asked for his opinions on what should be done. Turner, at that time Ford's Director of Public Affairs, had no executive responsibility for motor sport policy, but could at least offer his unofficial views on future policy. After Christmas, in the few quiet days that a busy Ford executive ever gets, he did just that.

Hayes listened, read, consulted, then acted. The result was that in March 1983 Karl Ludvigsen's tenure came to an abrupt end, and Turner returned to run Motorsport in a position he had relinquished as long ago as 1975. According to his reminiscences, he accepted the renewed challenge:

> as Director, European Motorsports, but on one condition: that I would have a completely free hand to reshape motor sport strategy.

Fortunately for Stuart, and for posterity, he got that assurance, took up his new post at once, and within days had recommended cancellation of both the Escort RS1700T and C100 programmes:

> Ford issued a press release stating that the two projects had been abandoned, and quoted me as saying that 'Having spent some time looking hard at

Stuart Turner

Although Turner's bestselling autobiography was titled *Twice Lucky*, there was no luck about his career. Already famous as BMC's Competitions Manager in the 1960s, along with Walter Hayes he was one of Ford's most influential motor sport characters from 1969 to 1990.

Turner initially trained as an accountant and broke into rallying at club level, after which progress as a club magazine editor, a 'works' co-driver, and the first Rallies Editor of *Motoring News* was logical. After winning three national Championship co-drivers' awards, and sitting alongside Erik Carlsson when he won the RAC rally of 1960, he then became BMC's Competitions Manager from 1961 to 1967, when the Mini was at the height of its powers.

Headhunted by Walter Hayes for Ford Motorsport in 1969 (where he succeeded Henry Taylor), his ruthless methods and sure eye for publicity stamped his authority on everything that Ford tackled in rallying.

After becoming Director of Motorsport in 1970, he then managed the AVO plant from 1972 until it was closed down in 1975. For the next seven years he directed the fortunes of the Public Affairs department, before returning as Director of Motorsport, Ford-of-Europe, in 1983.

During his 21 years at Ford he was a prime mover in the Escort RS1600/Mexico/RS2000 programme, in the Mk 2 versions of those cars, in the Escort RS Turbo, the RS200, the Sierra RS (and RS500) Cosworth and, finally, in the Escort RS Cosworth.

Retiring from Ford at the end of 1990, he then turned to his next career as a superb and much-in-demand after-dinner and conference speaker, and was still enjoying this 'hobby' as the 2000s opened.

---

our existing plans, I have become convinced that we are not moving in the best direction if we are going to resume our former position in international motor sport. This does not means we are giving up … Make no mistake – we shall be back, although not with the cars we have under development at the moment.'

From that moment on, however, the only way was up. Having cleared the slate in Motorsport, he had to start all over again. Having established the later-legendary 'Ladder of

Opportunity', he looked around for new products and discovered to his joy that Mike Moreton, an experienced product planner from his days running the AVO operation at Aveley, had already been seconded to Boreham (originally to help urge the Escort RS1700T into production). Later known as one of the most able wheeler-dealers/fixers/negotiators/facilitators in Ford's corridors of power, Mike would be the right man to have at his side in the difficult months ahead.

Difficult months? This is what he later

Looking rather like the Sierra XR4i, the Merkur XR4Ti was sold almost entirely in the USA and used a turbocharged Ford-USA engine. As an interim motor sport machine, it served Andy Rouse and Eggenberger in 1986 until the Sierra RS Cosworth was ready.

wrote in his bestselling autobiography *Twice Lucky*:

Way back in January 1983, when I had written down my thoughts, and concerns, for Walter Hayes, I suggested that Ford-of-Europe urgently needed a new race-winning Group A saloon car. The old-type Capri 3.0-litre cars couldn't win races any more – in fact it was embarrassing to see them being plastered by the big Rovers – and I wanted to know if he would support me in inspiring the birth of a new car to stop the rot.

Given a free hand to develop my strategy, two steps were taken – one immediately after I arrived in March 1983, the other later in 1983. One was to produce an upgraded version of a new Sierra-based production car which was already coming along – the car which would be badged as the Merkur XR4Ti, and sold almost entirely in the USA – the other would be a totally new model.

But it wasn't as easy, or as clean-cut as all that – this was Ford, after all. Even by mid-1983 we were still discussing the option of radically-modified 3.0-litre V6 Sierras, turbocharged 2.3-litre Sierras, 5.0-litre V8-engined Sierras (which eventually went into production in Ford-South Africa), and Sierras with different engines that hadn't even been finalised. However, we were all agreed on one thing – which was that we needed to win, and not just to show up to make up the numbers.

As I wrote in Motorsport Committee minutes in July 1983: 'The end product will be seen as a European car and must be capable of winning against all opposition from Rover, BMW and Jaguar – BMW for Germany and Rover/Jaguar for Britain. This would probably need 300bhp … The Sierra race car programme is only to be done if the car *will* win.'

Mike Moreton and Peter Ashcroft, it seems, had already done some lobbying. Mike Moreton once told me that:

The Capri was out of date, there was nothing else coming, so we needed a new car for Group A. Peter, as usual, went straight to the power/weight calculation, and it was blindingly obvious to us that we needed a turbocharged engine.

Peter and I worked out that if we had a Sierra, and we turbocharged this engine [that we knew Cosworth was developing …], we could get an enormous power output.'

Later, according to Stuart:

In the meantime, Walter and I had spent a miserable day standing on an embankment at Silverstone, seeing the Rover Vitesses charging round and humiliating the Ford Capris. Six Rovers faced up to three Capris: the fastest of the Capris was ninth in practice, and ninth in the race.

Walter, who had been away from the touring car scene for some time, was disgusted: 'Is this the best we can do?', he wanted to know. Without a stirring performance by Richard Longman's RS1600i, in his class, I might even have gone into a corner and shot myself.

Fortunately, when it came to taking action, Ed Blanch, Jim Capolongo and Walter Hayes were all on my side. [Blanch and Capolongo were respectively, chairman and president of Ford-of-Europe, the most senior executives on this side of the Atlantic. Further, they were Americans, with a mountain of corporate experience, and had the ear of their even more senior colleagues back in Dearborn.]

Purely by chance (I promise, there was no fell intent), we needed to go to Cosworth to see what was brewing on the Formula 1 engine. At my suggestion, I took Ed and Jim along to Northampton on a nice sunny day, to meet Keith Duckworth.

Ed and Jim had never before been to Cosworth, and had never before been exposed to Keith's personality (everyone ought to be, at least once in their lives – the effect is like electric shock treatment, I can tell you), so they came away impressed. While walking through one assembly shop, towards the Formula One area, we saw one Ford Pinto-based engine, on a stand, which had been given a 16-valve twin-cam conversion (As far as Keith was concerned, I'm sure it wasn't an 'accidental sighting', by the way – as Mike Moreton's early comments confirm).

In passing, we asked: 'What's that for?'

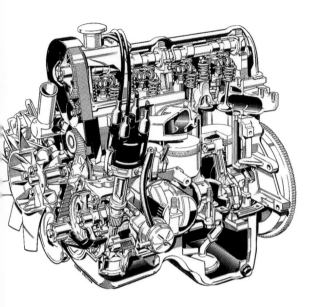

Cosworth's original idea was to develop a 16-valve 'kit' to upgrade the single overhead valve 8-valve 'Pinto' engine.

Keith's comment apparently was:

> We think we can find a market for 200–300 kits, just as private-venture performance items of our own.

Nothing more was said. After the tour was over, the group went off to the local pub for a ploughman's lunch, where everyone sat round a rustic table in the sunshine, and started talking about they had seen, and what Ford might do in the future. It was Turner, he insisted, who eventually came up with the most important comment of the day:

> If we could find a way of putting that 16-valve engine into a Sierra, and turbocharge it, Rovers wouldn't win another touring car race. But we'd have to build 5,000 of them.

New Start

At a stroke, as they say, the concept of the Sierra RS Cosworth took shape. New cars at Ford don't just happen like that, they're never conceived at one meeting, but I'm still convinced that this was the trigger for what became the Sierra RS Cosworth programme. Up to then the company had started homing on the idea of racing the Merkur XR4Ti, whose USA-based 4-cylinder engine could, at best, produce about 320bhp on the race track). The Sierra RS Cosworth project, in any form, simply did not exist.

Stuart told me:

> Looking back, that has to be one of the most enjoyable pub lunches I have ever tasted. Cosworth, maybe, had already talked unofficially to engineers at Dunton on a 'why don't we …?' basis, but I know that Jim and Ed had not been briefed before that day.

It must have struck a spark, because few people – except the manufacturing engineers, who eventually had to find ways of building the cars among other Sierras at Genk – found flaws in the concept. It had to be analysed, costed, designed and tested, and Rod Mansfield's SVE (Special Vehicle Engineering) team had to take on much of the work, but they did a great job.

SVE's first encounter with this project came in April 1983, when Rod Mansfield and marketing chief Bill Camplisson met with Turner, Peter Ashcroft and Mike Moreton. Turner effectively demanded approval for a 5,000-off 'homologation car', Camplisson agreed that the new Sierra was already in need of a boost to give it a 'halo effect', and *everyone* agreed that Cosworth should be asked to provide the engine.

Even though it took months for paper studies to be completed, and approval to come through, engineering work got going at once. Early pie-in-the-sky estimates – that 5,000 cars could be built in 1984, and a new car could go racing in 1985 – were soon abandoned, but development still went ahead at a remarkable rate.

Without Cosworth's uncanny expertise and without Ford's SVE I don't think this car could ever have been developed. Even so, SVE was already very busy ('short of "head-count"', as

---

Special Vehicle Engineering

Rod Mansfield was an early AVO member and was also responsible for setting up Ford's Special Vehicle Engineering department in 1980.

At AVO from 1970, Mansfield worked for Bob Howe, replaced Henry Taylor in 1972, and later engineered all AVO products until that project closed in 1975. Later, and after five years in relative obscurity, he was suddenly asked to set up Special Vehicle Engineering.

SVE's brief was to develop cars that were more sporty and more specialized than those normally covered by Ford's engineering team. Like AVO before it, SVE was really a team within a team, though liaison with all other departments was maintained.

SVE's first successful projects were the Capri 2.8i and the original Fiesta XR2, these being followed by the original Escort XR3i and the Sierra XR4 × 4. Although 'SVE' then worked on finalizing the still-

born RS1700T, the next to go on sale (in 1984) was the first-generation fuel-injected Escort RS Turbo.

Other cars like the Escort Cabriolet and the Sierra RS Cosworth were also important SVE projects, but serious work on the Escort RS Cosworth was a vital responsibility after 1989, and included several little-publicized 'why-don't-we ...?' dabbles with rear-drive Escorts, some driven by Cosworth (Scorpio-type) 24-valve V6 engines.

Mansfield himself then enjoyed a colourful 1990s, which included spells at Aston Martin, setting up an SVE-like operation at Ford-USA, and even spending a short and turbulent period as managing director of Lotus. Later he took an interest in an engineering consultancy before retiring to live in his charming farmhouse only a few minutes' drive from Ford's Dunton Technical Centre.

The most powerful Ford-developed version of the single overhead camshaft Pinto/T88 engine was this 140bhp derivative, as used from 1974 in Group 1 motor sport by the Escort RS2000.

Ford used to measure such things), so Motorsport at Boreham loaned three engineers – John Griffiths, Bill Meade and Terry Bradley – to help on this project.

By autumn 1983 Cosworth had been asked to go ahead with the new 2-litre engine, based on the Pinto/T88 cylinder block. Initially they were asked to produce a 180bhp road car power unit that could be race-tuned to more than 300bhp; when they subsequently found that 200-plus bhp was easy to achieve for road cars, this was also agreed. Experience later proved that race car engines could produce up to 350bhp, but the big leap to 500–550bhp would not come until the RS500-style YBD power unit (*see* Chapter 4) was developed.

Coded YAA (YB, the productionized variety, came later), the original Pinto/16-valve conversion had been designed by Mario Illien in 1982/83, originally with a very free-breathing cylinder head, a complex inlet manifold and very long, tubular, exhaust manifolding, all optimized for tuning to a 300–400bhp race car power unit, with full-throttle breathing in mind, and no thought of driveability or refinement.

By the time ex-Weslake/ex-Lotus engineer Paul Fricker joined Cosworth at the end of

Mario Illien

Although it was Mike Hall's road car engineering office at Cosworth that was tasked with working up the YA/YB series, the original 16-valve twin-cam engine kit of 1982/83 was designed entirely by Mario Illien, who really counts as the 'godfather' to the entire project.

Swiss-born Illien started work for race driver Jo Bonnier in 1971 as a technical draughtsman, working on Bonnier's old McLaren F1 car. After Bonnier was killed at Le Mans, Mario eventually moved on to the Biel University Engineering School and after graduation joined Mowag in Kreuzlingen to design diesel engines for tanks and armoured vehicles.

He first joined Cosworth in 1978, concentrating on F1 design work, and on the related turbocharged DFX Indycar V8. Having been responsible for much of the work that changed the DFV into the DFY F1 engine of 1982, as a different challenge he was then tasked with producing the YA conversion kit for the Pinto engine.

Having completed that job, he left Cosworth, together with his friend and colleague Paul Morgan, to found his own company, Ilmor Engineering. Not only did that company produce successful turbocharged V8s for Indycar racing, but by the 1990s they were producing race-winning V10s for Mercedes-Benz, for use by McLaren in F1 racing.

1983, Illien had left the company (to found Ilmor with Paul Morgan) and Ford had awarded Cosworth a contract both to complete the engine and to erect a manufacturing facility to produce at least 15,000 power units. As the newly appointed project manager, Paul was pitched into the deep end, with everyone from Keith Duckworth downwards expecting him to deliver:

> My job was to make sure that everything got done to put the engine into the car. It was going to mean a complete redesign for road car use. We needed the long exhaust manifold for a 4-into-2-into-1 layout, but we also had to install the turbo and get the exhaust pipe out to the back of the car!

Paul Fricker managed the redesign, with Mike Hall's 'road car engines' office handling the actual detail work, while Paul Squires and Pete Rogers did much of the work on the dynamometer. It had to be reoptimized to make it road-durable and road-driveable, but at no point was the competition potential to be degraded.

Twenty years on, Paul remembers the pressures. Firstly there was the original contract for 15,000 engines to be considered ('At one time Ford talked of ending the project after the first 5,000, but luckily they never did that …'), then

there was a change of mind over the fuelling system. Originally that was to be with Bosch, but following good experience with F1 engines a change was made to Weber-Marelli of Italy ('There we had three people who were working for just two clients – Ferrari and ourselves!').

Much of the work went into respecifying the turbocharger. Because the Garrett T3 was really a whole family of units, Cosworth eventually changed the inlet (compressor) volutes and then had to match the performance of the compressor to the turbine. As Paul recalls with a grin:

> The fact is that we did something like 400–500 hours on the performance test-beds at Cosworth. The first time we put one on the durability bed, it lasted for just 35 minutes before it blew up.

Compared with the Pinto/T88 engine, from which the new turbocharged YB evolved, almost everything was changed. Except for the cylinder block itself, the front cover and the jackshaft (retained to drive the oil pump and the distributor), all was new – new cylinder head and valve gear, new steel crankshaft, steel rods, pistons, sump and, of course, the internally cogged camshaft drive belt. Interestingly, the use of hydraulic valve lifters was a 'given', and no engine tuner appears to have suffered from not being able to use old-style conventional lifters. Fricker admits that:

> they did weigh more and there was always a small amount of air in the oil. We did end up changing the tappet design so that they couldn't deflate overnight! On the original engine, if you had a hot engine, then left it parked for a week, the tappets would go down!

Chassis Changes

While engine design was going ahead, Ford made great progress with the Sierra's structure. Although the original proposal was that the new car should be based around the unique three-door style of the Sierra XR4i, this did not progress far. This, on reflection, was wise, for the XR4i was not a simple three-door car, but had a three-side window layout, along with a 'biplane' rear spoiler that was definitely for 'show' rather than for 'go'.

Even so, original aerodynamic development and testing (including calibration in the MIRA wind tunnel) was carried out with an XR4i car during October and November 1983. Rod Mansfield, SVE's manager, recalls assessing more than 90 different layouts, some very extreme indeed. Gordon Prout, his aerodynamics expert, took charge of these investigations, with ex-F1 driver John Miles (whom Ford knew for his work on the contemporary Tickford Capri) also consulted from time to time.

The best results were obtained with extreme layouts involving endplates, but these were never likely to be acceptable to Ford's designers. Mansfield once told me:

> Ken Kohrs said: 'Do you *really* need this?' Uwe Bahnsen [Design chief] thought it was horrible. We kept on saying it *had* to have those sections, it was their job to make it look nice. His guys then set to, and in my view did a brilliant job. We lost a little bit of downforce in the reshaping, at the front end mainly. I think it is sculptural now, from being bloody awful to start with.

This was the lightest version of the new Sierra body shell, complete with three doors: the slatted grille was for 'fleet' cars only. This was the shell chosen as the basis of the Sierra RS Cosworth.

Cosworth's founder, Keith Duckworth, was always proud of the work his team did to create the Sierra 'YB' engine, and ran a three-door Sierra RS Cosworth for some years in the 1980s.

After all the arguments had raged for weeks, the matter was finally settled when a senior manager commented:

Well, after all, Porsche have a wing like this, so what's new? Why don't we have one?

The finalized 'aero' package not only included the vast rear aerofoil, a large front-end 'chin' spoiler, and plastic wheel arch and sill extensions, but an extra air intake in the nose (between the headlamps). Design studies of prototypes had certainly not included such an air intake (exclusive 1984 pictures from Ford Design in Germany are shown on page 38), but after Bill Meade had carried out hot-weather tests at the high-speed Nardo proving grounds down on the toe of Italy, this was added to the final specification.

Not all the Top Brass were impressed, as Walter Hayes told me:

I must say that I *never* liked the big tail. Absolutely not. Neither did Alex Trotman [who had taken over from Bob Lutz] – we both wanted unstated elegance and unstated performance. I always thought that what we really wanted was the fastest pussy-cat in the world.

But we were both persuaded, simply because all our people said it had aerodynamic importance. It worked.

Although he stood back from the detail, once he had gained approval for the project, Stuart Turner kept in close touch with progress:

Although our designers were adamant that a big rear wing was needed to trim the high-speed handling, many non-believers were horrified with its size, and where it was placed, effectively halfway up the line of the hatchback. Why, some of them said, could we not settle for the bi-plane

As Stuart Turner, Ford's new Director of European Motorsports, is reputed to have told his bosses: 'If we could put that 16-valve conversion into a Sierra, and turbocharge it, Rover's wouldn't win another touring car race…'

Boreham

Until the Second World War Ford's Boreham site was a peaceful orchard near Chelmsford. It then became a USAAF airfield in the 1940s, a motor racing circuit in 1950, a proving ground for Ford trucks from the mid-1950s, and the home of Ford Motorsport from 1963.

Boreham opened as a military bomber airfield in March 1944. It was speedily decommissioned after the war and then from 1950 it was used as a motor racing circuit by the West Essex Car Club.

Ford took over the site in the mid-1950s for use as a heavy truck test and development centre, and installed many special facilities.

When Walter Hayes arrived at Ford in 1962 he decided to revitalize Motorsport. On a budget of just £32,000 (other sources say £47,000), a new centre was built at Boreham, where Motorsport operations began in mid-1963. Then, as later, the 'works' team could use the airfield for test and proving purposes. For more than twenty years Boreham was shared between Motorsport

and Truck Development (later the Ford New Holland development facility), but all truck activity ended in the late 1980s. Motorsport then moved into the former Truck Development offices.

Motorsport originally operated 'works' Cortina GTs and Lotus-Cortinas. The original Escort Twin-Cam was designed there in 1967, and the first of the 'works' Escort rally cars followed in 1968. Hundreds of victories and Championship successes ensued. A number of 'works' race cars – Capris and Escort RS1600s – were also based in the same workshops.

Design and development of several limited-production Ford cars, notably the RS200, the Sierra RS500 Cosworth and the Escort RS Cosworth, was also carried out at Boreham along with (in the final years) the Escort WRC and the Puma Racing types. Having announced its imminent closure in 2003, Ford finally pulled out of Boreham early in 2004, breaking a fifty-year presence on that pleasant site.

rear wing already in use on the XR4i? It took time to convince those people that the package really worked.

The first time I saw the model, I was startled, and I remember saying that it was ideally designed so that if a police car was following, you would be able to see the blue light above the wing, and the main 'Police' sign below it. Three years later, when on my way to a silver wedding party in an RS500 Cosworth, I proved the point, as my driving

licence will confirm. Bob Lutz, in the end, approved the layout on a styling model in March 1984, and no more criticism was ever heard.

Even so, the project did not always go ahead with total approval:

Notice anything? This was Ford Design's first attempt at styling the new Sierra RS Cosworth in 1984, when the extra front-end air intake had yet to be included.

Right *Later in 1984 Ford design, in Cologne, had almost finished shaping the still-secret Sierra RS Cosworth …*

Below right *… with the massive rear spoiler already finalized.*

There was one particular occasion when the Sierra Cosworth project was still not approved and needed every encouragement it could get. There was an occasion when it was still on 'life-support' (as Walter Hayes used to call it), when Chairman Sam Toy spoke to me in the boardroom one day. Looking across at a large painting of Jim Clark three-wheeling his Lotus-Cortina around a race track, he asked me:

'Will the Cosworth do for the Sierra what Jim Clark's Lotus-Cortina did for the Cortina?'

'Yes', I said, with fingers firmly crossed, and more besides.

This was the original official press release picture of the brand-new Sierra RS Cosworth, as previewed in March 1985.

Sierra RS Cosworth and RS500 Cosworth (1986–87)
[RS500 Cosworth differences, where applicable, in brackets]

Layout
Unit construction steel body/chassis structure. Two-door plus hatchback, front engine/rear-wheel drive, sold as four-seater sports hatchback.

Engine

Type	Ford-Cosworth YB Series
Block material	Cast iron
Head material	Cast aluminium
Cylinders	4 in-line
Cooling	Water
Bore and stroke	90.82 × 76.95mm
Capacity	1993cc
Main bearings	5
Valves	4 per cylinder, operated by twin overhead camshafts, via inverted bucket-type tappets, with the camshafts driven by cogged belt from the crankshaft
Compression ratio	8.0:1 (nominal)
Fuel supply	Weber-Marelli fuel injection, with Garrett AiResearch TO3 turbocharger [TO4 turbocharger]
Max. power	204bhp @ 6,000rpm [224bhp @ 6,000rpm]
Max. torque	205lb ft @ 4,500rpm [206lb ft @ 4,500rpm]

Transmission
Five-speed manual gearbox, all-synchromesh

Clutch	Single plate, diaphragm spring

Overall gearbox ratios

Top	2.93:1
4th	3.64:1
3rd	4.86:1
2nd	7.05:1
1st	10.75:1
Reverse	10.03:1
Final drive ratio	3.64:1

22.98mph (36.97km/h)/1,000rpm in top gear

Suspension and steering

Front	Independent, by coil springs, MacPherson struts, track control arms, telescopic dampers and anti-roll bar
Rear	Independent, by coil springs, semi-trailing arms, anti-roll bar and telescopic dampers
Steering	Rack-and-pinion (with power assistance)
Tyres	205/50VR-15in radial-ply
Wheels	Cast alloy disc, bolt-on fixing
Rim width	7.0 in

Brakes

Type	Disc brakes at front, discs at rear, hydraulically operated, with hydraulic ABS anti-lock control
Size	11.1in front discs, 10.8in rear discs

Dimensions (in/mm)

Track	
Front	57.1/1,450
Rear	57.7/1,470
Wheelbase	102.6/2,610
Overall length	175.5/4,460
Overall width	68.0/1,730
Overall height	54.2/1,380
Unladen weight	2,690lb/1,217kg

UK retail price
(at launch in 1986) £15,950 [1987: £19,950]

Although Motorsport had wanted to use the new turbocharged Sierra from 1985, quite early in the programme this was seen as impractical. Cosworth's very first road car YB engine prototypes did not start test-bed work until June 1984, and the first test cars did not go over to Weber-Marelli in Italy (for calibration) until September 1984, by which time SVE's development programme was swinging into gear.

Even though it was not nearly ready to go on sale, the very first public showing of what soon became known as the 'whale tail' Sierra RS Cosworth was made at the Geneva Motor Show in March 1985, and a suitably liveried race car by Andy Rouse Engineering followed later in the year.

This caused a sensation, not least among the management of BMW. Although the Bavarian company had already decided to make an ultra high-performance version of their 3-Series (it would be badged M3 when it went on sale in 1986), this car was to have a normally aspirated engine. Competitive in road car tune, maybe, the M3 looked likely to be outgunned by a turbo-boosted Sierra RS Cosworth on the race track. And so (as detailed in Chapter 7) it was, for after mere months of face-to-face competition the M3 had to slip in behind the fleets of race-ready RS500 Cosworths!

By comparison with all the effort that went into finalizing the style, SVE found that sorting out the transmission, and the chassis, was a more predictable business. We now know that the bulk of their original development work was completed in double-quick time – mid-1984 to the end of 1985 – although, as we shall see, there was then a flurry of extra work connected with gearbox failings.

Because Ford's existing Sierra T9 five-speed gearbox was not strong enough to withstand the torque of Cosworth's new engine, a new main gearbox had to be sourced. Although both ZF and Getrag of Germany could have

By mid-1984 Paul Fricker's project team had built the first turbocharged Sierra engine, the YAB prototype. Developing up to 180bhp at this stage, the YAB still used a fabricated, tubular, exhaust manifold and its own unique style of camshaft cover. When YA became YB, both these features would disappear.

provided suitable five-speed transmissions, these were thought to be too expensive, and in the end the chosen unit was the North American Borg Warner T5 box.

This was a modern, all-synchromesh, mass-production unit, already well known to Ford-USA since it was being used in the newly announced SVO Mustang of the period (as well as in such cars as the Thunderbird), and was also employed in many different high-performance General Motors, Jeep and Nissan products. At the rear, Ford matched it to a new sub-frame mounted '7½ inch' final drive, as scheduled for use in Granada/Scorpio types (but not in other Sierras, except the Merkur XR4Ti), and fitted a rather 'softly' specified viscous coupling limited-slip differential. In fact some perceptive Ford engineers thought that the viscous settings were so slight that this fitting was almost superfluous – although it was undoubtedly a good selling point!

Automatic transmission, naturally, was never even considered for this model.

The suspension and steering, though thoroughly worked over, were all closed based on the new Sierra layout, beefed up, and with new

The principal architecture of the YAB prototype engine of mid-1984 would be carried forward into the YB of 1985.

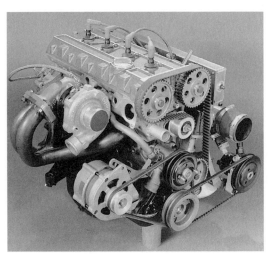

Enough space, but only just enough, to install the YAB turbocharged engine in the engine bay of the Sierra. The packaging of the Garrett AiResearch turbo and the complex exhaust manifold is explained by the torque requirements of this power unit. This installation is still incomplete, for the air cleaner, the inlet passage piping and the air/air intercooler are still to be fitted.

suspension/steering geometry at the front. Compared with the conventional Sierras, there were stiffer front and rear springs, uprated dampers, and anti-roll bars at front and rear (that at the rear being surprisingly slim at 0.55in/14mm diameter).

A raised front roll-centre, and carefully developed negative camber wheel settings at front and rear, along with 7.0in alloy rim wheels by ATS/Rial, and Dunlop D40 tyres of 205/55-VR15 (those sounded big and fat twenty years ago!), all transformed the handling.

The first cars, even those pre-production cars prepared for the press launch in December 1985, had very 'nervous' steering, but after several influential journalists complained about this the system was slightly 'de-tuned' by

This 'exploded' drawing of the YBB production engine (both the inlet manifold and the exhaust manifold/turbocharger have been withdrawn laterally from the cylinder head) shows just how much of a redesign had been carried out in an astonishingly quick time.

This display unit shows the production standard YBB engine, complete with Borg Warner T5 gearbox, plus the intercooler, all laid out in the way in which they were installed in the car.

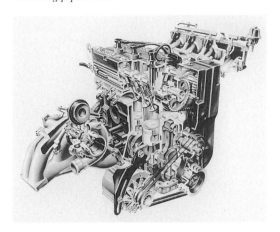

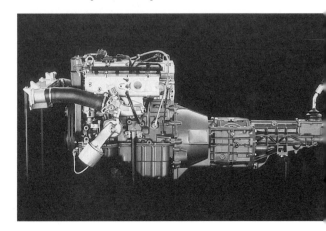

Compare this YBB engine bay installation of a Sierra RS Cosworth production car with that of the YAB prototype of 1984 (shown opposite on page 42). Much has changed, some dictated for styling reasons, in less than a year.

changing some suspension pivot and rack-and-pinion steering settings.

Brakes, all disc of course, with a Teves ABS anti-lock installation, were like those of the soon to be launched 'Mark 3' Granada/Scorpio range. At 11.1in (front, ventilated) and 10.7in (rear, solid) these were adequate (but no more) for standard cars. Once these cars started to be used in motor sport with up to 300bhp, however, speed shops made haste to find larger discs.

Inside the car there was a mixture of Sierra Ghia-style fittings (trim, carpets and facia layout in general), with a special instrument cluster that included a 170mph speedometer, a 7,000rpm rev counter, and the tiny turbocharger boost gauge that had first been seen in the Merkur (Sierra) XR4Ti. Fabulous fig-

In December 1985 seven of the press launch cars were handed over to competitors in the Securicor Sierra Challenge of 1986. Competition manager Peter Ashcroft is on the far left, next to marketing chief Bill Camplisson.

C235 HVW, which became familiar as a BRSCC official circuit car at Brands Hatch in later years, shows off the lines of the original three-door car at the launch in Spain towards the end of 1985.

This was the facia/instrument panel layout of the three-door Sierra RS Cosworth, showing off the Recaro seats, and the turbo boost gauge in the corner of the instrument display.

ure-hugging Recaro front seats made all the difference to the driving compartment's ambience, while other standard fittings included the manually operated tilt-and-slide glass sunroof, electric window lifts and a high-quality radio/cassette installation.

Even though this was to be the most expensive Sierra by any measure, it was only to be available, from standard, in one of three colours (Diamond White, Moonstone Blue and Black), all cars having the same trim colour and package. There were to be absolutely no options, for which Ford saw no need.

When the car was unveiled, Ford talked confidently about a 'Job One' date (when the first true production cars would be produced) in September 1985, and for a time both SVE and Cosworth made good progress towards that deadline. Because the car had been officially previewed at Geneva in March, there was no longer any need for disguise to be applied when the cars were out on road test, all the performance claims (including a 149mph/240km/h top speed) were verified, and except

A properly set-up three-door Sierra RS Cosworth always seemed to ride slightly nose-down, this being due to the big, low, front spoiler and the high rear spoiler.

for continuing discussion about steering and handling settings the rest of the car was well up to expectations. Motorsport's morale brightened, for there seemed to be every chance of achieving sporting homologation by mid-1986, half-a-season ahead of what BMW was likely to achieve with the M3.

Delays then set in, to the great frustration of one and all. Unhappily, Cosworth was only just able to start building off-line YBBs by that time, though Paul Fricker denies, smilingly, that this was caused by the time it took Ford Design and himself to agree on the colour the 16-valve cylinder heads should be painted:

When we started off, we had always done sand castings, but as we were going into bigger volumes we could go to die casting, with a very nice surface finish. The problem was that Ford's styling gurus wanted the engine to show a feeling of Italian exotica, so they actually wanted to make it red, and to make it look sand cast! So I then had to buy the paint with lumps in it. It took me the longest part of anything else on the job

to specify the right red paint, with the right amount of bits in it … It took about six months!

'Job One' was late – and actually delayed until March/April 1986. This was mainly due to early problems with the Borg Warner gearbox. Once pilot-build cars were available (towards the end of 1985), SVE soon found that continuous high-speed durability trials at Ford's Lommel proving ground encouraged premature gearbox bearing failure. Although the box had an adequate torque rating, in its North American specification it was by no means ideal for use at continuous high speeds. Borg Warner had to provide specially developed bearings and improved lubrication, pinpointing those special versions purely for the Sierra RS Cosworth (and the 'Sapphire' Cosworth that followed).

Above *When the Sierra RS Cosworth was first shown to the press at the end of 1985, several writers clocked up to 150mph (241km/h) on Spanish motorways and were astonished by the performance of this new Ford.*

Below *All three-door Sierra RS Cosworths had a monstrous rear spoiler that was not there merely for show. Much wind-tunnel development had gone into shaping it, to provide significant downforce at high speeds.*

Whale Tail on Sale

By the spring of 1986, and once the Borg Warner transmission's testing problems had been settled, Ford was finally ready to put the car into production at Genk. Cosworth's Wellingborough factory had been churning out 'red top' engines for months, and was well ahead of the game (they were tooled up to build more than 150 engines every week, and soon achieved that target), so there would be no hold ups in that department.

One of the most precious artefacts in my archive is the computer print-out of Sierra RS Cosworth production that Ford prepared for the homologation inspectors from FISA

(Fédération Internationale du Sport Auto-motive), the Paris-based body that governed rallying, on 4 December 1986. More than 5,000 cars had already been produced (actually it was 5,052 at that time; this number, of course, included the 500 cars earmarked for conversion/upgrading into RS500 Cosworths in 1987 – *see* Chapter 4), and it is fascinating to see when series production started and how the build rate then notched itself up.

A diligent search shows that the first car appears to have left Genk on 12 March 1986 for a German destination, the next two were for the UK and Norway (14 April), and the fourth was for Belgium (30 April). One more British car left on 7 May, the next German machine on 10 June, after which series production began to build up more regularly.

Those early cars and several others, I think, were almost all sent to Ford's concessionaires in those countries – *Autocar*'s road test (of D789 PVW) was published on 13 August 1986, which means that the car must have been assessed in July. More and more cars followed in July, all of them slipping down the same assembly lines as other 'mainstream' Sierras. By October and November several hundred Sierra RS Cosworths were being completed every week. The same document

Who owned Cosworth – and when?

In the beginning Keith Duckworth and Mike Costin were the only shareholders in Cosworth: family members took a small shareholding as the years passed, with Keith Duckworth always the dominant member.

Cosworth sold out to United Engineering Industries in 1980, this company itself being taken over by Carlton Communications in 1989. Less than a year later (in March 1990) Carlton then sold off the Cosworth business to the Vickers engineering conglomerate.

It is important to understand that Cosworth's successive owners allowed Cosworth to 'do their own thing' for many years (Keith Duckworth remained as chairman until 1988, Mike Costin from 1988 to 1990), and that Ford had no financial interest whatsoever in Cosworth throughout these manoeuvrings.

Vickers sold off the Cosworth operation in 1998, at which point two separate businesses emerged. Cosworth Racing was absorbed by Ford, while Cosworth Technology (the 'production car engines' side of the operation) was taken over by the Audi arm of the massive VW Group.

In November 2004 Ford sold off Cosworth Racing to two North American entrepreneurs, Kevin Kalkhoven and Gerry Forsythe, who already owned the Champcar racing series in North America, where Cosworth was the standard engine supplied to all runners. After a 24-year run of ownerships by large groups, the racing side of Cosworth was once again in private hands!

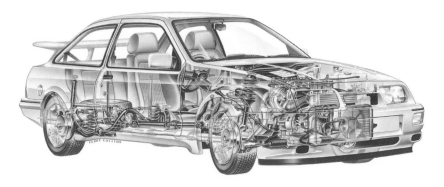

Compared with the bread-and-butter three-door Sierra on which it was based, the Sierra RS Cosworth had a complete mechanical transplant – with its turbocharged engine, its Borg-Warner T5 gearbox and its larger rear axle, plus special brakes and wheels.

confirms that the 500 right-hand-drive cars earmarked for eventual conversion into RS500 Cosworths (*see* Chapter 4) were assembled in a concentrated eleven-day period in November 1986. In the following weeks all were shipped from Belgium to Essex, where they were put into store at Ford's 'Frog Island' storage area.

No sooner had the homologation inspection taken place than Sierra RS Cosworth assembly closed down, and shortly afterwards all the original Sierra pressing and welding facilities were torn apart so that modified tooling for what Ford called the '87½' model Sierra could be installed. By that time a total of 5,542 Cosworth-engined cars had been produced, of which 500 were in store for eventual conversion to RS500 Cosworths.

Priced at £15,950 in the UK (with no extras – especially no 'compulsory extras' – to be added), the 'whale tail' model was immediately popular, as it also was in other speed-happy European countries like West Germany and France. As forecast, more than half of these cars would eventually be sold in the UK, with 847 of the first 5,000 units going to Germany,

Cosworth was adamant that the YB engine needed a long exhaust manifold to help produce the right sort of torque. On production engines this manifold was in two separate castings, with the T3 turbocharger positioned high and close up to the cylinder head itself.

564 to France, 281 for Italy, 223 for Spain and 197 for Austria.

Even so, the introduction into service was not without drama. Proud owners in the UK

This view of the YBB engine shows clearly the way in which the exhaust manifold was accommodated.

The definitive YBB engine featured a neat plastic front cover to hide the camshaft drive belt, and a simple plenum chamber connecting the throttle body and the inlet manifold.

found that the new car was embarrassingly easy to steal, so anyone who parked his car in the open, or out of sight of his home, ran the risk of having it lifted and never seeing it again. In Germany the problem was not one of theft, but of engine head gasket failure on the autobahns, something that was highly embarrassing to both Cosworth and Ford. This was so serious that a fully warranty recall went out to all German owners – among a total of 2,300 cars in all territories.

Paul Fricker told me how Cosworth learned the bad news:

> The fundamental issue was that our sign-off testing was at constant speed, and the cylinder head was designed to be a rigid structure. When we came to the driving cycle of that car, especially in Germany, it gave us a significant problem.
>
> You could accelerate hard until someone pulled out in front of you, you would then lift off, and what was actually happening was that every time you accelerated the head expanded, and every time you lifted off the head contracted again. This gave the design a very hard time – the head around the exhaust ports was expanding and contracting, that then moved the gasket, and the head joint would then fail. The cure – we eventually chose to go with Reinz – was to come up with a gasket design that allowed a metal Omega ring in the gasket.

Rod Mansfield confirmed that analysis:

> In addition, a new cylinder head bolt design involving tapered (or, more correctly, yield) bolts was employed, along with extra meat in the gasket to accommodate different heat expansion rates. Such changes were introduced in mid-1986, when more than 4,000 Sierra Cosworth engines had been completed.

Fundamentally, of course, this was a remarkably sturdy engine. This, incidentally, was period when Cosworth's F1 team was developing the turbocharged 1.5-litre GB engine, which eventually used phenomenal boost, and produced up to 1000bhp. When the team was investigating all the latest 'rocket fuel' mixes for that engine, it ran YB engines for fuel evaluation, sometimes above 300bhp with very weak fuel ratios, to assess detonation resistance, as Paul Fricker recalls:

> They were cheap and reliable for that … and we had a cupboardful of them to carry on testing if we had a major blow up!

How to sum up this remarkable engine and remarkable machine in one sentence? Perhaps it would be best to quote what my friends on *Autocar* had to say in their road test:

> The Ford Sierra RS Cosworth is quite an extraordinary car, for we cannot think of another car that combines such a high degree of practicality with 150mph performance and has a price tag of just a little under £16,000 attached to it.

In his editorial column, published in the same week, Editor Matthew Carter noted that:

Seen from the front end, the YBB engine mounted its throttle body, plenum chamber and inlet manifold on the right, with the distributor and the power steering pump, its exhaust manifold, turbocharger and alternator on the left.

YB engine assembly at Cosworth's Wellingborough factory in 1986, showing what was a series-production power unit by any standards. This line would be modified, expanded and relocated more than once, before the last engine of all was built ten years later.

There was a time when the kind of performance offered by the Ford Sierra RS Cosworth would be exclusive to those who could afford the stratospheric prices for membership of the Supercar club … By those standards, a shade under £16,000 represents good value for a road racer. It may be somewhat unsubtle, but there is no argument against those impressive performance figures.

The public – or, rather, those members of the public who believed in high-performance road cars, and didn't mind everyone else knowing what they drove – obviously agreed

Even at a casual glance there must be twenty-five engines in this Wellingborough assembly shot – 5,000 horsepower at least! This was about one day's production since, at its peak, Cosworth was producing more than 5,000 engines a year.

This is what the Cosworth YB engine project was all about – providing Ford with peerless racing saloon cars. They were that, and more. This is Spa-Francorchamps in 1987, with the two Eggenberger Sierras leading the rolling start of a World Touring Car Championship event.

with this verdict. Although Ford did not put the car on sale officially until mid-July 1986 (just in time, as it happened, for UK dealers to have cars to sell ahead of the registration letter change on 1 August), the new extrovert Sierra sold briskly for the rest of the year. More than 1,000 cars were registered before the end of 1986 (some, no doubt, made acceptable high-

value Christmas presents!), while 1,761 (including all the RS500s – *see* Chapter 4) followed in 1987. By any standards that made the original RS Cosworth a one-year sell-out, which must surely have been very profitable.

By 1987, however, the three-door cars had come and gone on the Genk assembly lines, and a new, rather more civilized, four-door variety was under development. Before then, however, Ford had a major surprise up its sleeve – one that would electrify the public, satisfy its motor sport users, and frighten the life out of all its saloon car racing rivals. After the Sierra RS Cosworth, the RS500 Cosworth was on the way.

4 Sierra RS500 Cosworth – the Ultimate Homologation Special

What Sierra enthusiasts may still not understand is just how quickly the RS500 was developed. Although first thoughts came in 1983, proper engineering work did not begin until the summer of 1986, engine manufacture took place early in 1987, and no fewer than 496 of the 500 cars were completed in a breathless six-week period in June and July 1987. Every single one of those cars had right-hand drive, and every single one was destined for sale by one of the ninety Ford RS dealers in Great Britain.

Way back in August 1983, when the original Sierra RS Cosworth was still no more than a paper project, Motorsport director Stuart Turner's determination to have an absolutely unbeatable saloon car racer in its future was apparent in this internal memo:

> We need to resolve our race Sierra specification as soon as possible. We need to do more than enough to be competitive …
>
> Boreham and Köln [Cologne] must think up ways of doing (a) 5,000 as a base car … then (b) evoluting 500 which could be turned into winners under Group A rules.

Apart from the horrible use of the English language (Ford Motorsport loved to talk about 'evoluting' things when no dictionary includes that word – 'evolving' was the only correct usage), Turner's recommendation was very

Mike Moreton (far right), with Stuart Turner next to him, explaining the rationale of the RS500 Cosworth at Boreham in 1987. Running the RS500 programme was Moreton's 'baby' in 1986 and 1987.

Ford built 500 Sierra RS Cosworths at Genk in late 1986, then shipped them over to Essex, where they spent the winter outdoors, well-waxed, but not needed until mid-1987, for conversion into RS500 Cosworths. There must be 200–300 cars in this shot, all of them black, which was taken as deliveries to Bedworth began.

clear. Put into layman's language, he wanted to see something even more special than the Sierra RS Cosworth made available, and that was special enough, so that all the motor racing opposition would be obliterated.

Except that he realized that it would have to be done briskly, and at minimum cost, at this time Turner had not gone into any detail. One is reminded of that famous throwaway remark by Winston Churchill, when he asked for the 'Mulberry' floating harbours to be constructed during World War Two:

> Let me have the best solution worked out. Don't argue the matter. The difficulties will argue for themselves.

Desirable, but Possible?

It was never going to be easy, as the international regulations defining FIA (Fédération Internationale de l'Automobile) Group A motor sport made quite clear. First of all, 5,000 mechanically identical cars of one saloon type had to be built, and after that (but not before homologation had been granted) a further 'Evolution' car could then be put on sale. To gain homologation for that 'Evolution' car, at least another 500 mechanically identical cars (10 per cent of the original run) had to be built. Ford had thought of everything for, well before it took shape, they had planned for the RS500 Cosworth. As with the previous 'RS200' model, there was no need to consult marketing gurus about a possible title – it more or less invented itself.

So far, so good – but according to the regulations there were strict limits as to what could be changed to produce an 'Evolution' car, and what could not. Changes could be made to the engine but not to its cubic capacity. No transmission changes were authorized. The suspension detail, but not its general layout, could be improved, while the aerodynamic trimming of the body shell (but not the body shell itself) could also be changed. Not only that, but the actual production of those cars (their numbers, and their specification) had to be verified, by one or more inspections by an FIA team, which usually included at least one member of a rival organization.

That was the theory, and as far as Ford was concerned no one had more experience, or was better qualified to push those rules to the

John Griffiths

Who was it who, many years ago, commented that a rally car was only as good as its homologation would allow it to be? This was certainly the case at Ford, where careful attention to planning and paperwork made good cars even more competitive.

Although Henry Taylor and Stuart Turner had laid the foundations, from the early 1970s it was John Griffiths who created some very inventive homologation papers, a job which he held down for the next thirty years at Boreham and at M-Sport.

John had already presided over the 'development' of the late 1970s 'Escort RS' (a near-mythical 400-off 2-litre/16-valve Escort Mk 2), and made sure that the RS200 had a 1803cc engine (instead of the originally planned 1786cc) so that it could be much enlarged in the next capacity class, before he turned his attention to the Sierra RS Cosworth and all its descendants.

Other people engineered and produced the cars, but John made sure that all the best pieces were available for motor sport, that the Sierra RS500 Cosworth had modified rear suspension at minimal cost, and that more than 2,500 Escort RS Cosworths had 'water injection kits' lying loose inside the cars when they were delivered. It was John who advised on the fitment and specification of such gizmos as the extra four fuel injectors on RS500 Cosworth engines (even though they were not working on road cars), and who was much involved in setting the vast choice of gearboxes, axle ratios, brakes and other details that stuff the options pages of the homologation forms.

John's influence at Ford outlived the Cosworth-badged models by some years, when he became heavily involved in the Focus World Rally Championship programme.

---

limit, than its homologation expert John Griffiths. Not only that, but after many years' experience at Ford, John also had a very good idea of what proposed changes would be acceptable to top management and to the assembly plant operators (in this case at Genk). John, after all, had masterminded the approval of the Escort RS1800 in double-quick time in 1975, of the flat-nose Escort RS2000, of the near-mythical 'Escort RS' of the late 1970s (a 2-litre BDA-engined type that Ford never actually built themselves), of the 200-off RS200 – and, most recently, of the Sierra RS Cosworth itself.

Time, of course, was never going to be on Ford Motorsport's side. By mid-1986 it was clear that more than 5,000 Sierra RS Cosworths would be built before the end of the year, but it was also clear that a further 500 'Evolution' cars would need to be built (or almost built – as will become clear shortly) before the end of the calendar year.

That much was essential. Quite simply, at the end of 1986 the original Sierra body shell was to be rendered obsolete by the introduction of what Ford called its '1987½' style, which not only involved new front end sheet metal styling, but the introduction of a four-door saloon style as well. It would not be possible for

five hundred 'new' 'Evolution' Sierras to be assembled in 1987, since by then the old-type jigs, fixtures and press tools would have been dismantled.

Pandemonium! Because Group A Regulations stated firmly that 'Evolution' cars could not be completed until assembly of the original 5,000 cars had already been finished, when (if ever) could they be built? Wasn't it inevitable, though, that the combined minds of Stuart Turner, Peter Ashcroft, Mike Moreton and John Griffiths would come up with a solution – not only one that complied with the letter of FIA regulations, but one that made business sense too. (Ford was, after all, in business to turn a profit, and its hard-bitten bosses were not about to approve so-called alternative schemes that made no financial sense. The RS500 Cosworth could indeed have been created on the Merkur XR4Ti lines at Karmann in 1987, but at horrendous cost, so this idea was discounted after a very short discussion.)

The solution was as neat as it was practical, and as cost-effective as it was sporting-legal. Instead of making sure that the Sierra plant at Genk produced just over 5,000 Sierra RS Cosworths in 1986, it would be asked to produce more than 5,500 cars instead. Late on in

This startling shot dates from July 1987, when conversion of RS Cosworths to RS500 Cosworths was in full swing at Bedworth. About twenty brand-new large-turbo YBDs, newly delivered from Cosworth's factory at Wellingborough, are ready to be craned into place. By the end of the day, almost all of them would be in a car – and another twenty to twenty-five engines would have arrived from Wellingborough!

the rush to built Sierra RS Cosworths, five hundred extra cars would be produced, then immediately shipped into safe storage in the UK, where they were waxed and thoroughly protected for winter storage.

In the meantime, Ford already knew what they wanted to achieve in uprating the basic car. On the race tracks, experience was already building up with the Merkur XR4Ti. With that in mind, Ford developed two main objectives: to provide the potential for a much more powerful engine, and to make the car more stable at high racing speeds. In double-quick time, Cosworth finalized the design of the engine upgrade, Aston Martin Tickford (at Milton Keynes) tackled chassis and body modifications, and aerodynamic development was headed by Ford-Germany Motorsport.

Engine

Ford's definite aim was to have a 500bhp race engine to obliterate all their opposition (it seemed like a pie-in-the-sky target at the time, but proved to be routine within a couple of years), so they needed a stronger cylinder

block, more turbocharged air into the engine, and more fuel for that air. Since this was the 'Evolution' car, Ford concentrated on these requirements without worrying too much about refinement, which explains why the road cars were neither as flexible nor even as powerful as the pundits would have liked.

Cosworth's engineering work, to evolve what came to be known as the YBD, was carried out by experienced F1 designer John Hancock. Once John had settled the details, Paul Fricker picked up the project and urged it into production at Wellingborough. Hancock specified a new and stiffer cylinder block (stiffer, and with more metal around sections identified as being close to their structural limits when 350bhp was being developed on the Sierra RS Cosworth, including the cylinder walls themselves and the top deck that mated to the cylinder head), remembering that, no matter what he wanted of a different casting, it would have to be cast and machined by Ford themselves, on existing or only temporarily changed production machinery.

This time there was a new, massive and larger Garrett T31/T04 turbocharger, while the

Comparing the power of the RS Cosworth with the RS500 Cosworth		
Feature	*RS Cosworth*	*RS500 Cosworth*
Peak power (bhp)/rpm	204/6,000	224/6,000
Peak torque (lb ft)/rpm	205/4,000	206/4,500

inlet and exhaust manifolds were both modified to deal with the much enhanced air-flow. A twin-fuel-rail eight-injector fuel injection system was specified and plumbed into the plenum chamber, although only the original four-injector rail was actually hooked up on the road cars. The electronics were much modified to take account of all this ('Weber-Marelli had to build 500 "specials"', Paul Fricker remembers), and if all eight injectors were coupled up a further ECU was also required. Other internal modifications included changes to the lubrication system.

As far as the road car specification engines were concerned, the differences were not very marked. According to Ford's official figures, seen in the accompanying table, although the peak power had gone up by 10 per cent, the torque had barely changed, but because the peak was recorded at higher speeds, that meant there was less usable torque lower down the rev range.

There was also a new, larger capacity air/air intercooler, positioned across the rear of the enlarged water radiator. All in all this was an integrated package, with much more potential than even the Sierra RS Cosworth had offered. It's worth recalling, at this moment, that a fully race-tuned RS500 Cosworth engine developed five times as much power as the T88/Pinto engine from which it had evolved.

The bad news for engine tuners was that it was not possible to convert or upgrade a YBB into a YBD – simply because the cylinder block itself was substantially different: in later years some individuals screwed many YBD pieces on to a YBB block/bottom end – and speedily discovered that this had been unwise.

Rear suspension

Right from the start Ford Motorsport tapped into the racing expertise being built up by both Andy Rouse Engineering and Eggenberger Motorsport (*see* Chapter 7) with their Merkur XR4Tis. Since the race-tune chas-

RS500 Cosworth assembly working flat-out at Bedworth. The five cars seen on the ramps have already had their 'standard' YBB engines removed, while those on the ground ahead of them have had new YBD engines craned into place instead. All cars in this shot are black; the white and Moonstone Grey examples followed towards the end of July.

sis/suspension layout of those cars was the same as that of the Sierra RS Cosworth, their opinions were of great interest.

Both teams agreed that the existing Sierra/Merkur type of semi-trailing link rear suspension put limitations on the grip, traction and poise of the race cars, especially if track conditions were not smooth and dry. (It wasn't long, incidentally, before Boreham's own experience with rally cars backed this up.) Maybe the handling of the cars was acceptable – just – with 350bhp and ultra-wide slick tyres, but an improved layout was needed.

Once again it was John Griffiths's careful reading of Group A regulations that helped provide appropriate advice to the development team. The best way to improve the rear suspension was to reduce the 'swing axle effect', and because the standard sub-frame crossbeam was to be retained, this was best done by providing alternative pivot points for the semi-trailing links.

Although Ford was not willing to make wholesale changes to the rear suspension, John's reading of the rules confirmed that extra mounting points could be provided on the otherwise unchanged tubular beam, so that race-type arms could hook up to them. Accordingly, when the time came to convert

RS Cosworths into RS500 Cosworths, these additional inner pivot mounting brackets (welded to, and ahead, of the standard brackets, as the picture on page 60 makes clear) would be provided during the build process. Even so, it is important to realize that the standard pivot/mounting brackets were retained, along with the standard rear suspension arms, for use on every standard RS500 road car. (In later years, RS500 road cars that required new crossbeams, perhaps after an accident that had distorted the original, have sometimes had 'standard' Sierra RS Cosworth beams fitted instead, and the extra forward-mounting brackets may no longer be present.)

Aerodynamics

Although these changes were of little importance to road car customers, they were vital to the balance of the RS500 Cosworth at high-speed racing speeds, since at circuits such as Spa and Brno the fastest Sierras might be exceeding 170mph (273km/h)!

At the front there was a new front bumper moulding, which was reprofiled and provided with enlarged air inlets, so that more air could be channelled into the cooling radiator/intercooler area. At the same time, the low-mount-

Not nearly finished yet, but well on the way to completion, the RS500s in the foreground already have YBD engines and new-type RS500 front bumper mouldings. Much work remained, including rigorous quality control checks, before the completed cars could roll out of the door.

The assembly hall at AMT's old factory at Bedworth was not cramped, but certainly quite small. The miracle was that, at peak, up to twenty-eight completed RS500 Cosworths would be wheeled out of the one building every day. It was not the sort of pressure that anyone, workforce and management alike, wanted to sustain for too long.

ed driving lamps were discarded in favour of wire-grilled holes, which increased the flow of cooling air towards the brakes, and an extra rubberized spoiler lip was fixed to the bottom of the new moulding. Although this reduced the ground clearance, it undoubtedly improved the front-end aerodynamic performance.

At the rear there were two further aerodynamic add-ons. One was a secondary rear spoiler, underneath the original, fixed on the rear corner of the hatchback lid. The other was what aficionados call a 'Gurney' flap (really an upward tilting edge, only 1.18in/30mm deep), fixed to the rear of the existing large spoiler. Once again, these had little or no obvious effect when the RS500 was being driven at normal road speeds, but were undeniably effective at high speeds in motor racing when an extra 220lb (100kg) of aerodynamic downforce was created.

Apart from the above, and the fixing of discreet 'RS500' badges on the sides of the front wings and on the tailgate, there were no other obvious differences. Nor was there any obvious external difference in engine specification, for the same exhaust system and outlet pipes were retained.

Building the Cars

With four prototype cars already being used for test, development and legal homologation work, Ford had to find a way of converting the balance of 496 cars from Sierra RS Cosworth to Sierra RS500 Cosworth. As ever, the problem had not been the desire to do so, but finding the most practical way to accomplish this.

If this had only been a matter of assembly, then Ford might have considered the possibility of sending all the cars down an existing Sierra assembly line at Genk, or maybe even down the line at Karmann, where Sierra-based Merkur XR4Ti cars were already being manufactured. Unfortunately, as already described, in order to produce the RS500 it was originally necessary to partially strip out an existing car, including the removal of the complete engine and of the front and rear spoilers.

As with the RS200 programme, therefore, Ford decided to let a trusted contractor do that job. Well before the end of 1986, what Mike Moreton once described as 'the usual suspects' were considered: all of them British, all independent of Ford, but all with the capacity, the ability and the hunger to get the job done. The result of a brisk and businesslike 'beauty con-

Mike Moreton

As a planner, organizer and schemer, Mike Moreton had no equal. In print, I once defined Mike as a 'fixer', and though he thought this was a touch undignified he never actually complained: I reckon he was proud of that description. Whether it was in planning new AVO products, or aiding and abetting Stuart Turner and John Wheeler to get the Escort RS Cosworth approved, he was peerless.

After working at Rootes in Coventry and at Vauxhall, Mike joined Ford in 1966. Within two years he had hitched his star to Bob Howe, and became AVO's product planner in 1972. After a period in mainstream Product Planning, where he wrote an influential paper suggesting that a 'Special Vehicle Engineering' department should be set up (it was!), he was then seconded to Boreham to make planning sense of the Escort RS1700T in 1982, although in the end that work was wasted.

He was an important mover and shaker at Boreham for some years, heavily involved in the development of the Escort RS Turbo and the Sierra RS Cosworth. He then became project manager of both the Sierra RS500 Cosworth and the demanding RS200 projects.

In 1988 and 1989 he was one of the founding fathers of the Escort RS Cosworth project, alongside engineer John Wheeler and director Stuart Turner, pushing it over every Product Planning hurdle and finding a production home for it at Karmann in Germany.

Mike's direct Ford connection was broken when he was 'head-hunted' by Tom Walkinshaw to work at TWR in Oxfordshire. During his decade at TWR he was Project Manager for the Jaguar XJ220, ran the Aston Martin factory at Newport Pagnell for a time, inspired the planning behind the Aston Martin DB7 and advised Walkinshaw on many other projects.

In 1999, in theory, he reached retiring age, but as 2000 opened he was still consulting with TWR and retaining his links with Ford, although he eventually retired to contented obscurity in rural France.

---

test' saw the deal going to Aston Martin Tickford (AMT), whose ancient, but well-equipped, factory at Bedworth was ideal for the job.

Although Mike Moreton was fresh from running the RS200 manufacturing programme at Shenstone, as Project Manager on the RS500 Cosworth programme he had to face a new set of challenges in the building of the 496 cars. Ford formally signed a deal with AMT in March 1987 and wanted to see all the cars completed by the end of July.

Why such a rush? For motor sport purposes Ford needed to get the RS500 Cosworth homologated as soon as possible, so that cars might compete in at least the latter part of the World, European and national Touring Car Championships. Then there were the marketing considerations, for although Ford was confident that every car would find a ready home with a British customer, if the launch date were to slip back beyond August, into September or even October, the peak buying season would have gone and the RS dealer chain would find their task that much more difficult. Finally, although only a few knew this at the time, Ford needed to clear the decks of all 'whale-tail' cars before the end of the year, because the next derivative of the design, the four-door saloon 'Sapphire' Cosworth, was due to be launched in January 1988.

At first glance Tickford's premises were not ideal for the assembly of high-performance cars – but their workforce most certainly was. The factory buildings, set back from a side road in Bedworth (a small town about five miles due north of Coventry), were long-established and old-fashioned. Way back in the early days of the twentieth century this plant had been used for the mass-market manufacture of automotive soft tops, side screens and other trim items for Coventry's booming motor industry (it had been called the Coventry Hood and Seating Company), but had only recently been swept into the AMT orbit. Used since then to manufacture the 100-off run of Tickford Capris, this factory had also tackled some of the conversion work needed to build Jaguar XJ-S Cabriolets (from fixed-head coupés), and work was also being carried out for Leyland Daf Vehicles (concerning the production of passenger-derived versions of the vans) and for the railway rolling stock industry.

AMT never possessed anything resembling a moving assembly line, for the cars always had to be moved from work station to work station. The main assembly area, however, was large enough to embrace more then twenty or thirty vehicles at once, and had at least six modern four-pillar vehicle lifts and five mini-production lines, each with four work stations. Outside storage and parking space, on the other hand, was very limited indeed.

No matter. Mike Moreton and Mike Goddard, one of his most trusted cohorts, were used to constraints like this and rapidly set up a working supply system. The Sierra RS Cosworths already stored at Frog Island in Essex would stay there until the very last minute, and would then be trucked to Bedworth (four at a time, on new-car delivery transporters) by a three- to four-hour journey around the M25 and up the M1 and M6 motorways. Newly converted RS500s would be delivered in the reverse direction.

Ford was indeed fortunate that the M25 was very new and not yet permanently jammed, and that Frog Island was only minutes from an M25 interchange, with Bedworth a mere three kilometres from Junction 3 on the M6. It was a transport strategy that just had to work, for there was no Plan B. Motorway jams might mean that Bedworth's assembly hall was in imminent danger of becoming empty – or that a day's production of RS500s had nowhere to be stored! But somehow it worked, and worked triumphantly.

For the RS500, Ford homologated an extended inner pivot location for the race-type (but not the road-type) semi-trailing suspension arms. This shot (as taken for the actual homologation form) shows how the extra pressed steel brackets were added ahead of the unchanged 'standard' pressings. Quite pointless for road cars (and actually never used), they were very useful indeed for the racing fraternity.

Because Cosworth built all 500 YBD engines in one sweep at Wellingborough between May and July 1987 – this factory was only an easy 40 miles away from Bedworth, and the job took less than three months – there was no hold up from that direction. It helped that Ford's foundries, which produced Pinto engines, had been persuaded to alter the casting moulds for a big one-off operation, and apparently manufactured all 500 YBD cylinder blocks, ready-machined, over one weekend in a single working shift!

The biggest hang-up, it seemed, was in sourcing plastic aerodynamic add-ons from Phoenix in Germany, where the quality was sometimes below standards. Because time was pressing, at one stage it was necessary to have new supplies flown in to Coventry airport nearby.

All Built in Six Weeks

Preparation to build RS500 Cosworths at Tickford took six months, but once the process began all 496 cars were completed in six weeks. If not a miracle of improvisation, it was a wonderful example of 'can-do' manufacturing. First of all, a squad of Tickford workers, who previously might have been working on Leyland Daf vehicles or on Tickford Capris, had to be trained. Next a simple but rudimentary 'flow line' had to be set up in cramped surroundings, and space had to found for the floods of YBD engines that Cosworth was ready to deliver. As can be seen (*see* page 55), sophisticated methods were not applied, for rows and rows of YBD engines were 'stored' on the workshop floor until they were needed.

Two cars arrived in Bedworth on 17 March and 9 April to help train the workforce, and eight more, intended as press appraisal cars or for validation testing, rolled up to the door on 22 April. From Thursday 18 June the floodgates opened: sixteen cars arrived for conversion on that day, eight on the Friday, sixteen on the following Monday, sixteen on the Wednesday – the pressure was relentless.

Tickford's own build sheets show that there was no question of converting cars in any strict VIN number sequence: later, when number-crunchers realized that engine number and

VIN number sequences bore little relation to each other, there was much confusion. Various conspiracy theories grew up (including one that far fewer than the necessary 500 cars had ever been built – what nonsense!), but the bare facts were that RS Cosworths were delivered from Frog Island in the most convenient way possible, and that the YBD engine fitted was usually that which was on the floor at Bedworth and closest to the hoist at the time!

What happened to the engines and clutches that had been craned out? The engines, for sure, were returned to Cosworth at Wellingborough for minor updating and any necessary refurbishment, after which they were used in 1988-Model-Year 'Sapphire' Cosworths. The clutches, they say, were returned to Ford and never used again, but I prefer not to know the actual (economic) truth of that one.

When Mike Moreton started planning in mid-1986 there were suggestions that all the RS Cosworth cars earmarked for conversion should be painted in a special colour (Strato Silver was proposed). That was refused, however, and as an alternative it was suggested that all cars should be painted black. In the end – and

E501 NWN was the only RS500 that could be spared for publicity shots in July 1987. Here seen with the bonnet removed, it shows just how neatly the enlarged Garrett turbocharger and its trunking, together with the much-modified eight fuel-injector plenum/inlet passages actually fitted into the engine bay. When cars were prepared for motor sport use, teams somehow managed to add strut and bulkhead/roll-cage braces into the same space.

This front end detail of the RS500 Cosworth not only shows off the use of the much larger turbocharger, but it also illustrates the revised front bumper moulding (which channelled more fresh air into the radiator area), and the fact that low-mounted driving lamps had been replaced by plain black grilles. The moulding itself had a lower extension, which acted as a 'splitter' for the onrushing air.

How to identify an RS500 from the rear? Not only by the badging on the tail, but by the use of two transverse aerofoils – the lower one, on the corner of the hatch lid, was new – and by the use of the additional, upward-flipped, 'Gurney' flap on the whale-tail itself.

such was the rush to get cars built at all – Ford had to accept whatever was available. Of the 500 cars, 396 were black, 56 were white (including the four prototypes) and 52 were painted in Moonstone Grey: each and every one of these cars had right-hand drive.

Early in the process a Sierra RS Cosworth could become an RS500 Cosworth in a week to ten days, but by the end of July, when the homologation inspection was looming, that process was often reduced to a mere two days. The last hundred cars for conversion arrived at Bedworth in the last week (the final twelve on Tuesday 28 July). Every car was given a brisk 8 mile road test before being signed off.

As to the conversion sequence, after de-waxing there were five phases for each car: roughly de-waxing, strip-out and rear-suspension modification, engine-removal and YBD engine installation, mechanical completion, quality assurance and road test. Somehow AMT found space inside the factory, and on the crowded Warwickshire roads, to do all that.

With each car, the truly major task was that the existing, not-yet-run-in YBB engine

This shot of the RS500 Cosworth from low down shows the new front bumper moulding, which was supplied with an extra rubberized lower extension that had a real aerodynamic purpose at high speeds. These were, however, vulnerable to kerbing, or 'sleeping policemen', and many road car owners removed them for everyday usage. The 'RS500' decals on the front wings, above and behind the wheel-arch cut-outs, were also new.

assembly had to be craned out (along with the radiator and intercooler), before a Wellingborough-fresh YBD was hooked up to a Borg Warner T5 gearbox and slotted back into its place.

Not really believing that they would see concrete evidence of this resourceful enterprise, the FISA homologation inspection duly took place later that week, but when the team arrived there was no doubt that the job had been done. So much had been achieved that some of the inspectors were reluctant to believe the sporting legality of what they were shown.

'They can't do that … or that … or that!', was heard repeatedly from a rival manufacturer's representative during this visit, to which an experienced and independent administrator eventually replied calmly:

Oh yes, they can – they have built the cars. We have just counted them.

Head on, low down – this is where the aerodynamic changes to create the RS500 become obvious: note the deeper front bumper moulding with its rubberized splitter extension, which reduced ground clearance even further.

Approval, of course, came just in time, for the newly homologated Eggenberger RS500 Cosworths duly competed in the Belgian Spa 24 Hour race on 1/2 August, leading impressively for the first twenty hours.

This programme came to a rapid end. Just as the Ford/AMT juggernaut had turned on the taps to produce RS500s in such a hurry, the process was speedily run down. A further 100 cars were delivered into the dealer chain over the last weekend and the final 'quarantined' cars (those that had been suffering from minor problems) were cleared out of Bedworth within days. The workshops, so frantically busy for weeks, suddenly echoed their emptiness – yet within months the space would fill up with a stream of RS200s being refurbished and finished off.

20bhp for £4,000 – Was it Worth it?

For the first two weeks the inevitable shortages (the lack of Phoenix parts was a real problem) held up despatches. As a result nearly, but not quite, complete RS500 Cosworths were jammed into every corner of the AMT Tickford complex. Even as late as 23 July only half of the production run had been despatched, leading to 'standing room only' at Bedworth, because up to twenty-five cars were being finished off every working day. On 19 July, for example, twenty-five Sierra RS Cosworths (all of them black, incidentally) arrived at Bedworth for conversion, although according to the records not a single completed RS500 left the premises that day!

Taken in July 1987, this shot links the ubiquitous RS500 press car, E501 NWN, with race driver Dr Jonathan Palmer, and the Camel-liveried Bell Jet Ranger helicopter. The location is Ford Motorsport's Boreham airfield.

Although Ford had not then made any announcements, by mid-July the sporting world seemed to know all about the imminent launch of the RS500 Cosworth. This duly followed on 22 July; within six weeks Ford was also able to announce that every car had been sold. All this, mind you, was at a retail price of £19,950 – which was exactly £4,000 more than the Sierra RS Cosworth had cost in 1986. Cynics priced this at £4,000 for 20bhp (£200 per horsepower), but the clientele didn't seem to mind at all.

One very active RS dealer boss told me recently:

> We recall negotiating an allocation of forty of the regular Cosworth three-door hatchbacks. As far as the RS500 was concerned, we put up our hands for as many as Ford would sell us, and were awarded with six White, and three each of Moonstone and Black. They sold out very quickly – and the claim of a six-week timespan for 'sell-out' sounds reasonable. We advertised regularly in *Motoring News*, and sold them all over the country at full

retail price … I made sure that each of the RS500s we delivered had the correct Tickford paperwork, with the build number of each one.

Purely in terms of performance figures, was the RS500 worth it? The test figures published by my friends on *Autocar* magazine indicate that there were some obvious improvements, but these were not startling. Even so, how can anyone measure enjoyment, prestige and character by a few statistics?

According to *Autocar*, their RS500 (E203 APU) had a top speed of 154mph (248km/h), which was 9mph (14.4km/h) better than their Sierra RS Cosworth had achieved in 1986, but there was very little difference in acceleration figures between one car and the next (for a comparison see the accompanying table).

Apologists, no doubt, might suggest that the RS500 (tested in August 1987, only days after the new model had been revealed) must have had a 'tight' engine and could have been better with several extra thousand miles under its belt.

From most angles there was very little to distinguish the 5,000 Sierra RS Cosworths from the much more exclusive 500 RS500 Cosworths – but the true enthusiasts could always pick them out. From this angle, indeed, the different front spoiler, splitter, wing badges and 'Gurney' flap on the rear spoiler, all tell the story.

Comparing the acceleration of the RS Cosworth with the RS500 Cosworth		
	RS Cosworth	*RS500 Cosworth*
Acceleration (sec)		
0–60mph	6.2	6.1
0–80mph	10.4	10.5
0–100mph	16.1	16.2
0–120mph	24.0	24.6
Standing start–¼ mile (sec)	15.5	15.1
Top gear acceleration (sec)		
30–50mph	8.8	12.0
50–70mph	7.0	10.1
70–90mph	8.2	8.6
90–110mph	8.9	9.9

Did the Sierra RS500 Cosworth always drive along slightly nose-down? On the evidence of this static shot, it did – just, but not a lot. The under-door sills were definitely down at the front, but the low front spoiler/high rear spoiler arrangement somehow exaggerates that.

Maybe so, and maybe not. The fact is, though, that the original RS Cosworth was faster in every single 'top gear' acceleration measurement, which seems to confirm that a slight gain in peak torque, at higher revs, had been made at the expense of lower

RS500s – real or fake?

Amazing, isn't it? No sooner had the Sierra RS500 Cosworth gone on sale, and sold out, than the first fakes began to appear. While it was easy enough for the low-life to produce the extra front and rear spoiler mouldings, although not necessarily to the same standard of precision, they could not replicate the different engine and suspension pieces described in the main text.

For today's buyers the important caveat is that they should never believe any of the claims that have been made for 'fake' RS500s:

• 'This is one of the very rare left-hand-drive cars.' Every RS500 had right-hand-drive.

• 'Oh yes, this one was very special: it was not built up at Tickford.' Except for the four development prototypes, all the production road cars were built at Tickford, although many competition cars took shape in specialized workshops: these were either converted Sierra RS Cosworths, or built up around a new body shell.

• 'This one was originally painted red [blue. or whatever] to special order.' All RS500 production cars were painted Black, White or Moonstone.

• 'This one had the smaller turbo to special order'. All RS500s were produced with YBD engines and the larger TO4 turbocharger.

• 'This one was built up in 1988 [or 1989] to special order.' Once the 500th car was completed at the end of July 1987, the RS500 programme was immediately wound down. No further RS500 road cars were ever produced.

and, most importantly, unless a Sierra has a VIN number in the span of GG38600 to GG39099 inclusive (which, please note, totals exactly 500 cars) then it is not, and could never have been, a Sierra RS500 Cosworth.

---

speed torque. Maybe it wasn't significant (for no sensitive Sierra Cosworth driver would accelerate hard from 30mph in fifth gear!), but by comparison the RS500 was definitely more sluggish from 30–50mph and from 50–70mph.

No matter. If the customer was ready to 'drive around' the latest engine's torque characteristics – he had to try to match the road speed to a chosen gear so that the rev-counter showed at least 3,500rpm – this was still a phenomenally fast road car, and its potential for race track (or, in later years, track-day) usage was quite awesome.

Well before the Sierra RS Cosworth was homologated, Andy Rouse Engineering had built its very first test car which, at that time, showed support from Ford's Motorcraft division.

Standing room only! This was the confined 'completed car' RS500 compound at Bedworth in July 1987, when RS500 assembly was at its height. When FISA inspectors visited the site and doubted whether as many RS500s existed as were claimed, Ford merely took them out to the cheek-by-jowl car park to prove their point!

Unhappily for many first owners, Britain's low-life soon found that the RS500 Cosworth was just as easy to steal as the RS Cosworth had already proved to be. Racing drivers Steve Soper and Jonathan Palmer, for example, both of whom had RS500 Cosworths as their road cars, left their cars parked outside and woke up the following morning to find that they had disappeared, never to be seen again.

Even so, for those who could guarantee to keep theirs intact (not a joke this, for a very significant proportion were stolen in the first year of the model's existence – where do you think some of the amazing but hard-to-find major components on eBay come from?), the RS500 proved to be an enduring delight as a classic car. Not an investment, for sure – values soared in the first two years or so, but once the bubble burst at the end of the 1980s they returned to more reasonable levels – but an enduring delight that still causes jaws to drop when a carefully restored example is seen at a classic car event.

Would I have one today? Damn'd right I would …

5   Sierra 'Sapphire' Cosworth – Ford's BMW-beater

It was Ford's Walter Hayes who gave me the best possible reason for the four-door 'Sapphire' Cosworth being put on sale in 1988:

> We wanted a car that would sit at traffic lights and look like any other car, except that other drivers would know that it wasn't. You didn't often see BMWs tarted up in strange ways, and the evidence was there to suggest that we were ready to take a share of that BMW market.
>
> When we were doing the original [whale tail] car, we always used to say that when the Sapphire came along we should also do it on that basis.

By that time, in other words, Ford's marketing gurus had concluded that potential customers had widely different views of the three-door car. One faction thought that the extrovert looks exactly matched the performance of the car itself, but the other faction made it clear that the looks actually put them off.

At the end of 1986, when production of original-generation Sierras came to an end at Genk, the three-door derivative (from which the Sierra RS Cosworth had been developed) was dropped. Henceforth Sierras would only

The second-generation Sierra RS Cosworth, which everyone now calls the 'Sapphire' Cosworth, was previewed in March 1987. Ford stressed its motor sport connection by posing the new car alongside the latest Ford-Cosworth (turbo) Benetton F1 car.

Three important Cosworth (and Ford) personalities of the late 1980s – left to right, Keith Duckworth, Mike Costin and Jackie Stewart – at the opening of Cosworth's new 'Costin House', where many Ford road car engines were engineered.

be produced as four-door saloons, five-door hatchbacks or five-door estate cars.

The arrival of a 'three-box', four-door saloon type with a conventional boot was a real novelty, the need for which had been flagged up by marketing staff in the early 1980s. By that time, of course, Ford-of-Europe was concentrating on the hatchback theme – hatchback Fiestas, Escorts, Sierras and Granada/Scorpios – but many influential fleet managers continued to ask for conventional saloons. Ford, for whom fleet business was always very important, listened, acted and began to reverse the trend. Even so, it was more than four years after the launch of the original Sierra until its four-door 'Sapphire' derivative came along.

Not only did the new four-door saloon types (badged 'Sapphire' in the UK, but by no means everywhere else in the world) have a revised rear-end body style, or structure, but the front of the car also had more fluid contours and a rounded headlamp profile. Unseen changes, to stiffen up the structure, included the use of reinforced chassis side rails and seat-support cross-members, with a fixed steel diaphragm behind the rear seat squab, while the windscreen glass was larger and the screen surround altered to suit. This, therefore, was the 'Mk 1½' Sierra body shell, which would continue until 1992, when the front-wheel-drive Mondeo would take over.

There was no chance, therefore, of producing any more 'whale tail'-derived cars, even if the demand was present, since the basic three-door body shell no longer existed and there seemed to be no 'business case' for reviving it. Bold (or, shall I say, wishful) suggestions from Motorsport, or from SVE, that Karmann could carry on building 'whale tails' alongside the Merkur XR4Ti, perhaps with the new front-end style grafted on to the old-type three-door shell, were briskly rejected. Motorsport, the marketing staffs decided, had indulged themselves in 1986. Accordingly, when the much changed/facelifted Sierra was revealed in February 1987, there was no immediate sign of a YB-engined version.

As confirmed by Walter Hayes, however, the first plans had already been laid to produce a second-generation Sierra RS Cosworth based on the new car, this time with a four-door saloon shell, but in the event it was not ready to go on sale until the first days of 1988. For Cosworth, which had a confirmed contract to build at least 15,000 engines, this was something of a relief, since by the end of 1986 they

had built fewer than 6,000 units in all: except for the period when 500 RS500-type YBDs were manufactured in the spring of 1987, the Wellingborough plant continued to churn out YBBs at the rate of up to 150 units every week. Because Cosworth had only limited facilities for long-term storage, these engines (still 'red-topped', of course) were delivered to Genk, where they waited for production of the new-shape car to get going.

As it happens, and because far more 'Sapphire' Cosworths were produced than the original three-door, Cosworth produced a grand total of 18,990 YBB types, before changing over to YBG/YBH Types for the Sierra Cosworth 4 × 4 variety (*see* Chapter 6). More than 5,000 had already been built in 1985 and 1986 for use in three-door cars (and for supply to other industrial customers), so the success of the 'Sapphire' Cosworth is obvious.

As ever, nothing happened at Ford as quickly as some enthusiasts would have liked. First thoughts on a revised type of Sierra RS Cos-

The very first Sapphire Cosworth prototype was photographed with these mocked-up bonnet louvres in place. According to SVE engineers, later testing showed that they were not necessary.

worth (the 'executive model' that Walter Hayes and his senior colleagues yearned for so much) had been discussed as early as 1984 – even before the first three-door cars had gone into production – but SVE could not find the time to get their teeth into any real development until they had finally 'signed off' the three-door cars in spring 1986. From mid-1986, however, it was all-systems-go on a new type that promised to be equally as fast as the three-door had ever been, but which it was hoped would be a 'softer', more gracious and more refined car then before.

Between them, SVE and Cosworth developed a host of minor improvements, which made the new car more civilized and driver-friendly than the original car had been. First of all, it was necessary to finalize the style. Because Motorsport and its customers showed no interest in using this model in world-class racing or rallying, there was no question of providing extrovert aerodynamic aids to provide truly positive downforce. At the front end, there was yet another new type of bumper moulding, still deep, still contoured to channel lots of fresh air into the engine bay, but subtly different in shape from that of both the other less specialized 'Sapphires' and the three-door variety. Headlamp wiper/washer mechanisms (as used in other top-of-the-range Fords of the period) were standard, as was a new style of cast alloy wheel, still with 7.0in rims and 205.50-VR 15in Dunlop tyres.

The aerodynamic novelty was at the tail, where there was no sign of a 'whale tail' but

instead there was a small and rather inconspicuous flat spoiler, bolted on the tail of the new boot lid. Was it effective? Only marginally, experts tell me, but at least it certainly made a discreet marketing point. Although bonnet cooling louvres were tried out at an early prototype stage, these were not used on production cars: they would eventually reappear in 1990 when the four-wheel-drive derivative took over.

At first glance, maybe, there was no change to the suspension, but in fact quite a lot of work went into the front-end geometry. The fundamental change was to lower the roll centre and the steering 'knuckle' of the original car: in fact the geometry of the new type was very close to that of other non-Cosworth-engined 'Sapphires'. At the same time, front and rear springs were all stiffened up, as was the rear anti-roll bar, although all the damper settings were softened up significantly. This was to be a much more driver-friendly – even gentlemanly – machine than its ancestor.

Although automotive drag coefficients should always be read in conjunction with the total frontal area of a car, a comparison between the first three Sierra RS Cosworth types, seen in the table bottom left, is interesting. This shows that the deletion of extrovert aero-aids made very little difference to the drag coefficient, though of course the 'Sapphire' did not develop anything like as much downforce as speeds rose.

Except that all the engines had the updated features that had been rushed through in 1986 to make the original YBB more reliable (*see* Chapter 3), the 'Sapphire' engine was much the same as before and was still rated at 204bhp, although Cosworth apparently found that power-tested engines often recorded up to 210bhp and more. Later engines had revised pistons and a revised turbo damper. The 500 'standard' YBB engines craned out of the RS Cosworths, when they were converted into RS500 Cosworths in mid-1987, were all returned to Cosworth to be freshened up, modified as

Comparing Drag Coefficients	
Model	*Drag Coefficient (Cd)*
RS Cosworth (3-door)	0.336
RS500 Cosworth (3-door)	0.351
'Sapphire' Cosworth (4-door)	0.33

appropriate and resupplied for use in 'Sapphire' models. As their average mileage was absolutely nominal in almost every case, this was an eminently practical strategy.

The very first prototype, still without the rear spoiler, which had yet to be finalized both in the German wind tunnel and with Design, ran in August 1986 and others soon followed. By summer 1987 there would be eight prototypes, others were committed to crash testing, and before the end of the year a run of no fewer than 70 pilot–built/production–specification machines were produced at Genk.

In some ways Ford found it easier to finalize the specification of the 'Sapphire' RS Cosworth than the original type, as Motorsport made it clear that they had no use for it and therefore had no special demands to make concerning the mechanical layout. For motor sport purposes, Stuart Turner and his colleagues made clear, they would stick with the three-door cars for all types of racing and rallying, although when the already forecast

One year before the Sapphire Cosworth went on sale, the first prototype, complete with bonnet louvres, was up and running. With four passenger doors, and only a small and very discreet rear spoiler, the new car's image was bound to differ from that of the original three-door model.

**Sierra 'Sapphire' RS Cosworth
(1988 and 1989)**

The specification was as for the original Sierra RS Cosworth 3-door, except:

Layout
Unit construction steel body/chassis structure. Four-door saloon, with front engine/rear-wheel drive.

Dimensions (in/mm)
Overall length	176.9/4,490
Overall width	66.8/1,700
Unladen weight	2,660lb/1,206kg

UK retail price
(at launch in 1988)   £19,000

four-wheel-drive version followed in 1990 they would certainly be interested in that!

Marketing could therefore concentrate on idealizing the four-door car as a BMW-beater and as something able to fight head-to-head with the Cosworth-engined Mercedes-Benz 160E 2.3 16.

Because Ford did not want customers to think they were abandoning the Sierra RS Cosworth concept, the forthcoming 'Sapphire' model was officially previewed, at a very early stage, in March 1987. Photographed alongside the latest turbocharged (by Ford-Cosworth) Benetton F1 car, this merely emphasised that the same chassis would be back 'towards the end of 1987'. Significantly, the new car was photographed from three-quarter-rear, which meant that the front end/grille/bumper moulding was not shown – just in case SVE got their way in enlarging the air inlets to the engine bay, and the brakes!

This cutaway drawing of the four-door model should be compared with that of the original (see page 47). Mechanically there had been very few changes, only details, although of course the body shell itself was much altered.

For this more 'executive' model, very little needed to be done to update the engine of the original three-door 'whale tail' model. This was probably just as well, since after December 1986 (when Cosworth's Wellingborough plant had delivered its 5,000th three-door engine) it then carried on producing engines ahead of the next model's launch.

Four-door Cosworth on Sale

Ford finally put the new 'Sapphire' RS Cosworth on the market in January 1988, immediately making it clear that there would be no abrupt cut-off in supply – either by time, or in numbers. Production, they emphasised, could be up to 7,000 cars a year, the limit being defined by the number of engines that Cosworth could supply. A few over-enthusiastic hotheads had said that many more such cars could be sold if they could be made, but cool Marketing advice prevailed. Demand, in fact, exceeded supply only for the first few months, after which sales settled down so that in two years around 14,000 such cars would be produced. In January 1988, at launch time, the new car retailed at £19,000. This was £3,000

All glossed up for this studio shot, the 'Sapphire' Cosworth, which went on sale early in 1988, was destined to sell in larger numbers than the three-door type.

more than the three-door 'whale tail' car's price, yet still significantly less than the £19,950 asked for an RS500 Cosworth, all stocks of which had, naturally, sold out.

Although SVE had worked on improving the refinement of the new car, rather than its road-holding and performance, this was still a very specialized machine. Some Cosworth characters now refer to the YBB as a 'surpris-ingly unsophisticated' power unit, but its 204bhp power output was still enough to make other manufacturers jealous – and redouble their efforts to match it in the future.

Behind the engine, the same sturdy five-speed Borg-Warner gearbox was used, along with the same sub-frame mounted differential, in which there was a viscous coupling limited-slip differential with a very 'soft' setting.

Although the 'Sapphire' Cosworth of 1988 was just as fast as the original three-door type had been, its character, that of a 'businessman's express', was entirely different.

When the 500,000th SVE-engineered Ford was produced in 1988, Ford set up this special photo opportunity on the test track at Dunton. The brand-new 'Sapphire' Cosworth is in the lead, followed by the Escort RS Turbo (left) and Escort Cabriolet (right), and with a menacing-looking RS500 Cosworth bringing up the tail.

Inside the cabin, the trim was a combination of Ghia-standard fixtures and fittings, with appropriate high-performance seats (from Recaro – the driver's side being height-adjustable), along with leather-rimmed steering wheel and gear lever knob. This, by the way, was the point at which Ford discarded the boost gauge that had always been present on three-door cars, reasoning that the quadrant gauge at the top-left of the instrument display was small enough, insignificant enough, and just not informative enough.

In the same week that the car was launched, Ford was highly embarrassed by sneak pictures showing that yet another future derivative of the Cosworth-engined range was already under development – the four-wheel-drive version of the car! All that, however, was still two years away, and Ford chose to ignore the scoop. *Autocar*, however, balanced their scoop with these wise words in an editorial:

> A 150mph four-door saloon in regular production, as much a part of Ford's range as an Escort Ghia, the new Cosworth has to be regarded as something of a milestone for Ford. There aren't many giants of the car world which can boast such a flagship …

A few weeks later, when their testers had tried out the new cars, *Autocar* added:

> A family Ford that's just two tenths slower than a Porsche 911 in the sprint to 60mph is the centre-piece of this week's issue. Whether this level of performance tells us that the Ford – of course, the Sierra RS Cosworth – is exceptionally fast, or that the Porsche these days is disappointingly slow, is open to debate.

Above *Experts, and all Ford enthusiasts, could pick out a 'Sapphire' Cosworth from other Sierras by the deep front spoiler and by the unique cast alloys …*

Below *… while at the rear the boot lid badges and the rubber-lipped rear spoiler gave the game away.*

The 'Sapphire' sold particularly well in Germany, where it proved to be a great Mercedes-Benz and BMW-eater – but, please note, there was no 'RS' badge for that market.

Britain's most authoritative magazine, in fact, had tried out a four-door Cosworth (E 489 CHK, one of the press fleet) against its obvious rivals, a BMW M3 (200bhp/2.3 litres) and a Mercedes-Benz 230E-16 (185bhp/2.3 litres). They concluded that the cars felt, indeed were, surprisingly different. Having established the Cosworth's top speed at 142mph (228 km/h), with 0–60mph in just 5.8 seconds, the testers made the following comments:

By ditching the original Sierra RS Cosworth's jumbo jet rear wing for its newest and possibly greatest RS, Ford has struck a blow against the boy racer it will surely never regret. Where that wing was all about racing, raw performance and track ride and handling, the new model's discreet spoiler tells a different story – one that sums up Ford's fastest-ever production car. With its sober three-box body, subtle body add-ons and quietly pur-

poseful air, the Sierra RS Cosworth gains a respectability that sees it in the forefront of high-performance saloons. Its hairy-chested one-off image has been discarded along with that giant rear wing …

The Ford's engine is neither mechanically quiet nor vibration-free, but let there be no doubt that it is the master of this group. There's more power throughout the range, spoiled neither by turbo lag or lack of low-down response, and it is willing and able, time after time, to record acceleration times that embarrass its German rivals.

The team, however, wasn't totally impressed by its high-speed, race-track handling:

These grouses aside, the car is marvellous. It has things that BMW and Mercedes seem to have forgotten about: decently quick steering, a firm and positive gear shift, a firm and reassuring brake

German-registered 'Sapphire' Cosworths could often be seen swishing along unlimited German autobahns at 120mph (193km/h) and more – it was an ideal car for those conditions. With air-conditioning and full four-seater comfort, it was a great car to own.

pedal and tyres – ultra-low profile, remember – that offer grip the other two cars can only approximate. Add the best driving position and most grippy seats of the trio, plus all that fast-acting turbo power, and you have the recipe for the performance and ability that make the Cosworth a real driver's car …

The Sierra RS Cosworth is the best car of the group. With the best performance, driving position, seats, brakes, ergonomics, steering and grip, plus sportily failsafe handling and the least road noise of the bunch, it could not be any other way. Plus it seats four adults in a way the others cannot

and costs upwards of £4,000 less. The best sports saloon in the business is British.

Once on the market in 1988 the 'Sapphire' settled down, not only as the flagship of the revised Sierra range, but as one of the most pricey of all new Fords of that period. Apart from the Cosworth, the most expensive Sierra saloon was the 2.0-litre Ghia model at £11,729, while the only rear-drive Scorpio retailing for more was the 2.9i Ghia at £19,918 (automatic transmission being standard).

It was no wonder, therefore, that sales of the 'Sapphire' RS Cosworth were limited by price rather than by engine availability. Helped along by the large quantity of YBB engines already in stock by the end of 1987, Ford churned out an impressive number of cars in 1988. At times 800 cars were being completed

Posed for the occasion, we hope, for this was a factory-registered car sitting on the side of the A12 near Ford's HQ. The Sapphire police car gave the Boys-in-Blue enough performance to deal with all but the most determined speeders. Love the registration number – 999. Geddit?

every month, and early in its career no fewer than 400 cars were sold in a single month in the UK.

Even so, the new car took on at the same time the unwanted title of Britain's 'most often stolen' model (it was some time yet before Ford would have an effective immobilizer/alarm system for their cars), which made potential customers think twice before taking delivery. Over in Europe, Ford managers in countries such as Germany and Italy, where the car sold particularly well, could not understand this phenomenon, since theft was much less prevalent there.

Interior details of the 'Sapphire' Cosworth of 1988 and 1989, showing the plushy but very supportive Recaro front seats, and the very well-equipped facia/instrument board. This was years before the arrival of air bags, of course.

Above *The 'Sapphire' aerodynamic kit – big front spoiler and flat rear spoiler – was not as extrovert as that of the three-door car, but still effective at high speeds.*

Below *The 'Sapphire' Cosworth from a different angle, up in the mountains, but where?*

In 1988 and 1989, when the 'Sapphire' Cosworth was on sale, Mike Costin (left) was Cosworth's chairman and Richard Bulman the managing director.

Although demand was strong, by the end of the first year all waiting lists had disappeared, and there was usually at least one unsold car in the showroom of every RS dealer in the UK or major sporting Ford dealer in Europe.

In the event, the 'Sapphire' was on sale for just two years, as it was to be supplanted by the four-wheel-drive derivative from early 1990. Few changes were made in that period – minor technical updates, but no style changes of any type – although the price gradually crept up along with other Ford prices of the day. By the end of 1989 the UK price of a 'Sap-

phire' stood at £21,300, which was still an astonishingly small amount for such performance, but expensive when compared with other Sierras, indeed all other Fords, in the existing range.

Was this rather an anonymous Supercar? Indeed it was, visually: many an owner tempted to push along at highly illegal road speeds gave thanks for its relative 'invisibility' in traffic. On the other hand some sales were lost because the 'Sapphire' lacked what one might call 'bragging rights' in the golf club or country club car park.

None the less, within two years about 14,000 such cars were sold all round Europe and its replacement, with a very capable four-wheel-drive chassis, was already on the way.

6 Sierra Cosworth 4 × 4 – Performance with Poise

Fascinating, isn't it? The best of all the Cosworth-engined Sierras was not even considered when the first of that line was being designed in 1983, and if Boreham had not desperately needed a fast four-wheel-drive car in which to go rallying, it might never have seen the light of day.

Sierra Cosworth 4 × 4s never took on the reputation that they deserved, and far too many people now see them as interim cars bridging the gap between the Sierra 'Sapphire' Cosworth and the Escort RS Cosworth. The fact that their first sales year was headlined by a spate of low-life thefts at home, and by poor 'works' rally performances out in World events, didn't help.

Although the record shows that the Sierra Cosworth 4 × 4 was officially revealed in February 1990 and that the first 5,000 cars were hustled through the Genk factory before the end of July so that motor sport homologation followed on 1 August 1990, Ford's own knowledge of four-wheel-drive cars stretched back a long way. Although concept engineering of the Sierra Cosworth 4 × 4 began in 1987, and real development began as soon as the rear-drive 'Sapphire' Cosworth had been signed off, other Ford four-wheel-drive cars had been produced as early as the 1960s.

The key to what happened, and when, was Harry Ferguson Research of Coventry. Buoyed up by the millions he had made from

Final flowering. Four years after the original Sierra RS Cosworth went into production, Ford put the four-door/four-wheel-drive Sierra Cosworth 4 × 4 on sale. This was much the most capable of the Sierra-based cars ever sold.

Sierra XR4 × 4 – Ford's first four-wheel-drive car

In the beginning, in 1982 Ford's Bob Lutz asked SVE to build a special Sierra 4 × 4 as a 'show-time special', to add a bit of glamour to the launch of the Sierra. Given six months to do that job in conjunction with HFR, Rod Mansfield's engineers were almost ready to show off the result, a five-door Ghia-trimmed Sierra with 2.3-litre V6 engine up front, when the Product Planners stepped in.

'Hold it', the edict came down. 'We don't want a one-off. We want a production car instead.' Given two years to do the job, Mansfield set Ray Diggins and a small team to do just that. Working around the more specialized XR4i chassis (but not the style), complete with fuel-injected 2.8-litre V6 engine, but with four-wheel disc brakes, the result was the XR4 × 4, which was introduced in March 1985.

Available in three-door (some markets), five-door and eventually in estate car styles, this chassis settled the formula that would serve Ford well when it came to develop the Cosworth-engined derivatives. Some, but by no means all, of the elements of the original Sierra four-wheel-drive system would be used in later years – and the last Escort RS Cosworth drive line certainly looked familiar in some ways – but a great deal of development would follow.

Although the original type of Borg-Warner Hy-Vo chain drive would always be used as a 'step off' for the transfer gearbox, the XR4 × 4's main gearbox (the T9) could not cope with the power of more powerful engines and would have to be changed, while the front differential (that which was mounted alongside the sump of the engine) would always be a worry.

Even so, XR4 × 4s, continually uprated and eventually fitted with the all-new MT75 gearbox, were in production until the early 1990s, sold steadily and made a definite profit for the company. Not only was the XR4 × 4 Ford's first four-wheel-drive car, but it was also the one that sold best of all. By the 1990s 4 × 4 transmission for Ford's 'mainstream' models was no longer a priority: although a few Escort RS2000 4 × 4s and Mondeo 4 × 4s were produced, by the end of the century the layout had gone back into the spares and heritage cupboard.

---

agricultural tractors, the Irish-born tycoon Harry Ferguson concluded that private cars needed to have four-wheel-drive systems, and set up a new business – Harry Ferguson Research – in Coventry to develop that technology.

Early systems were eventually seen, in public, in the P99 single-seater racing car of 1961, and eventually in the Jensen FF limited-production car of 1966. It was about this time that Ford-UK became involved when technical chief Harley Copp, who also colluded with Walter Hayes in getting Ford into Grand Prix racing in 1965, encouraged Harry Ferguson Research to convert a Mustang 'just for fun'.

Four-wheel-drive Zodiacs and four-wheel-drive Capris soon followed, and the Advanced Vehicle Operation (AVO) was much involved in refining the system. None of these cars, however, made it into quantity production. Police and emergency services were apparently interested until they saw the cost of the installation. While Boreham's 'works' Capri 4 × 4s made plenty of headlines, AVO could never quite work out how to keep a complex system simple enough that they could be made, in numbers, at attractive prices.

Nor were they behind the times, for in this period the only four-wheel-drive 'cars' on sale in Europe had a dual agricultural purpose. The only up-market, relatively high-performance 4 × 4 on the UK market, for example, was the lofty Range Rover.

Enter the Quattro

In 1980 the arrival of the four-wheel-drive Audi Quattro changed everything. Starting from scratch, and grafting its own interpretation of four-wheel-drive under the front-drive Quattro Coupe, not only did the German company prove that it could produce a refined, commercially attractive, four-wheel-drive road car, but that it could then be developed into an outright rally winner. Within three years, and after Audi had made it clear that they intended to add four-wheel-drive to other cars in their range, other manufacturers were ready to follow suit.

In 1982 Ford's SVE team was invited to build a four-wheel-drive Sierra 'concept' car, and chose to adapt the latest iteration of the Harry Ferguson system (now known as the FF – Ferguson Formula – system) to do that job. Behind closed doors everything was looking good, and within months there was a change of management heart that turned 'concept' into 'serious project'. As a result SVE carried out a rapid development programme. The launch of the Sierra XR4 × 4 production car, originally a hatchback (some three-door, the big majority five-door), although a Ghia-specified estate car would be added later, came in 1985.

Hampered by an old and asthmatic 'Cologne' V6 engine, and able to use only a conversion of the existing T9 five-speed main gearbox, the XR4 × 4 was never likely to become a supercar. On the other hand, SVE proved that it could engineer an extremely capable and well-balanced machine that thousands of enthusiasts (including the author) drove with great relish. Within months, those with more money, and the need for an even larger car, could also buy the sleek new Granada/Scorpio 4 × 4, which used the same V6/5-speed/FF running gear in a large monocoque.

Although the XR4 × 4 was selling very fast in 1986, Ford still had no concrete plans to produce a four-wheel-drive version of its Sierra RS Cosworth. Because this would need a new main gearbox (or a heavily re-engineered Borg Warner T5 installation), and changes to the bottom end of the existing YB engine to accommodate the drive shafts to the front wheels, even the most enthusiastic engineers shrugged their shoulders and mentally filed the idea under 'Good Idea, Too Complicated, Not Yet …'.

Group B Tragedies

In 1986, though, a series of tragic rallying accidents changed everything. First, Joaquím Santos's Group B RS200 left the road in the Rally of Portugal, killing three spectators, then in May Henri Toivonen's Group B Lancia Delta S4 crashed on the French Tour de Corse, killing the driver and his co-driver Sergio Cresto. Within weeks the world motor sport authority, FISA, had announced the cancella-

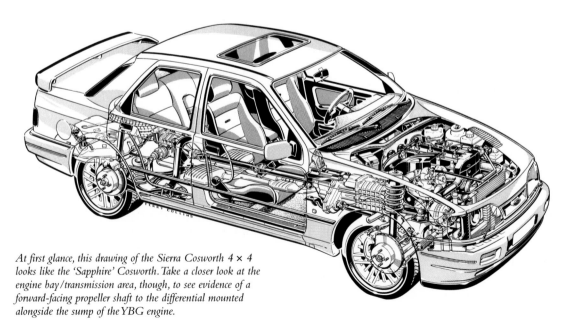

At first glance, this drawing of the Sierra Cosworth 4 × 4 looks like the 'Sapphire' Cosworth. Take a closer look at the engine bay/transmission area, though, to see evidence of a forward-facing propeller shaft to the differential mounted alongside the sump of the YBG engine.

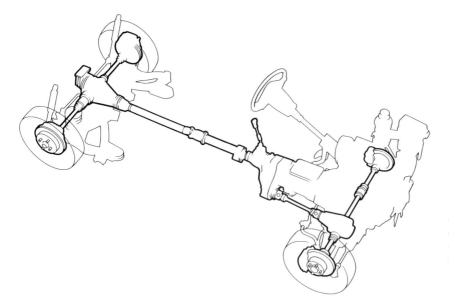

This schematic drawing shows how the four-wheel-drive versions of all Sierra and Granada/Scorpio models (and, later, of the Escort RS Cosworth) were laid out. The key was the use of a transfer gearbox behind the main gearbox, and a front propeller shaft running alongside the sump of the engine, with a cross-shaft running through the sump of the engine to feed drive to the left-side front wheel.

tion of Group B, laying down an edict that from 1987 top-class rallying would be for Group A cars.

As described in detail in the next chapter, this immediately threw Ford's rallying strategy into turmoil, for they would no longer be able to user the specialized RS200s. In the short term, a choice would have to be made between Sierra XR4 × 4s (for loose surface rallies where good traction was essential) and Sierra RS Cosworths (for tarmac events, where there was plenty of grip for rear-drive-only machines).

From that moment, it seems, Motorsport started nagging away for a new model, one that would combine the best features of both models with a further-developed YB engine mated to a full-time four-wheel-drive transmission system. As already described in the previous chapter, this marriage would have to be located under a four-door saloon, or five-door hatchback version of the face-lifted Sierra body shell – and at least 5,000 such machines would be needed to secure sporting homologation.

Although Ford management could see Motorsport's dilemma, the development of a four-wheel-drive Cosworth YB-engined car could not be pushed through in a great hurry. Recent experience had proved this, for the 'whale tail' Cosworth had taken nearly three years to progress from 'good idea' to 'showroom' status. In any case, although it was easy enough to sketch out a 'wouldn't it be a good idea' brief for such a car, there was one very important problem: a new main gearbox would be needed.

The basic layout of Ford's four-wheel-drive installation, then still a novel design, is made clear by accompanying drawing. Mounted in its conventional position, up front, the engine drove through the main gearbox to a transfer casing behind it, which included a centre differential. This transfer casing also included a sophisticated 'HyVo' chain, which drove a cog, offset several inches to the right side of the car. From that cog, an open propeller shaft led forwards towards the front differential, which was bolted directly to the cast alloy engine sump pan. After threading an intermediate cross shaft through that sump (but below the level of the crankshaft), there were exposed drive shafts to the front wheels.

Rear-wheel drive was provided by a rear

propeller shaft from the transfer casing to the rear differential, and in Ford's case there were viscous coupling limited-slip differentials in the centre and rear differentials; the set-up led 34 per cent of torque to the front wheels, 66 per cent to the rears. Maybe this all sounds complicated, but a visual study of the layout makes everything seem more logical.

Existing Ford systems, though, used the T9 transmission, so until and unless action wes taken to replace it nothing could be done about a Cosworth derivative. Help, however, was already at hand, for by the mid-1980s Ford had a major development programme underway to provide a new corporate gearbox. What emerged was not one, but a family of five-speed manual transmissions, coded MT75 (Manual Transmission, 75mm between main

and lay shafts), which were eventually manufactured in the UK and Germany.

Designed to be practical for all longitudinally positioned/front-engine/rear and four-wheel-drive Fords (current and future models including Transit commercial vehicles), it had a ribbed aluminium casing, was five inches (127mm) shorter than the T9, 16lb (7.25kg) lighter, and had synchromesh on all forward gears and reverse. (Later, in the 1990s, an MTX 75 derivative suitable for use in transverse-engined cars, such as the Mondeo, would also be announced and derivatives continued to appear until the 2000s opened. It was not until an even heavier-duty six-speeder was launched in the early 2000s that it was supplanted.)

As early as 1987, and even before it was offi-

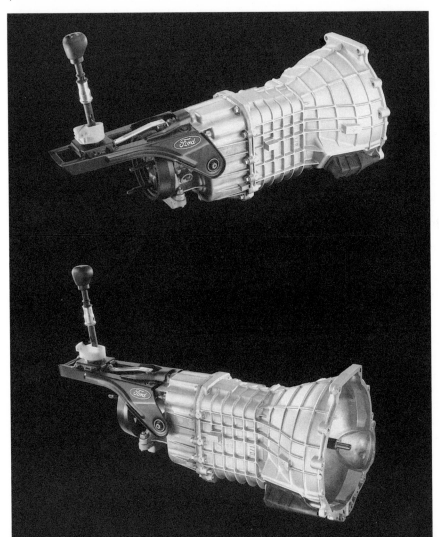

Ford's all-new MT75 gearbox was a vital new 'building block' for the late 1980s and beyond, for it was much more robust than the old Sierra-type transmission that it replaced. This particular study is of a rear-wheel-drive assembly, but in modified form it also formed part of the complex 4 × 4 transmission of Sierra Cosworth 4 × 4 and Escort RS Cosworth models.

cially launched, Ford Motorsport began using the MT75 in its 'works' XR4 × 4 rally cars. Rod Mansfield had no doubt as to its worth:

> MT75 was an essential part of the Cosworth 4 × 4 programme. Borg-Warner actually did a conversion for us [of the T5] to show how they could do it, but that was never considered. MT75 saves an awful lot of money.

With the rear-drive 'Sapphire' RS Cosworth committed to production at Genk, development work on the new four-wheel-drive car could start in earnest. Coincidentally, ace Motorsport planner/project manager Mike Moreton extricated himself from the demanding Sierra RS500 Cosworth project at about the same time and was let loose on the four-

When Ford updated the 'Sapphire' Cosworth saloon into a four-wheel-drive car, the only style change was to fit discreet 4 × 4 badges on the front wings, just ahead of the A-Pillar.

wheel-drive concept, enabling him to start expertly nagging for features that would make a 'works'-prepared car even more suitable for International rallying.

(It is worth recalling that Ford's Motorsport Centre at Boreham was still wedded to the idea of cars developing positive downforce at high speed, and had always wanted to retain the three-door hatchback complete with its huge aerofoil. This request was turned down flat – even though management at Karmann, where related XR4Tis were being built, had said they were willing to take on the job. As a result the only four-wheel-drive three-door type ever built was D373 TAR, which underwent extensive testing at Boreham in 1989.)

Before long, therefore, the new Cosworth 4 × 4 model began to take shape around the existing four-door body shell, with near-identical aerodynamic features. Although SVE (and Ford Motorsport) were allowed to look at every aspect of the existing rear-drive car, there was no guarantee that proposed changes would be cost effective.

Cosworth 4 × 4 in Detail

Engine
For this application there were two much-modified YBs – YBJ being a 'red-headed' type

This rear view of the Sierra Cosworth 4 × 4 is nearly identical to that of the 'Sapphire' Cosworth it replaced, except for new-type tail lamps, and minor changes to the bumper moulding close to the number plate recess.

and YBG being a 'green' variety – of which series production began at Wellingborough in October 1989. Although these looked superficially like the YBB that they replaced, many changes, and any amount of work on reliability and durability, had quite transformed them. At launch time, in February 1990, Ford stated that 80 per cent of the engine parts were either new or significantly modified from before.

Not only did Ford provide a stronger cylinder block (really an RS500 block, but with normal-sized core plugs), but Cosworth provided a stiffened cylinder head, a much more compact exhaust manifold, a modified/slightly enlarged turbocharger, a larger capacity oil pump and changes to the inlet manifold. All this was matched by a heat shield atop the turbo itself, and by an enlarged air/air intercooler, which Ford claimed had 'greatly improved efficiency (78 per cent)'.

Because of the need to provide a mounting face for the front differential (this being fixed to the right side of the assembly), and to pro-

vide a tube through which the intermediate drive shaft could run, there was a brand new aluminium sump casting, too.

In the beginning YBJ 'red top' engines were fitted to cars destined for territories demanding compliance with what the industry knew as '15.04' emissions regulations, while YBG 'green top' engines, slightly different in many ways and able to run on lead-free fuel from the very beginning, went to countries requiring compliance with more stringent '83US' emissions standards, and for where catalytic converters were needed in the exhaust system.

Why green? Whimsy really, as Paul Fricker confirms:

> I had to identify the engine [YBG or YBJ], so we decided to keep the red cam cover for the 15.04 (J) types, and in development, so that people knew what the engines were, and didn't put the wrong fuel in them, we made the YBG cam covers green. There was a bit of mickey-taking going on – oh yes, a 'green' engine, so it had to have green cam covers …
>
> Incidentally, I was not about to spend another six months of my time negotiating the green colour with Ford Design. So when I saw the engineers, I said 'this is the green we've got, you like it, don't you?' They went downstairs to the styling people, told them this was the green that everyone had approved, so the styling people signed off on it.

Once re-engineered (as YBG and YBJ types), the production process settled down, for this had become an extremely reliable and durable engine. Over time the general refinement level was steadily improved, and there is no doubt that durability increased at the same time. Paul Fricker insists that there were never any serious problems thereafter.

Although the twin objectives for the Sierra Cosworth 4 × 4 engines – increasing durability and improving refinement – were both achieved, the modified turbocharger also delivered a small, but welcome, boost to the power rating, shown in the accompanying table (below).

The joy of this engine, though, could not be spelt out in peak figures, but in experiencing the sheer flow of consistent torque. Although there was still a noticeable 'hump' in torque at about 3,000rpm when turbocharger, camshaft and air flow all began to work together, Ford rightly claimed that 80 per cent of peak torque had already been achieved when the engine passed 2,300rpm, and it stayed above this level all the way to 6,500rpm.

Even so, this did not mean that there would be a major improvement in performance, for although peak power and torque were up by 7.8 per cent and 4.4 per cent, the vehicle itself was heavier (by 180lb/81.6kg, or 6.7 per cent).

The net result was that, although the traction was astonishingly improved, and the handling was now at a peak for a Ford passenger car, the straight-line performance was much the same as before.

Transmission

This was where the big changes could be seen. Behind the engine there was the brand-new

Comparing the power of the 'Sapphire' with the Sierra Cosworth 4 × 4		
Feature	*3-door/'Sapphire' RWD cars (YBB)*	*Sierra Cosworth 4 × 4 (YBG/YBJ)*
Peak power (bhp)/rpm	204/6,000	220/6,250
Peak torque (lb ft)/rpm	205/4,000	214/3,500

MT75 main gearbox, and behind that was the centre differential and the 'step-off' transfer gearbox.

The rear axle unit was now the 7.0in, rather than the 7.5in, corporate design (as the torque it had to deal with was so much less than on two-wheel-drive cars, Ford could save a significant amount of money in this manner), while at the front, bolted to the Cosworth-designed engine sump casting, was a 6.5in differential, which split the drive to the front wheels. Loosely set-up viscous coupling limited-slip differentials were included in the centre, and rear axle casings, the FF-engineered items being built in series production by Viscodrive, which was a joint GKN-ZF enterprise. The normal torque split was 34 per cent to the front and 66 per cent to the rear. So well-balanced was the car's handling that some engineers think that these VCs needed to be tweaked up a lot more before they would have any noticeable effect on the Cosworth 4 × 4's traction.

Suspension and chassis
SVE chassis guru John Bull (along with Peter Gregory) was tasked with finalizing the chassis of this new four-wheel-drive car, and he confirms that there was significant component commonization with the Sierra XR4 × 4, which by this time was also inheriting the new MT75 transmission and, of course, the latest 2.9-litre V6 engine.

Because this was a car that drove all four wheels, the front suspension had to absorb significantly more stress than before. This, and the sheer spatial challenge of routeing a cross-member around the sump, the front differential and the front-drive shafts, meant that this cross-member was in cast aluminium (on previous models it had been made of fabricated steel).

Other changes were in detail, for front and rear spring rates were as before (although both front and rear anti-roll bars were slightly beefed up), Bridgestone tyres replaced Dunlop D40s, and the rear brake discs were ventilated (they had been solid on previous Sierra Cosworth types): the 7in rim alloy wheels were as used on the 'Sapphire' model.

Body
Outwardly, at least, there appeared to be little change, especially to the aerodynamic specification, where the front-end spoiler and the rear boot-lid spoiler were carried over. The most obvious aerodynamic tweak, of course, was the reappearance of cooling louvres in the bonnet panel itself (these, you may recall, had been standard on three-door RS and RS500 types, but not fitted to 'Sapphire' production cars.). Even so, although the Cosworth 4 × 4 looked almost identical with the older 'Sapphire' model, there were many detail changes.

In the shell itself, inner wings had been beefed up and there were reinforced mounting points for the rear dampers. At the front of the shell, changes were made to the chassis rails to allow for the articulation of the front drive-shafts. Visually, and style-wise, there were 'black' rear tail lamp clusters, and 'white' front flashers, while there were discreet little 4 × 4 badges on the front wings, immediately ahead of the front doors.

Fixtures and fittings
Those who had known, and maybe owned, the 'Sapphire' model, which dropped out of production as soon as the four-wheel-drive car came along, would soon be familiar with the interior of the latest car, for little had been changed, but much had been enhanced in detail.

Central locking, a tilt-and-slide sunshine roof (not on competition cars, though), electric window lifts and mirror adjustment, high-quality radio/stereo equipment, Recaro-style front seats and that familiar three-spoke steering wheel were all present, but now there was an adjustable steering column, while leather upholstery and air conditioning were both options.

Air conditioning, in fact, did not become generally available until Cosworth had worked

---

Six-cylinder YB?

Early in the 1990s Rod Mansfield, who had moved up from Ford's SVE division to become Engineering Director of Ford's newly bought subsidiary, Aston Martin, approached Cosworth to discuss the new Aston Martin DP1999 project. This was the much-discussed 'smaller Aston Martin' that would make little progress before finally being displaced by the Jaguar XJS-based DB7 project.

At that time Mansfield was searching for a suitable engine, and one idea being discussed with Cosworth was whether they could, and should, produce a straight-

six version of the YBD/YBG – effectively a Sierra engine with two extra cylinders. Clearly this was likely to be a very limited-production engine, but Cosworth knew that it could cope with such numbers.

On the basis that they could make a turbocharged 3-litre 'six' produce at least 350bhp, which would be ample for the DP1999 to behave reliably and relatively smoothly, Cosworth drew up schemes and lashed up a mock-up by cutting and shutting YB blocks. That was as far as it went, however, and no further prototypes were ever manufactured.

---

yet another packaging miracle around the front of the YB engine, for an extra pump and its drive belt had to be incorporated, and various other engine 'add-ons' relocated. Not for nothing, therefore, did Cosworth have to allocate new Type designations – YBG (AIR) and YBJ (AIR) – to their famous engine.

Cosworth 4 × 4 on Sale

Especially for those of us who were in the know, the Sierra Cosworth 4 × 4 seemed to be a long time a-coming. Already under development in 1988, it was scooped in the motor sport press at that time and quite persistently forecast throughout 1989. Officially launched in February 1990, it went on sale across Europe from March 1990 and almost immediately began to sell faster than any previous YB-engined car.

That in itself was a miracle – admittedly a short-lived miracle – since years of inflation and a positively aggressive market pricing policy meant that it went on sale for no less than £24,995, with an extra £500 asked for the optional leather-seating package. At £25,495, therefore, a leather-equipped Cosworth 4 × 4 (my second example was so equipped) was an eye-watering 60 per cent more expensive than the original three-door 'whale tail' model had been.

Since the European sales trend graph was just about to turn downwards, it was indeed a

miracle that more than 5,000 cars were completed in advance of the 1 August 1990 sporting-homologation deadline. That figure, too, was quite genuinely achieved, for Cosworth's Wellingborough factory had been churning out the new-specification YBG/YBJ types since October 1989; they would actually deliver 7,570 during the calendar year 1990.

In the week the new car was launched, *Autocar & Motor's* John Barker swooned over its abilities:

If, at the end of that 25 mile ribbon of tarmac there had been a 16V Lancia Integrale, warmed up and ready to go, and the option of either car for the return run, I'd have taken the Sierra …

In the 220BHP Cosworth, the two-thirds rear torque is more fully exploited. 'On rails' isn't a description that springs to mind: it's far more entertaining than that.

The Cosworth remains confidently composed and allows its driver to modify the plan of attack just before or even during a corner. Approach a turn too fast, and a sharp tug of the wheel drifts the tail out. If the road tightens after the apex, throttle back, or even apply the brake. But if the

Opposite *In production from 1990 to 1992, the Sierra Cosworth 4 × 4 was one of the most sure-footed (and fastest) family cars that Ford had ever put on sale. Even after the Escort RS Cosworth took over, these cars still held their reputation in 'classic' circles.*

exit is clear, hit the throttle instead and emerge on a twist of opposite lock, without crossing the white line. That's how adjustable it is …

Understeer or oversteer never exceed a handful of steering lock and the turbo lag – still evident but not so pronounced – can be driven around. Only an Integrale could have covered the ground as quickly and been as economical with road space.

There was, however, a veiled bite in the summary:

> Some will see spending £25,000 on a Sierra with a raucous four-cylinder engine as an unsound proposition. But at the price there is no other car with the Cosworth's blend of brilliantly fluid and responsible handling, searing performance, and five-seat comfort. This Sierra isn't simply the most desirable Ford or most accomplished Cosworth, it's the best 4wd saloon car you can buy.

That price tag, however, was soon to become a millstone. By May 1990 it had already risen to £25,960 and it was the most expensive Ford in the lists. Compare that, for instance, with the Granada Scorpio 4 × 4 (£25,350), and with the next most expensive Sierra saloon, the £16,230 2000E. The obvious German competition (both rear-drive only) came from the BMW M3, £24,200 at the time, and the Mercedes-Benz 190E 2.5-16, which cost a whopping £32,940. To keep on moving the metal, Ford RS dealers knew they had a problem. Although they were struggling by the end of 1990, they kept on moving cars out of the door.

Not even an adulatory full road test or two could convince everyone. *Autocar & Motor*'s report, published on 11 April 1990, quoted a top speed of 144mph (232km/h), at least 6mph (9.6km/h) down on earlier forecasts, 0–60mph in 6.6 seconds, and a standing start ¼-mile figure of 14.3 seconds, which was really no advance at all on the three-door 'whale tail' car of four years earlier. Although they described it as 'the world's first housetrained

Sierra Cosworth', commented that the traction was 'awesome', and that the handling was simply astounding, they were also distinctly sniffy about the noise levels, the finish and the equipment levels.

The good news about that report, however, was that it ended with these remarks:

> in anything less than ideal conditions, the 4 × 4 Cosworth is the fastest saloon on sale, and an astoundingly accomplished ground-coverer by any standards. And if you have a family, yet still wish to enjoy Supercar-style performance in total security, there is nothing that can compete.

By 1991 Ford, without a doubt, was in a philosophical cleft stick. On the one hand it needed to charge such high prices because this was an expensive car to build, but on the other the demand for all its cars – not merely the Cosworth 4 × 4 – had gone into a decline. Price cuts, it concluded, were not part of its long-term marketing agenda, although the dealer chain resorted to making more and more trade-in concessions. One is reminded of yet another of Walter Hayes's famous aphorisms:

> Anyone who thinks you can have a 'loss leader' in the car business is quite securely out of his mind.

Once Motorsport had secured their sporting homologation on 1 August 1990, they perhaps did not worry too much about the Cosworth 4 × 4's looming marketing problem, but it came home to them in 1991 when they tried to induce private owners to run Group N rally cars.

Under the title 'Ten by N', in a special cut-price deal that the author was invited to administer, ten British private owners would be provided with a brand-new Cosworth 4 × 4 (without a sun roof) and a complete kit of Group N motor sport parts – several thousand pounds worth of springs, dampers, bushes, seats, safety belts, safety switches and related items – for the same price as a showroom car.

Sierra Cosworth 4 × 4 (1990–92)

Layout

Unit construction steel body/chassis structure. Four-door saloon, front engine/four-wheel drive.

Engine

Type	Ford-Cosworth YB Series
Block material	Cast iron
Head material	Cast aluminium
Cylinders	4 in-line
Cooling	Water
Bore and stroke	90.82 × 76.95mm
Capacity	1993cc
Main bearings	5
Valves	4 per cylinder, operated by twin overhead camshafts, via inverted bucket-type tappets, with the camshafts driven by cogged belt from the crankshaft.
Compression ratio	8.0:1 (nominal)
Fuel supply	Weber-Marelli fuel injection, with Garrett AiResearch TO3/TO4B turbocharger
Max. power	220bhp @ 6,250rpm
Max. torque	214lb ft @ 3,500rpm

Transmission

Five-speed manual gearbox, all-synchromesh, and four-wheel-drive incorporating 34%/66% front/rear torque split

Clutch	Single plate, diaphragm spring

Overall gearbox ratios

Top	3.02:1
4th	3.62:1
3rd	4.96:1
2nd	7.58:1
1st	13.13:1
Reverse	11.85:1
Final drive ratios	3.62:1

22.2mph (35.72km/h)/1,000rpm in top gear

Suspension and steering

Front	Independent, by coil springs, MacPherson struts, track control arms, telescopic dampers and anti-roll bar
Rear	Independent, by coil springs, semi-trailing arms, anti-roll bar and telescopic dampers
Steering	Rack-and-pinion (with power assistance)
Tyres	205/50ZR-15in radial-ply
Wheels	Cast alloy disc, bolt-on fixing
Rim width	7.0 in

Brakes

Type	Disc brakes at front, discs at rear, hydraulically operated, with hydraulic ABS anti-lock control
Size	11.1in front discs, 10.7in rear discs

Dimensions (in/mm)

Track	
Front	56.8/1,440
Rear	57.5/1,460
Wheelbase	102.7/2,608
Overall length	176.9/4,490
Overall width	66.8/1,700
Overall height	54.2/1,380
Unladen weight	2,870lb/1,305kg

UK retail price

(at launch in 1990) £24,995

When it was first proposed in 1990 this sounded attractive, but when the cars became available the following year it became almost impossible to sell them at full retail price. Competitors reasoned that if they secured a cut-throat deal from an RS dealer, they could then afford to buy the parts themselves or through other sources. The Ten by N challenge soon faded into obscurity.

The author has many fond memories of the two years (1991–92) when he ran Sierra Cosworth 4 × 4s (the first being in 'basic' specification, the second having leather upholstery and air conditioning). Not only were the cars – each of which completed more than 20,000 miles in a year – unfailingly reliable, but they were also sweet-natured in heavy traffic. Coming, as they did, within memory of the RS200s that had occupied his life in the late 1980s, this was a peaceful interlude.

Even so, these cars were awesomely capable, especially on roads not well known to the driver. The author will not forget one drive back to Boreham from an RS dealership in Grimsby – late at night, in the dark, in the rain – trying hard to keep up with rally driver Gwyndaf Evans, who had a near-identical car. A journey not to be forgotten, though it is perhaps advisable that no mention is made of the journey time via Lincoln, Newark, the A1 and the M25.

Along with those of all other contemporary Fords, Cosworth 4 × 4 retail prices continued to rise in 1990 and 1991. By the end of 1990 the 'sticker' price was £26,854, but that proved unacceptable to all except rabid enthusiasts,

and sales drooped yet again. All Sierras received a new and less angular-looking instrument package, along with generally improved trim and a different style of alloy road wheels, but this provided only a temporary lift.

The combination of air conditioning, the new facia and generally improved Sierra quality in cars assembled at Genk was still very appealing, but as the Escort RS Cosworth (*see* Chapters 8 and 9) was known to be on the way – it would hit the market in spring 1992 – there was really no come-back.

Even so, British sales figures held up well: 1,227 in 1990 (1,093 rear-drive 'Sapphire' models were also delivered in this year); 1,424 in 1991; and 1,010 in 1992.

During 1992, in fact, the Sierra Cosworth 4 × 4 reached full maturity, and no major improvements were made during that season. Ford could not deny that a 'new-generation Sierra' was on the way (this, in fact, was the car we came to know as the original Mondeo), the Escort RS Cosworth was now on sale, and the

The author's Sierra Cosworth 4 × 4s gave fast, flawless and, above all, reliable motoring for two years in the early 1990s. Note the bonnet cooling louvres and the headlamp wipe-wash fittings, both of which were standard on this model.

Above In 1962 Keith Duckworth rejuvenated the Lotus-Ford twin-cam engine that powered the Lotus-Cortina of the 1960s. This was one of his first ever links with Ford.

Below Keith Duckworth (right) and Mike Costin (left) founded Cosworth in 1958, and formed strong links with Ford that would last for more than forty years.

Above In the late 1960s British Saloon Car Championship rules allowed Lotus-Cortinas to run with Ford-based FVA F2 engines. Cars like the Alan Mann Racing machine of 1968 were startlingly successful.

Left Designed in 1967–68, Cosworth's Ford-based BDA engine was the first 16-valve twin-cam engine to power a Ford road car – the Escort RS1600. In concept the engine layout was very similar to that of the later YB.

Above *16-valve BD-engined Escorts were the most successful Ford competition cars of all in the 1970s: this was Russell Brookes's car on the way to winning the Manx International rally of 1979.*

Left *The original Sierra RS Cosworth of 1986 set new standards. With a 150mph (241km/h) top speed, and extrovert aerodynamic features, it was a stunning concept.*

Below *Ford built exactly 500 Sierra RS500 Cosworths in the summer of 1987 to allow this model to go motor racing. Compared with the standard car, the inlet manifold had eight fuel injectors instead of four, and a much larger turbocharger.*

Below *How to identify a Sierra RS500 Cosworth from the rear? First of all, by noting the two rear spoilers, and then (if you are quick) by seeing the 'RS500' badge on the tailgate.*

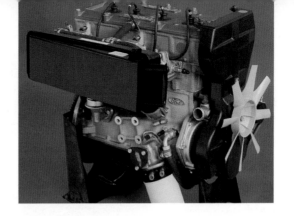

Right *Later model BDAs had a light-alloy cylinder block, but this was an indulgence denied Cosworth when they came to develop the YB in the mid-1980s.*

Above *The original Sierra RS Cosworth had a three-door body shell, the turbocharged YBB engine up front, and a massive hatchback-mounted spoiler. More than 5,000 were built in 1986.*

Right *When previewed in 1985, to power the Sierra RS Cosworth, the Ford-Cosworth YB engine broke new ground. With 204bhp it was the world's first road car power unit to offer more than 100bhp/ltr.*

Below *This display model of the Sierra RS Cosworth engine/gearbox assembly shows its considerable bulk. The air/air intercooler sat atop the water radiator up front, and the gearbox itself was a Borg Warner T5 unit.*

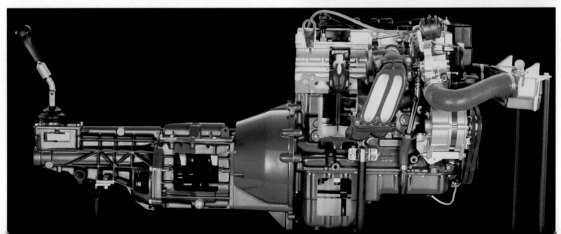

Right *Worm's-eye view of the Sierra RS500 Cosworth, differing visually from the original Sierra RS Cosworth in having an extra low front spoiler, and two rear spoilers instead of one – all of which provided more downforce at high speed. This was the basis of the world's most successful racing saloon car of the period.*

Below *Under the skin the 'Sapphire' Cosworth was much the same as the 1986 Sierra RS Cosworth, but had a totally different body shell style.*

Above *The Sierra 'Sapphire' Cosworth of 1988 looked very different from the original three-door model, for it had a different nose, a four-door saloon body shell and only a small rear spoiler.*

Left *The four-wheel-drive Sierra Cosworth 4 × 4 of 1990 looked almost the same as the 'Sapphire' Cosworth that it replaced, except for having extra bonnet cooling louvres, and discreet '4 × 4' badges on the front wings.*

Four-wheel-drive and proud of it – this was how Ford showed off the all-wheel traction of the Sierra Cosworth 4 × 4 in 1990.

The combination of François Delecour and his 'works' Sierra Cosworth 4 × 4 was a formidable combination in World Rallying in 1992.

Didier Auriol drove his 'works' Sierra RS Cosworth to a stunning outright victory in the 1988 Tour de Corse rally.

Below Two of the world's fastest RS500 Cosworths faced up to each other at the Silverstone TT race of 1988: the Texaco-liveried Eggenberger racing car of Soper/Dieudonné, against Dick Johnson (from Australia) in his Shell-sponsored machine.

Above *Open wide, please! Apart from the blue-painted camshaft covers, the engine bay of the original Escort RS Cosworth looked much like that of the Sierra Cosworth 4 × 4 on which it was based.*

Below *The Escort RS Cosworth of the early 1990s came with this new facia/instrument panel style, with Recaro-type front seats and twin airbags.*

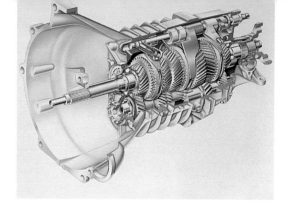

Ford's sturdy new MT75 transmission was the core of the four-wheel-drive layout used in Sierra Cosworth 4 × 4s from 1990 – and the Escort RS Cosworth that followed.

From mid-1994 the Escort RS Cosworth engine was retuned, and made to look subtly different, with a smaller (T25-type) turbocharger, Ford EEC IV engine management system, and these novel camshaft and drive belt covers.

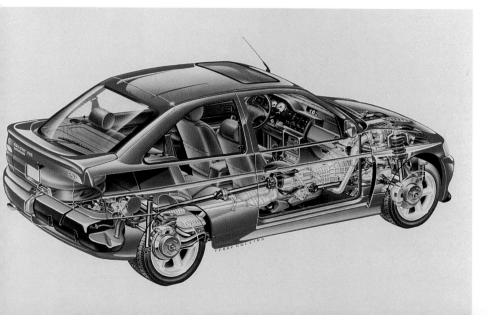

The Escort RS Cosworth of 1992–96 was available with or without a large rear spoiler: under the skin was a shortened, and further improved, Sierra Cosworth 4 × 4 platform.

Top *The proposed 'Acropolis' version of the Escort RS Cosworth was a specially painted and equipped limited edition, although mechanically standard. Would it have sold?*

Above *Perhaps the Escort RS Cosworth's most notable achievement came in January 1994, when François Delecour won the legendary Monte Carlo Rally.*

Above *Sisters, sisters ... the 1995 Escort RS Cosworth parked ahead of three low-powered Escorts of the day, M606 WOO being an Escort RS2000.*

Left *'Works' Escort RS Cosworths won several World Championship rallies in their debut year, 1993. This was Miki Biasion on his way to victory in the Acropolis.*

Below *A famous occasion. The very first Escort RS Cosworth prototype won its very first rally, the Talavera of Spain, in 1990. It was the start of a great motor sport career.*

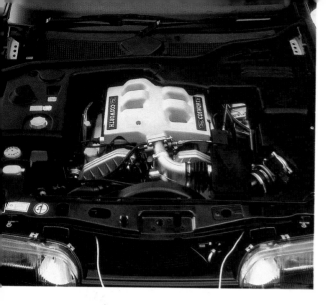

Above The Escort World Rally Car was a strictly limited-edition machine, made with motor sport in mind in 1997 and 1998. It was the last Ford to use a version of the YB engine.

Left Maybe it's not obvious, but this Cosworth engine is a 24-valve, twin-cam per bank, 2.9-litre V6 engine, which powered the Scorpio 24V so successfully in the 1990s.

Above Famous opera singer Dame Kiri Te Kanawa posing alongside the Cosworth-engined Scorpio 24V when it was introduced in 1991.

Left The Scorpio 24V was initially available in five-door hatchback or (as here) four-door saloon car form. A five-door estate car soon joined that range, too.

Happy Christmas! – especially if that late-model Sierra Cosworth 4 × 4 (note the different badges on the flanks) was one of the presents.

company admitted that it had no further plans to prolong the life of its charismatic four-wheel-drive saloon.

In 1991 and 1992 soaring insurance premiums, which were never convincingly backed by insurance company risk statistics, threatened to kill off the Cosworth 4 × 4 before its time, and not even a massive price cut (to £20,063, in February 1992) could counter that.

Even so, assembly ambled along, at no great rate, until the end of 1992, when all Sierra pro-duction at Genk ended in favour of the all-new Mondeo, which was to be launched early the following year. After about 12,000 4 × 4s had been produced, this rounded off the seven-year career of the Cosworth-engined Sierras. Now it was up to the smaller, more nimble and altogether more extrovert Escort RS Cosworth to take over instead.

7   Sierra in Motorsport

As already related in Chapter 3, the Sierra RS Cosworth took shape through a series of coincidences: the fact that Stuart Turner was recalled to run Ford's European motor sport programme in 1983; that he and Walter Hayes were depressed by Ford's lack of a 'winning' touring car racer; and by that chance encounter with Cosworth's 'private-enterprise' YA 16-valve engine.

Yet although Turner's reaction to the new engine was immediate, at first he thought this could be used only for racing, and not rallying. Even so, if a Cosworth-powered Sierra was to go motor racing, Boreham and its associates (particularly Ford-of-Germany) would have to start work on the new project at once.

The time was absolutely ripe and there was an element of good fortune here. Because one of Turner's first decisions in March 1983 had been to cancel the Escort RS1700T project – cancelled at just one phone call's notice – Boreham's design and development staff found themselves short of work. Rather than let them play football on the sports field, and even though there was then little interest in Sierras for motor sport use, Peter Ashcroft set John Wheeler's team to work on a 'why don't we ...?' exercise.

First of all they spent time on the Sierra chassis, working out how the MacPherson strut front end and the semi-trailing link rear suspension could be optimized for use on the track. This was the time – playtime, we might even call it, since there was then no urgent purpose – when the basic layout of the Group A front struts was established and the concept work on the rear suspension geometry, which

would be so valuable in the mid- and late 1980s, took place.

Not only did Boreham's team turbocharge the existing single-cam 8-valve Pinto engine (in the end that work would not have any application in motor sport), but they also assessed other Group A transmission and chassis components that 'might be useful, one day'. In particular, they concluded that the most viable alternative gearbox (in Group A an entirely different main gearbox could be listed) would be the sturdy German Getrag five-speeder.

Even so, by the autumn of 1983, just when the Sierra RS Cosworth project was starting to take shape, most of this work had to be put on

Peter Ashcroft was Ford's successful Competitions Manager from 1972 to 1991, and saw the best of the Sierras and the Escort Cosworths that followed them.

Boreham, the home of Ford Motorsport from 1963 to 1993, conceived the Sierra RS Cosworth in 1983, and administered its successful subsequent race and rally programmes.

ice and the drawings stored, all because Boreham's effort then had to go into the brand-new four-wheel-drive, mid-engined, Group B RS200 project.

As a regular visitor to Boreham at this time, I can confirm that little 'works' motor sport development went into the Sierra RS Cosworth until 1986. Although John Griffiths kept a close eye on what should, and could, be homologated for the car, it would be the Sierra-based Merkur XR4Ti (as raced in the UK by Andy Rouse, and in Europe by Eggenberger Motorsport) that flew the flag on the race tracks at first. That XR4Ti, of course, used a turbocharged 2.3-litre Ford-USA 'Lima' engine, a single-cam engine fairly closely related to the Pinto/T88 on which the Sierra RS Cosworth engine was also based.

All this changed in May 1986, when the FIA abruptly put Group B rallying under sentence of death and decreed that from 1987 onwards World Championship rallying would only be for Group A cars. Suddenly, therefore, Boreham turned back to the Sierra – in the forms of both the rear-wheel-drive Sierra RS Cosworth and the four-wheel-drive Sierra XR4 × 4 (which, of course, used the ageing Ford-Cologne V6 engine).

Behind the scenes, however (and did you expect anything else?), Stuart Turner had been thinking hard and been as Machiavellian as usual. Although he could never personally warm to motor racing (rallying was always his first love), he had already realized that most of the European markets for which he was responsible were anxious to see competitive Fords back on the race track. Apart from the Merkur XR4Ti, which was only to be sold in the USA and Switzerland, the only real contender was the Sierra RS Cosworth.

In the meantime Turner, looking well ahead, had been laying long-term plans for Ford's high-profile return to the race tracks.

Not only did he direct Ford-Germany, where the motor sport operation was managed by Lothar Pinske, to push ahead with a new race car programme, but he encouraged Pinske to look around for an independent team to race those cars in European Championship events.

Turner also knew that BMW was working hard on a compact new Group A project – even in 1984 BMW revealed their intention to put a new car on the tracks in 1986 (this would eventually be labelled the M3). Even though this was to be a normally aspirated 2.3-litre car, Ford certainly had to raise its sights further if the Sierra was to stay on top of the heap for several seasons.

Back in Britain, Turner then called on Andy Rouse, already known as 'Mr Touring Car Racer' for winning many Championship races in a variety of cars, not only in Ford Capris, but also in the new Rover Vitesse. As Stuart told me:

> I called Andy Rouse and asked what it would need for us to get him back into a Ford car? 'Simple', he replied. 'I need 350bhp in a rear-wheel-drive car to beat all the Rovers and BMWs.'

And he was right. To beat the 300bhp Rovers, and the projected 300bhp BMW M3s, Andy needed more of the same, in a nimble package. A super-powerful rear-wheel-drive Ford – and the Sierra RS Cosworth showed every promise of being one of those – was surely right for the job.

For Andy, therefore, Motorsport reacted positively, and Stuart Turner took him into his confidence. First, as an interim measure, Andy was asked to race the Merkur XR4Ti in 1985 and 1986, and the Sierra RS Cosworth race car programme would soon follow.

Andy's XR4Tis were totally dominant in the UK, outpacing all rivals and winning most of their races (he won nine races and the Championship in 1985, and won five more races in 1986). This racing experience was invaluable in developing the chassis and transmission. In particular, Andy's cars always used Getrag five-speed gearboxes and AP Racing 'paddle' clutches, which would directly 'read across' to the Sierra RS Cosworths in 1987.

Sierras were first seen in rallying in the Securicor Sierra Challenge of 1986. This car, driven by Phil Collins, won that series.

Peter Ashcroft

Peter Ashcroft, 'Mr Nice Guy', was one of Ford's most famous motor sport personalities and seemed to be respected by everyone, being involved in the development, or rallying, of almost every Escort RS model.

Originally a mechanic with the Gilbey Engineering racing team, he joined Ford Motorsport in 1962. Except for a short period when he worked with Brian Hart at the Peter Sellers Racing Team, Boreham was his workplace from 1963 to the end of 1991.

First as an engineer, and soon running the engine development and test department at Boreham, he spent two winters at Ford-Cologne, where he inspired the improvement in Capri RS2600 engines that turned those cars into Touring Car winners, before becoming Ford-UK's Competition Manager in 1972.

He ran the development and build programmes for the 'works' Escort Twin-Cams and RS1600s, as well as shaping the 1.8-litre engines, which used the 'Ashcroft' block, and developing the 140bhp London–Mexico engines of 1970.

From 1972 until the end of 1991 he led the victorious 'works' Escort teams, led the department through the confusion of the RS1700T, the front-drive RS1600i, the RS200 and the rear-drive Sierra RS Cosworth eras, before observing the original concept of the ACE, the Escort RS Cosworth project. He retired at the end of 1991.

It was Peter's strategy that let his successor, Colin Dobinson, enjoy such a successful tenure of office in 1993 and 1994 with the 'works' Escort RS Cosworths, which used a chassis based on the Sierra Cosworth 4 × 4.

Years later Andy agreed that this had been a very busy and happy time for him and for his business, Andy Rouse Engineering. Not only did he win many races in the XR4Ti, but he had demonstrated his 'can-do' skills: although the Ford deal had been sealed only in September 1984, his first car raced (and won) at Easter 1985. By the time his long-running Sierra race programme was completed in 1990, Andy's Coventry-based business had built 30 complete RS500 Cosworth race cars, and more than a hundred 500/550bhp full-race engines to power them.

Merkur XR4Tis using some Boreham-designed chassis components started to race in Europe in 1985, and when Eggenberger Racing of Lyss, Switzerland, joined in for 1986 they were among the fastest Touring Cars of all. Even so, because series production of Sierra RS Cosworths was delayed and Group A homologation was not achieved until 1 January 1987, the long-term aims of this programme also had to wait. The only piece of good news was that BMW's M3 was also delayed, for although previewed in 1985, it did not go on sale until the spring of 1986 and similarly would not be raced until 1987.

The rear-drive Sierra RS Cosworth was never meant to be a rally car, but the cancellation of Group B in mid-1986 meant that Boreham had to turn it into one for 1987. At that moment Ford had no 'Plan B', since they had already developed their future rallying strategy around the RS200 and RS200E types. Now they had to face up to developing rear-drive Sierras (and four-wheel-drive Sierra XR4 × 4s) as a stopgap measure until something purpose-built could come along: a four-wheel-drive Sierra Cosworth would not be ready until mid-1990.

Peter Ashcroft was pragmatic about the challenge:

> Nobody at Boreham liked it very much, but I told them that we would have to develop the Sierra RS Cosworth – the alternative being to close down completely.

Some tentative work had already begun. In 1986 Ford-UK had promoted the Securicor Sierra Challenge for seven dealer-owned RS Cosworths, which were used in National rallies well before homologation could be achieved. Those cars, incidentally, had all been used as Press Launch vehicles at the end of 1985.

Boreham was never more than peripherally involved, but three times in only five 'Nation-

Good gimmick, doubtful result? A downhill-skier tried out his stance, at Bruntingthorpe airfield, on the roof of the Brooklyn Motorsport Sierra RS Cosworth rally car in 1986.

al' outings (all of them on tarmac), the Brooklyn Motorsport car, driven by Phil Collins, took a second overall and two third places behind four-wheel-drive Group B cars. These were very simply developed Sierras, with standard transmissions and 280bhp engines, but it was very promising. These cars showed up the Sierra RS Cosworth's frailties – engine durability, the need for an alternative gearbox, and proof that the standard rear axle could not cope with any more than 300bhp.

The first 'works' rally cars were made ready

Didier Auriol, famous only in France before his Sierra career began, astonished everyone with his pace in 1987 and 1988. This was Didier, well-sideways, in the Scottish rally of 1987.

Boreham built this much-modified Sierra RS Cosworth to compete in the 1987 Safari rally – but it became famous only for hitting a cow and being written off just before the start!

for the Monte Carlo rally of 1987. What followed was a traumatic period. On the Monte, Kalle Grundel's car struggled for grip on the ice (it set one fastest stage time) and could not match the Lancias' pace. Power was never a problem (first from Terry Hoyle, later from Mountune): the lack of rear-wheel grip was the enemy.

Out in Europe, the Sierra RS Cosworths soon started to win. RED ran cars for Didier Auriol in the French Championships, and Mike Little Preparations supported Carlos Sainz in Spain. Both won their respective series and within a year the drivers would be in the World Championship team.

Back home, Jimmy McRae ran an RED-prepared car in the British Rally Championship, winning two rallies outright (Circuit of Ireland and Manx) and the Drivers' Championship; Mark Lovell's car won the Ulster.

Boreham then made a special effort to win

the East African Safari, with two heavily reinforced Cosworths for Stig Blomqvist and local hero Johnny Hellier. Even so, the best-laid plans all went wrong. Ford elected to complete their preparation in Mombasa and then drive the cars back up the main road overnight to ease the running-in process. But … when mechanic Bill Meade was halfway to Nairobi in Stig's new car, a bus running close ahead of him suddenly twitched off line, leaving the new Cosworth facing the obstacle of a cow fast asleep on the still-warm tarmac! The Sierra was launched into space, rolled and effectively wrote itself off.

In just two days the hard-working mechanics rebuilt a training car, using undamaged components from the wreckage, and sent Hellier out to do his best. Stig was allocated the other car. It was all in vain. Although Stig led up to the fifth control, both cars were eliminated with insoluble electrical problems. Three weeks later, in Corsica, things got even worse, when Grundel's car went off on the first special stage, and Blomqvist's car was withdrawn with major transmission problems.

For a time there was talk of closing down

After 1986 Andy Rouse retired his Merkur XR4Tis in favour of brand-new Sierra RS Cosworths. Once the teething troubles had been sorted out, Andy's RS and RS500 Cosworths won many races in the British Touring Car Championship. That is his team-mate/sponsor Pete Hall in the sister car.

the Sierra programme, and some acrimonious meetings took place. Grundel was dismissed, and it was not until late August that Ford competed again.

What a difference a three-month lay off could make. For the Finnish 1000 Lakes, the 'works' cars got new livery – exactly like that of the Eggenberger RS500s, which had started to dominate World Touring Car racing. Stig Blomqvist was joined by 1981 World Cham-

pion Ari Vatanen! No-one expected them to win – or to finish second (Vatanen) and third either. When Didier Auriol's French-Championship car finished fourth in the San Remo, this was a real fight back.

On the RAC rally, Blomqvist was backed by Jimmy McRae (RED) and Carlos Sainz (MLP/Ford-Spain). Hampered by their lack of wet-track grip, Stig took second place, with McRae third, and newcomer Sainz eighth.

Ford's 'works' rally team ready to tackle the Finnish 1000 Lakes rally, with two Sierra RS Cosworths for Stig Blomqvist (left) and Ari Vatanen; they finished third and second respectively.

Stig Blomqvist flying over one of the many humps of the Finnish 1000 Lakes rally of 1987, in which he finished third.

By this time Group A YB engines could deliver well over 300bhp, Getrag gearboxes were normal wear, and specially engineered (by FFD) massive rear axles with 9in ring-and-pinion sets were also available.

Out on the race tracks the RS500 Cosworth that Mike Moreton and John Griffiths had done so much to urge towards homologa-tion had proved to be outstanding. The Swiss-based Eggenberger team, which was as near to a Ford-Germany 'works' operation as could be arranged, could now be expected to win almost any race it entered.

In the brand-new World Touring Car Championship of 1987 there were to be twelve rounds, eight of them in Europe, the

In 1987 and 1988 the Texaco-sponsored Eggenberger RS500 Cosworths were stunningly fast and reliable, winning the World series in 1987 and the European Championship in 1988. This is the Ludwig/Niedswiedz car at Silverstone in 1988.

Not only did the Eggenberger RS500s dominate almost every race they started, but usually circulated in line-astern.

final races to be in Australia, New Zealand and Japan. Eggenberger Racing always entered two startlingly liveried black/Texaco red cars: these were RS Cosworths at first, but became RS500 Cosworths on 1 August when the new car was homologated. With 340bhp at first, as RS500s they produced more than 500bhp. Early in the season, Eggenberger was nervous about unleashing the torque through the hard-pressed rear axles, so Ford was relieved when WTCC events were given a rolling start.

This World series was a triumph for Ford, but was only a one-season wonder. The RS500s started ten times, and enjoyed five victories, plus one extremely dubious post-event disqualification after a sixth victory, all backed up by other podium finishes. Ford easily won the Manufacturers' title, with Klaus Ludwig and Klaus Niedzwiedz finishing second in the

Drivers' tables, just one point behind BMW driver Roberto Ravaglia.

Yet this was an unhappy series, torn with jealousies and inter-company politics. To quote Joe Saward of *Autosport*:

> You are left with one conclusion – someone did-n't want a World Touring Car Championship to happen, perhaps because they had other interests elsewhere ... Within a few short months ... it was shot down by the guardians of the sport. The whole affair was a disgrace.

The interpretation of regulations was always a problem. The season began chaotically at Monza, with the Sierras withdrawn after arguments over their electronic engine management systems, while the BMWs (not being Italian, you understand) were also disqualified over bodywork infringements. Surprise, surprise – 'victory' was then handed to the Italian Alfa Romeos, which never won again.

The season then settled down. When it was

dry the Sierras could only lose on reliability grounds: in the wet the BMWs were on terms. Second in the next two races, the Sierras then won at the Nürburgring in July, for the first and only time as RS Cosworths. With the same cars, re-homologated and re-equipped as RS500 Cosworths, they then became class-of-the-field and always outpaced the BMWs.

Texaco-liveried RS500s also won at Brno (Czechoslovakia), Calder (Australia), Wellington (New Zealand) and Fuji (Japan). But it wasn't a complete massacre: the team failed to finish in the Spa 24 Hour race, while awful weather and electrical problems foiled them in the Silverstone Tourist Trophy race.

Then, of course, there was the shambles of Bathurst, the high-profile Hardie 1000 Australian event. After nearly seven hours of racing, the Soper/Dieudonné RS500 crossed the line a dominant first, with Niedzwiedz/Ludwig second; a locally manufactured 4.9-litre Holden Commodore was three laps adrift in third place.

The Australian scrutineers (surely they cannot have been thinking of national glory?) then disqualified the Sierras, stating that their rear wheelarches had been illegally modified to accommodate ultra-wide tyres. These, by the way, were the self-same cars that had raced all season without any complaints so far. The fact that an Australian Holden then just happened to 'win', and that the Australian-built Dick Johnson RS500s had earlier been humiliated by the Swiss cars, must have had nothing to do with this, of course. Even so, in this case it was not 'Whinging Poms' who caused trouble, but the 'Whinging Aussies'.

Protests were in vain, and the Sierras lost their valuable Championship points. Undaunted, Eggenberger changed the arches, ran narrower tyres and won all three remaining races, which proved their point.

Boreham's finest hour with the Sierra RS Cosworth came in May 1988 when Didier Auriol won the World Championship Tour de Corse rally.

If Andy Rouse had not also tried to win races in the World Series in 1987, he might have done better in the UK, where Cosworths won six of the twelve races (Andy's cars winning four of them) – and once the RS500 was homologated the British series effectively became 'Formula Ford'. Even so, for the first season there was much detail development trouble to be solved, notably around the turbochargers themselves and the troublesome cylinder head gaskets.

Boreham's front-line rally team for 1988 was Stig Blomqvist, Carlos Sainz and Didier Auriol. Blomqvist's fifth place in Portugal was low key, but there was then a mighty assault on the Tour de Corse, where Didier Auriol shocked the rallying establishment with a fine win. Seven years without a World Championship rally win, this was an emotional moment for everyone at Boreham – and not only for Ford. Five minutes after the cars had arrived at the final service point, Lancia's team boss, Cesare Fiorio, rushed up to Peter Ashcroft with a big grin on his face, and stuck out his hand in a genuine greeting:

If we couldn't have won, I'm glad it was you!

When the Cosworth's battered back end had to be repaired, a helicopter full of mechanics arrived, just minutes ahead, at a service point. With nowhere to land, except on the main road, the chopper did precisely that, with Ford staffers standing out in the road to halt the 44-ton trucks that would otherwise have been thundering past! Auriol was French, after all.

Morale back at Boreham was now as high as ever. In that spirit, Auriol took the self-same (but rebuilt) ex-Corsica car to Finland, where he achieved an astonishing third place overall, backed by Blomqvist (fifth) and Sainz (sixth).

In 1988, too, RS500 race cars still dominated every Championship they entered. Foiled in their ambition to win the World title for a second time (there was no second time!), the Eggenberger team turned to the European Touring Car Championship with three brand-new Texaco-backed Sierra RS500 Cosworths.

The 1988 European series was effectively a rerun of the 1987 World Championships. Sierras were demonstrably faster than any of the BMWs, though the M3s were always

Even in 1986 Boreham's motorsport department had developed new Group A components to use under the Sierra RS Cosworth, these being front suspension pieces.

Not only to stiffen up the rear suspension linkage, but to provide adjustable camber, Boreham developed these special magnesium semi-trailing arms. Updated versions would be used in the Escort RS Cosworth era, too

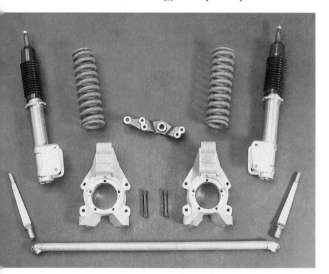

Andy Rouse re-liveried one of his cars in 1988 to compete in – and win – the RAC Tourist Trophy race.

competitive, usually reliable, and able to keep going in ultra-long races where the Fords, which now used a day-in-day-out 550bhp, might wilt. TWR's Holdens appeared occasionally, and the mention of Maserati Biturbos might bring on fits of nostalgia, but there was no other serious competition.

The 1988 season was almost a whitewash for the red-and-black Fords, which won seven of the rounds (and Andy Rouse an eighth). Problems? At Donington Park there was one axle and one engine management failure, while at Zolder in August a downpour led to the Sierras crashing out of contention. In the Spa 24 Hours crashes and electrical problems handed the race to BMW.

Yet here was another series that was cancelled before it had truly established itself. The RS500s, it seemed, were far too good to be tolerated by the authorities, or by the spectators, who wanted to see closer racing. By mid-season the series was already in deep trouble: its cancellation was announced just after the end of the 1988 championship. At a press conference Stuart Turner later commented:

What more could we do? We developed the Sierra to win races, which it did. We won the World

Championship, so they killed that. Next we won the European Championship, so they killed that too. The national Championships will be next …

And he wasn't joking.

In the TT, apart from the almost inevitable Sierra success at Silverstone, there were two significant occurrences at the Northamptonshire circuit. One was that Andy Rouse won the race, beating the Eggenberger cars, and another was that the Australian Dick Johnson brought two Shell-backed RS500s all the way from the other side of the world, planted his own car on pole, and only lost the race when a water pump failed!

Not that it was easy to race an RS500 to its limits, as Eggenberger star driver Steve Soper once admitted:

What a lot of people don't realize is that the RS500 is a very difficult car to drive really quickly. Anyone can hop in and drive one so that it looks spectacular. To drive it fast, though, to make it give you a time, is an art. You have to have grip everywhere, be early on the accelerator, have the car pointing straight, and be very, very, late turning into a corner, kill all the speed down to almost nothing by the middle of the corner, and then

The Rouse/Sierra RS500 Cosworth, with Kaliber (alcohol-free lager) sponsorship, won many British touring car races in the late 1980s.

point it where you want the damn thing to go and put the power down again without an oversteer or an understeer out.

It sounds easy, but every now and then it kicks its tail out in a massive power oversteer and you've suddenly just lost half a second.

Even while the Eggenberger team cars were completing their European Championship steamroller performance, their drivers took part, in other non-Texaco-liveried cars, in the German series. In 1988, to no-one's surprise, Klaus Ludwig won the German Championship outright, with Armin Hahne's Sierra third overall. No matter where it raced, it seemed, the Sierra RS500 Cosworth could always deliver.

But not always – not in the UK, at any rate. In 1988 Andy Rouse's RS500 won nine of the twelve rounds, while Jerry Mahoney, Steve Soper (in a newly built, Texaco-liveried Eggenberger car) and Gianfranco Brancatelli (in another Eggenberger car) won once each. Rouse's dominance was clear and he certainly seemed to have more power than the Swiss cars – up to 550bhp with excellent reliability.

It was a season, indeed, when the Sierras

could do no wrong, for Andy Rouse's RS500s were class-of-the-field in the UK, as were Dick Johnson's Shell-backed machines in Australia. All of them, of course, sourced their special Motorsport parts from Ford's motor sport centre at Boreham.

Meanwhile the end-of-the-year drama continued. In the Italian San Remo rally Sainz slaughtered the entire field on tarmac, only to drop back, inevitably, when the rally turned to gravel stages on the final days. Fifth overall was cruel indeed: for Auriol it was even crueller, since he totally destroyed his ex-Corsica-winning machine after only nine stages.

At European level, heroes like Robert Droogmans, Auriol and Sainz could often win on the National tarmac events. Jimmy McRae once again won the British Rally series, while Gwyndaf Evans won the Group N category in a Brooklyn car.

By this time, for sure, Boreham needed a competitive four-wheel-drive rally car even though the race car teams were still convinced that they didn't need four-wheel-drive for their Sierras: except when track conditions were truly awful, and monsoon-like, the Eggenberger, Rouse and Dick Johnson

Above *Even though his car was desperately short of financial support in 1990, Robb Gravett won the British Touring Car Championship in this ex-Dick Johnson RS500 Cosworth.*

Below *Using Shell Gemini-sponsored cars, Jimmy McRae won the British rally championships in 1987 and 1988: the Sierra was a supreme 'tarmac' car, but lacked traction on gravel.*

organizations were quite happy to push up to 550bhp through one set of carefully located rear wheels. At least team insiders knew that the Cosworth 4 × 4 was on its way – but would not be ready before mid-1990.

At the end of 1988, though, Boreham's people were positively bubbling over with enthusiasm. Wherever the Sierra RS Cosworth could get its power down, it could win – and it did so, all over Europe. Jimmy McRae won the British series, Didier Auriol the French, Carlos Sainz the Spanish, Mark Lovell the Dutch and the Irish Tarmac, and there were many more. Of the forty-seven European

Championship rounds, eleven were won by Sierra RS Cosworths.

Out on the race tracks, Boreham-inspired Sierra RS500 Cosworths had obliterated all their opposition. Using parts supplied from Ford, the Eggenberger team dominated the European series (the World series having been killed off after just one year): the Texaco-liveried cars won eight of the eleven events, finished twice in two others, and failed to score only once. In the British series, RS500s won twelve races (nine of these victories went to Andy Rouse), and it was a similar story all round the world.

Boreham then suffered a double loss. With no competitive four-wheel-drive car to use, Didier Auriol signed up for Lancia and, after much agonizing, Carlos Sainz joined Toyota. During 1989, therefore, there were few 'works' outings, none of them successful.

In 1989 Andrews Sykes sponsored the two-car team of Russell Brookes and (shown here) Mark Lovell in a high-profile British rally championship programme. Good, but not quite good enough, they had to fight against a new generation of four-wheel-drive cars.

Above *As an interim measure, rear-drive Sierra 'Sapphire' Cosworths were used in British rallying in the first half of 1990, this being Malcolm Wilson in a car later converted to 4 × 4 specification.*

Below *Colin McRae won the first British rally championship event of 1990, the Cartel, in this rear-drive 'Sapphire' RS Cosworth.*

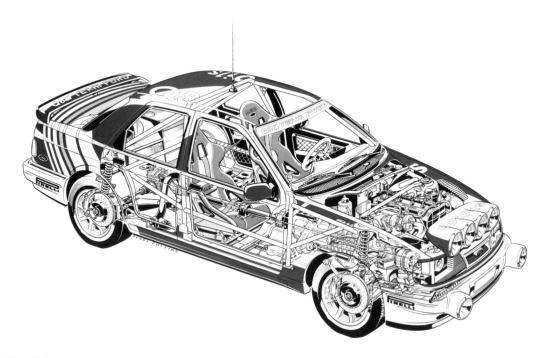

*Terry Collins's remarkable cutaway drawing shows the layout
of the 'works' specification Sierra RS Cosworths of the early
1990s. All top-grade rally cars of this era had left-hand drive,
even when used in the UK.*

It was a different story in Britain, where
Boreham supported cars for Jimmy McRae,
Russell Brookes and Mark Lovell. McRae won
the Circuit of Ireland, Gwyndaf Evans (driving
the lurid pink 'Mr Tomkinson' Brooklyn–Ford
car) the Ulster, and Brookes the Manx. In
Europe Robert Droogmans, Erwin Doctor,
Jean-Pierre Van der Wauwer, Christian Jacquil-
lard and Joachim Santos all won events, three of
them winning national Championships, too.

In 1989 and 1990, as Stuart Turner had pre-
dicted, the authorities seemed determined to
get rid of the RS500s from motor racing –
somehow, anyhow. With no World series and no
European series to contest, in 1989 the Eggenberger RS500s mainly played at home, in Germany, or in selected races in Europe, where
they were as competitive as ever. Even so, here
was another Championship under threat, for
German manufacturers in the high-profile
DTM (German Touring Car) series didn't like

being beaten by a 'foreign car' (originally built
in Belgium, of course), so new regulations concerning minimum weights were progressively
introduced to hamper turbocharged cars (such
as the Sierras), whereas normally aspirated cars
(BMWs and Mercedes-Benz – surprise, surprise) were not affected.

Eggenberger soon tired of this (Reudi's
office in Lyss shows one cartoon with his race
car being laden down by concrete being
poured into the boot!) and went off to win the
Spa 24 Hour race in a re-liveried car, before
gracefully withdrawing.

In the meantime, Boreham got on with its
four-wheel-drive work. Their first 'lash-up' car
was an old 'works' Sierra RS Cosworth car,
carved about, with a complete Sapphire-type
front end, and with the forthcoming Sierra
Cosworth 4 × 4 running gear under the skin.

Boreham came back to life for 1990, at first
with four-door (rear-drive) 'Sapphire' Cosworths in the British Championship. Colin
McRae won his first-ever International rally,
the Cartel, Malcolm Wilson notched up two
second places (Circuit of Ireland and Welsh),
while Gwyndaf Evans won the Group N

Championship. Russell Brookes then had his own Cosworth 4 × 4 private car prepared and won both the Manx and the Welsh-based Audi Sport events outright.

In the 1989 British Touring Car Championship there was a new team winning races, Trakstar, their leading driver being Robb Gravett. Together with TV personality Mike Smith, they set out to beat Rouse by buying up two of Dick Johnson's year-old Australian RS500s. Engines, originally supplied by Dick Johnson, were eventually developed and rebuilt by Mountune.

Even though the workshops were not immediately ready, the Trakstar team produced handsome cars that were always on the pace. Andy Rouse, previously so dominant, had a rude shock in this particular season, since,

The 'works' Sierra Cosworth 4 × 4s of 1991 had this well-equipped, but very starkly furnished, facia/instrument layout.

although he won six races, he found that Robb Gravett also won four times, while the Labatts team (using Rouse-built cars!) won twice.

Storm clouds then gathered for 1990. British motor sport's governing body, the RAC MSA, realizing that no other car could beat the Sierras, elected to run a parallel class in 1990 – for 2-litre, normally aspirated cars – and put the RS500 under sentence of death. Ford made great play of this dominance in one of its display adverts. Showing a series of different Sierras with naval descriptions, saloons were called 'Cruisers', the estate cars were called 'Carriers', while the Texaco-livered RS500 was brutally dubbed 'Destroyer'!

Among the rampaging Sierras, from Oulton Park in April to Silverstone in October, the principal battle was between Robb Gravett's Trakstar-prepared car and Andy Rouse's ICS-sponsored machine: Gravett won nine races, and Rouse only four. In a straight line there was little to choose between the cars, the difference effectively being in the choice of rubber.

This, though, was the end of the RS500's four-season racing career, forced out of motor sport by rule changes. At home, in the BTCC, the MSA adopted a normally aspirated 'Super Touring Car' formula, in Germany the DTM effectively became a silhouette formula for normally aspirated German machines, while in Australia the authorities soon turned back to promoting the Ford-versus-General Motors V8-engined monsters that the enthusiasts seemed to love so much.

Back at Ford Motorsport, in any case, the staff, mechanics and planners were no longer interested in two-wheel-drive cars. Well in advance of homologation, Sierra Cosworth 4 × 4 rally appearances came quickly. Boreham sent a development car for Pentti Airikkala to drive in the Welsh and Scottish rallies, where he headed the non-homologated category by colossal margins.

This, though, was only a prelude. With the car safely homologated, the first chance came in August 1990 in the 1000 Lakes, but this out-

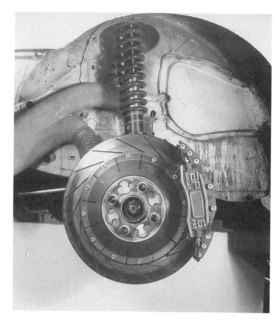

This was the complex new, seven-speed main gearbox, complete with its chain-drive transfer gear, as used in the 'works' Sierra Cosworth 4 × 4 from mid-1990 onwards. In developed (and later six-speed) form, it would be used in Escort RS Cosworths and Escort World Rally Cars until 1998.

'Works' Sierra Cosworth 4 × 4 rally cars used these sturdy AP Racing brakes, and air-cooling ducts from 1991 onwards.

ing was a fiasco, since none of the cars finished. After more than a year away from serious competition, new models were still giving trouble. On the tarmac-based San Remo fortunes improved, but only just: one car finished, but down in eleventh place.

Although it eventually became durable, and competitive, the Sierra Cosworth 4 × 4 was really only an interim rally car – for the Escort RS Cosworth was already on the way. Peter Ashcroft later admitted:

> The 4 × 4 was a lot too heavy, but we couldn't do much about that. Except for the Mk II Escort, all our rally cars have been too heavy.

There was, of course, the on-going problem of the Lancia Delta Integrale, which was at its peak when the Cosworth 4 × 4 came along. Take away the might of Lancia, its bottomless Martini support and its (yes, I'll spell it out,

In the early 1990s the 'works' Sierra Cosworth 4 × 4s used totally special front strut, vertical link and disc brake installations. With more than 300bhp to be dealt with, this was all very necessary.

because others have done so) tendency to push the regulations beyond their limits, then look again. In 1992 the 'works' Cosworth 4 × 4 would then have won four rallies outright – Portugal, Corsica, Greece and San Remo – and the World Rally Championship as well.

For 1991, under the skin the 'works' Sierras Cosworth 4 × 4s of the early 1990s were upgraded as far as the regulations would allow. The YB engine produced at least 340bhp, the 9in rear axle was bomb-proof, FFD viscous coupling limited-slip mechanisms were available for all three differentials, and now there was a brand new FFD-designed Type MS90 seven-speed non-synchromesh manual transmission linking it all together.

Acropolis 1991. François Delecour of France was the sensation in Ford's rally team in the early 1990s. François seemingly knew no fear, and regularly drove a Sierra faster than its designers could ever have hoped.

For the last of the 1990 events, the British RAC rally, Ford released Franco Cunico, replacing him by the Italian driver Alex Fiorio. All went well from the start in Harrogate, and after the first day Pentti Airikkala was third and Malcolm Wilson fourth.

Pentti then crashed at very high speed, Wilson's engine cam drive belt let go at half distance, which left Fiorio to take ninth place; young Colin McRae's RED-prepared Cosworth 4 × 4 took sixth place. The really good news was that Gwyndaf Evans's Group N car easily won the entire Group N category.

For 1991 there was much media talk when Ford signed up François Delecour, relatively unknown outside his native France, who was initially lined up to do only five World Championship rounds.

The biggest disappointment came right at the start. On the Monte Carlo rally, Delecour astonished everyone by setting 11 fastest stage times and was all set to win outright – until the final test. Halfway through the Col du Turini stage a rear suspension joint broke, the car became virtually undriveable, and the Sierra slipped to third place, more than five minutes adrift. Delecour wept, as well he might.

It didn't get any better as the season progressed. Much of the time the four-wheel-drive transmission gave trouble, often with an axle or a drive shaft letting go.

All three team cars went off the road in Portugal, yet Franco Cunico took a fine third place in Corsica. Ari Vatanen managed seventh in the 1000 Lakes, while Delecour took fourth place in San Remo, then went one better – to third place – in Spain, notching up fifteen fastest stage times. There was not even any luck on Ford's home ground, the RAC rally.

Privately entered Cosworth 4 × 4s won the important Group N category in Monte Carlo, San Remo, Spain (Catalunya) and the RAC events. Robbie Head was at the wheel of the RAC-winning Group N car, while Louise Aitken-Walker drove an ex-Boreham Group A car into tenth place to secure the Ladies' Award and gained huge applause from the sentimental British crowd.

Although François Delecour stayed on board for 1992, everything else seemed to be new. Mobil and Autoglass (or Carglass, depending on the country where the rally was held) were major sponsors, Michelin replaced Pirelli as tyre suppliers, and twice World Champion Miki Biasion arrived to replace Alex Fiorio.

Unhappily Peter Ashcroft was obliged to

retire, his health no longer robust. His successor was Colin Dobinson, a long-serving Ford sales, marketing and product planning expert with a ruthlessly logical mindset:

> I had previously been involved with RS products and performance Fords, but never with motor sport. Vice-President, Jack Brinkley, told me that he now thought Boreham needed someone with a marketing background, to try to make it as efficient an operation as possible.
>
> I went down to Boreham the next day after my appointment, to look round, and it was no more than two weeks before I took over. I guess the real handover came when Peter and I both went off on the 1992 Monte Carlo rally!

The Mobil-liveried Sierras raised spirits at Ford in 1992, for they were lighter, more nimble and a lot more reliable than before. Not only did the engines produce a reliable 300+ bhp, but the entire drive train – seven-speed main gearbox, and massive special front and rear differentials – was now solid enough to cope with anything. 16in or 17in wheels, two different patterns, all manner of rim widths, and superb service from Michelin made the Sierra a formidable, and adaptable, platform. So, what might the Escort RS Cosworth do in the future?

Although the record shows that the Sierras never managed to win a World event, they led several events for many hours, set many fastest stage times, and took four podium places. The methodical, cool and calculating Biasion proved to be the best test driver, while the fiery Delecour brought real excitement to the team. Off-season testing improved the cars even more. If only they had been smaller.

It all started disappointingly in Monte Carlo, where Delecour finished fourth, but fortunes soon improved, as Dobinson told me:

Opposite *Malcolm Wilson tackled the 1991 San Remo rally in this Q8-sponsored Sierra Cosworth 4 × 4. In the same period Malcolm was busily involved in testing and developing the forthcoming Escort RS Cosworth.*

Everyone was trying as hard as they could with the Sierra, but it was very apparent even to the uneducated, like me, that the Sierra was by no means the perfect rally car. The good news, of course, was that the Escort RS Cosworth was already well on the way.

I got to know the drivers quite well, quite soon – and found François very different from Miki.

On the very next event – Portugal – Biasion took second place. Fastest stage times were building up, and they did so even more rapidly in Corsica, where Delecour took another second place. Colin Dobinson began to smile more often. This was all taking place at the same time as Malcolm Wilson's prototype outings in Escort RS Cosworths had also looked encouraging and Boreham's workforce perked up markedly.

So near and yet so far. In 1992 the Mobil-sponsored 'works' Sierra Cosworth 4 × 4s regularly took second place in World Championship rallies, but couldn't quite make it to the top step of the podium. François Delecour in the San Remo rally, where he finished third overall.

In the Tour de Corse, though, the weighbridges told the story, for it was here, where every kilogram would tell, that the Sierras were seen to be 110lb (50kg) heavier than the Lancias, which was enough to tip the balance. Although Delecour took second place, and notched up seven fastest stage times, with twelve other 'podium' times, he lost out to Auriol's flying Lancia by just 86 seconds. Later, on the hot, dusty, battering-ram surfaces of the Acropolis, Miki Biasion finished third overall behind – guess what? – two 'works' Lancias.

Clearly the rough-road cars were still too

Posing at Boreham in November 1990 were two Sierra Cosworth 4 × 4s, all ready to tackle the RAC rally – with support coming from two trucks, ten Iveco-Ford service vans and two four-wheel-drive Sierra estate 'chase' cars.

heavy, yet Biasion took fifth place in the 1000 Lakes, and Delecour was actually ahead of him before he had a serious accident.

Then came San Remo, for which Ford had spent much time stripping weight out of two ex-Acropolis cars, which had been ruthlessly gutted and simplified. Official weighing showed that they were now as light as the Lancias – if

only they could have been shrunk in the wash to make them smaller, too. In a real head-to-head battle, on both tarmac and gravel stages, the Sierras were fastest on six of the 24 stages – and always on the pace. Third and fourth places, behind two 'works' Martini Lancias on home ground, was a stupendous performance.

Four weeks later, in Spain, Delecour looked even more determined. Even more weight seemed to have been thrown out, making his newly shelled Sierra now within 40lb (18kg) of the minimum. These savings included deleting most of the instruments and running without a spare wheel most of the time. When questioned about the lack of instruments, François apparently replied:

Well, I never have time to read them, anyway!

Maybe he could have won, yet this time he crashed the car.

The last event of the year, the RAC rally, was also to be the Sierra's final fling. Ford entered two cars: for Miki Biasion and Malcolm Wilson. Amazingly, although Biasion finished higher, in fifth place, it was Wilson who made such an impact. Seven fastest stage times,

compared with Biasion's three, caused a real stir.

After that, however, it was really all over for the Sierras. Back at Boreham the fleet was speedily parked outside in the yard, for the workshops were already filling up with brand-new, still-to-be-homologated, Escort RS Cosworths for the 1993 season. Boreham never used the Sierras again, although private owners enjoyed them for some years to come. And, whatever happened to all the special registration numbers – A1 FMC to A10 FMC, inclusive? I don't think they were ever seen again.

8 ACE – Boreham's Escort RS Cosworth

When Stuart Turner retired from Ford at the end of 1990, his greatest achievement had just been revealed. Although no Ford project was ever approved without a great deal of thought, lobbying and analysis, the seemingly impossible had been achieved. A car coded 'ACE 14' – the Escort RS Cosworth as we later knew it – was on the way.

Stuart himself once told me how it all started:

> Peter Ashcroft, Mike Moreton, John Wheeler, John Griffiths, Bill Meade and I used to get together at Boreham regularly, for meetings about the future. We used to meet up after hours, at Boreham, so that we wouldn't be disturbed, and could talk in private.

Way back in the early months of 1988, before Motorsport had even built its first Sierra Cosworth 4 × 4 development car, thoughts began to turn to a really radical car to take over in the 1990s. Everyone at Motorsport was irritated by the way that Lancia seemed able to turn out new model after new model, to ensure that they were always competitive, and to be thoroughly up-to-date with every rallying trend.

Maybe it was easier for Cesare Fiorio's Lancia motor sport operation to be indulged (for making money seemed to be less important to Lancia than winning at all costs), but Turner and his colleagues were determined to match that trend. As Turner told me:

> I think we were all agreed that whatever our next rally car would be, it had to be based on the platform and the basic layout of an existing main-

stream model … This time we wanted to plan well ahead, for the 1990s, and we wanted to start at once.

Only a year earlier the Sierra Cosworth 4 × 4 was seen as the trail-blazer, but as soon as its weight and bulk became clear the promise faded significantly:

> I think it was one of my comments, thrown into the conversation, that encouraged a breakthrough: 'Why don't we see if we can take the platform and running gear from a Sierra Cosworth 4 × 4, shorten it, then see if an Escort body will fit on it?'
>
> I suppose it's the sort of lunatic thing a non-engineer would suggest, and I can remember the laughter at the time. But the more we analysed our options, the more sense it seemed to make.

Romantic? Yes. Fictional? No. This really was how the Escort RS Cosworth was conceived. The elements of a new front-wheel-drive hatchback shell were somehow made to fit the shortened platform of an entirely different four-wheel-drive saloon. It all happened in 1988, though the production car would not go on sale for another four years.

I suppose I should have known that something important was brewing at Boreham at this time. On my regular visits I noticed that Mike Moreton used to tidy up his office and cover a flip chart before I was even allowed in through the door, and engineer John Wheeler began floating around with that familiar Cheshire Cat ('I'm working on something big and secret') smile on his face. I'd already seen that expression before: once when the Escort

RS1700T was being designed, and once when the famous RS200 was on the way.

But there was a protocol to be observed. At Boreham, when great schemes were coming together, you didn't ask questions, or take sneak pictures. At best you'd get a rude remark, and at worst you might find that you were not even allowed through the gate next time around.

With Stuart Turner's permission, I am now able to quote from his autobiography *Twice Lucky*, as it details what happened in that period:

> Whatever our next rally car would be, it had to be based on the platform and basic layout of an existing mainstream model. Also it would have to be built in a mainstream factory because of the 2,500-production rule for Group A homologations.
>
> There was one seminal meeting, early in 1988, when we concluded that we had to stop playing 'catch-up' – reacting to new regulations instead of planning ahead of them. We'd been last in the field with a four-wheel-drive Group B car, we'd not so far had a four-wheel-drive Escort of any type, and

we'd never get enough power out of the Sierra XR4 × 4 to make it competitive.

Mike Moreton had already been briefed to delve into Ford's forward model plan, and he reported that every new-generation Ford would be a transverse-engined, front-drive car. At the same time, we had got hold of drawings of cars like the Lancia Stratos, and of the current Lancia Delta Integrale, just to remind ourselves of packages that were competitive.

This was all a forerunner to late 1988, when a minor miracle had been achieved. Not only had Boreham thought out what it would like to use for rallying in the 1990s, but it had actually built a running car to prove that point.

I will never forget the day I arrived at Boreham to see a rather odd-looking white Escort RS Turbo in the main workshops, with mechanics fussing all around it. I wasn't encouraged to get too close at first so, was it an RS Turbo or not? Somehow, it stood more four-square than normal, with a wider track, with bigger wheel-arch flares … and there was something else. Yes! The wheels, subtly, were

John Wheeler (engineer – right) and Mike Moreton (product planner – left) were two of the most important personalities who inspired the birth of this famous 'mule' at Ford Motorsport in 1988. The main body superstructure was that of an Escort RS Turbo, but under the skin there was a shortened Sierra Cosworth 4 × 4 platform, its YB engine and its four-wheel-drive transmission.

not in their normal positions – the wheelbase was longer than usual. The tumblers finally dropped into place when I heard the engine being fired up and recognized the unmistake- able drone of a Sierra Cosworth engine.

This was, in fact, the original 'mule' for the car we now know as the Escort RS Cosworth, a one-off prototype that combined a neatly shortened Sierra 4 × 4 platform with a con- temporary white-painted Escort RS Turbo body shell – the Turner/Wheeler/Moreton way of making a smaller and more nimble car than the Sierra Cosworth 4 × 4!

But why build such a car, with an obsolete style? Simply because it is easier to convince management about a concept they can drive than a car that they can only study on paper. I think it was Ford's Bob Howe who once told me that:

One running car is worth a hundred meetings.

Convincing top management that such a car should be built was never going to be easy. The breakthrough, perhaps, came on a day when the original mule (E386 YVX, a unique

machine that has certainly been scrapped) was prettied up and, according to Stuart Turner:

Then we took it to Warley, and offered it to sever- al people, from the Chairman downwards, to take for a drive. They all went up and down the A12 and, to a man, came back with silly grins on their faces. Then, I have to say, every one of them made much the same sort of remark: 'Marvellous, great fun. Now go away and think of something more sensible.'

Concept

Boreham, however, had already done a lot of thinking and this, in their opinion, was 'some- thing more sensible'. This 'Escort-Sierra', in fact, was the result of a mountain of analysis. By the late 1980s John Wheeler knew that all World Championship-winning rally cars needed four-wheel-drive to be competitive. There were many precedents.

By 1988 the Lancia Delta Integrale was dominant in World Championship rallying, and Ford didn't enjoy that. They didn't like it at all. In a way, the 'works' team was still feeling cheated, for no sooner had the RS200 been turned into a winning car (and, make no mistake, it was all set to start winning World Championship events in 1986) than Group B cars were banned. Was it just coincidence that Group A was then imposed for 1987 and that Lancia happened to have an ideal machine ready to compete in that Group?

In the beginning, Wheeler and Moreton sat down to talk. Their object, quite simply, was to make Ford the world's most successful rally team. To do this, they needed to inspire the birth of a new car for Group A motor sport. At the end of the working day they found time for a series of legendary, feet-on-the-table, sketching sessions.

Designing a competitive car was going to be demanding, but forcing it through Ford's management labyrinths was going to be very difficult. The best man for the job was already in place, for, more than anyone at Motorsport, Mike Moreton knew how to do that. A veteran of AVO and SVE planning, he knew that it would have to survive committee meetings, presentations, driving demonstrations and a lot of good, old-fashioned lobbying.

Before approaching 'the Sixth Floor' (Ford-speak for the directors' principal area at the Warley HQ building near Brentwood), Wheeler considered every possibility. There were obvious constraints: 5,000 identical four-seater cars would have to be built to gain homologation (that number, which applied in 1988, would eventually be halved to 2,500 for homologation in 1993 and beyond, making Ford's job that much easier), and the new car would have to be based on a lot of existing Ford hardware. To win in motor sport more than 300bhp was needed, it needed four-wheel drive, and as a rally car it had to be as suitable for the Safari as the RAC rally, for Corsica as well as the Monte.

Any new Ford, therefore, needed to be better, a lot better, than the Lancia Integrale – and capable of improvement in the years that followed. In basic form it also had to be a practical road car: Ford would not approve the production of 5,000 identical cars if these could not be sold, and not make a profit.

Wheeler's analysis, given so often to Ford management teams, and later used as the basis of the presentation to the press, was masterly. Rejecting the new-type Fiesta as a basis, because he considered it as physically too small to accommodate the in-line engine, transmission and massive wheels that would be needed, and the forthcoming Mondeo because it was too large and still too far into Ford's future, he settled on the cabin 'package' of the next Escort, which was known by insiders as the CE14.

Right from the start, too, he was determined to have a car that was aerodynamically stable – and if this required features even more extreme than those of the Sierra RS Cosworth, so be it. The vast rear spoiler that transpired (at roof top rather than mid-hatch level) proves that his point was made. Nor would this purely be a styling exercise, but one that occu-

---

John Wheeler

London-born John Wheeler has always been interested in automobile engineering and spent years with Porsche before arriving at Ford almost by chance in 1980. He was a rising star in the chassis area at Porsche (this included work on racing sports cars) when he answered an advertisement in *Autosport* for a job at Boreham.

Once there he led the team that designed the still-born Escort RS1700T and lobbied in vain for a four-wheel-drive version to be developed. Later his concept for the RS200 evolved into the 200-off supercar, after which he became chief engineer on the rally-improvement of Sierra RS Cosworth cars and made remarkable detail improvements to the rear-drive rally cars.

From 1988 he was one of the prime movers behind the concept, evolution and progress towards production of the new ACE (Escort RS Cosworth) project. In the mid-1990s he had a spell as Aston Martin's chief engineer, during which the V12-engined DB7 was developed. After returning to Ford's technical HQ at Dunton, he began the 2000s working on a variety of secret projects.

pied Ford's German wind-tunnels for 200 hours, taking into account drag, downforce, and air flow into and out of the engine bay.

The CE14 was larger and longer than the Lancia, but no heavier. The fact that there was a lot more space in the engine bay was considered important, for Wheeler wanted to eliminate under-bonnet heat-soak problems, to cater for all high-speed service and rebuild needs – and find space for a lot of wheel movement in the bigger wheel-arches.

Although the Lancia and other current rally cars all used transverse-engine layouts, Wheeler rejected that idea completely. An in-line engine, with a gearbox behind it, offered more, not only in terms of accessibility, but it idealized the weight distribution.

For such a new car, which Wheeler and Moreton coded ACE 14 (Group A CE14), developed versions of the Sierra Cosworth 4 × 4's platform and proven running gear would be ideal. Was it coincidence, or was it the sort of divine fortune that gifted designers always need, but rarely encounter, that the Sierra running gear fitted so well and allowed development time to be telescoped?

Above *In 1989 the very first ACE prototype, SV701, which we would come to know as the Escort RS Cosworth, looked like this. At that stage there were different bonnet louvres, different grille, different front moulding, different wheels, no front splitter and no rear aerofoil – for these were still to be settled. (Courtesy: John Bull)*

Below *Mangle gears? No, something much more sophisticated than that. This is the innards of the MT75 gearbox, which, matched to the YBT engine, helped make the Escort RS Cosworth such a formidable tool in the 1990s.*

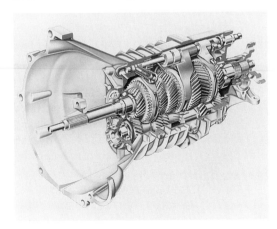

After much wind-tunnel test work, this was the finalized Escort RS Cosworth style, complete with a massive roof-level rear aerofoil, 16in road wheels and air outlets at the rear of the front wing pressings to help keep the brakes cool.

Development

Even though they didn't really have a budget, programme approval or any spare time, Wheeler and Moreton then started on a very expert scrounging process. Although the Sierra Cosworth 4 × 4 was still more than a year away from production, they acquired an engine and four-wheel-drive transmission from that car, along with the floor pan and suspension of a Sierra XR4 × 4.

Working in secret, with expert help from TC Prototypes (who built this car in Northamptonshire), the RS Turbo-based ACE 14 'mule' was completed in a matter of weeks. Without anything as formal as drawings, John Thompson's team shortened the Sierra floor pan, inserted the RS Cosworth engine and transmission, grafted the modified Escort RS Turbo body superstructure onto it – and the original ACE was born.

This was the strangely different 'Escort RS Turbo' I had seen, and which was demonstrated to every decision-maker at Ford's Brent-wood HQ and eventually convinced even the ditherers.

The rest is history. But doesn't it take a long time to turn a Good Idea into a production car? Although the Escort RS Cosworth rally car was officially previewed in September 1990, when Mia Bardolet won the Spanish Talavera rally on its world debut, and production cars went on sale in May 1992, it still took four years for the brainwave to be turned into the metal – for motor sport homologation was not achieved until 1 January 1993.

Every day, even so, was full of action and negotiation. Once approved, the project was turned over to Special Vehicle Engineering for completion, Wheeler moving from Boreham to Dunton to join them as the chief project engineer. At the start there was a tiny team working on the car, four or five at first, and never more than a dozen or so SVE personnel, though more than twenty engineers across the company soon had an input.

Along with Ford's stylists in the design department (and with consultants MGA Developments of Coventry taking on much of the work), SVE developed the hugely effective aerodynamic package ('I knew we needed a rear wing as big as that,' Wheeler recalls, 'but I wasn't sure management would "buy" it at first'), chose the 16in road wheels and produced a remarkably successful ride and handling package.

Inevitably, the original romantic notion that a new-type Escort body shell could be enterprisingly cut-and-shut on a slightly shortened Sierra Cosworth 4 × 4 platform and rolling chassis had to be modified, as more and more structural and aerodynamic imperatives were identified. In the end, the Escort's doors, roof, tailgate and glass were still recognizable, but front and rear wings, bonnet and other major pressings were all changed or unique and 50 per cent of the body shell was new: in fact there were 400 unique components, many of which were modified by Karmann from standard Escort parts.

It's worth noting that those five-spoke Ronal wheels were not only one inch larger in diameter than those of the Sierra Cosworths, but were to have eight inch rim widths, and would run on soft-compound Pirelli P Zero tyres. As dynamics engineer John Bull reminded me, the choice of wheels and tyres at Ford was influenced as much by styling requirements (and customer expectations) as by engineering ideals.

Those Escort RS Cosworth tyres, in fact, were so bulky that they could not be fitted into the existing spare wheelwell bequeathed to the project by the Sierra Cosworth 4 × 4 floor pan, and capital was not available to alter that part of the structure. On road cars, the only spare provided was a puny 'get-you-home' tyre on a steel rim, rated only for 50mph (80km/h), and looking quite ridiculous when fitted. How do I know? Because one of my cars (I ran two Escort RS Cosworths, in consecutive years) suffered a blow-out on the M5 on a wet Sunday evening – the resultant 100-mile crawl home on the 'get-you-home' tyre being one of the most depressing journeys of my life!

Continuity with the Sierra Cosworth 4 × 4 project shone through at SVE, where one or two minor projects had to be shunted aside, or deferred, so that the ACE 14 project could have full priority – the Fiesta RS Turbo, and air-conditioning installations in more than one car were typical examples. John Bull, John Hitchins and Mick Kelly looked after the ride, handling, chassis and general dynamics 'package', and other SVE personalities took a full role in transferring known Sierra engine and drive line technology to the new car.

Along the way, SVE also oversaw the development of an even more powerful version of the famous YB engine and chose those unique instruments. The engine, by the way, might

In the winter of 1991/92 cold-climate testing was carried out close to the Arctic Circle. This is senior chassis development engineer John Bull with a finalized prototype. This car ran on steel wheels for the occasion, so that the appropriate spiked tyres could fit under the wheelarches. (Courtesy: John Bull)

One of the unique Escort RS Cosworth features was the array of back-lit instrument dials. Note, too, the auxiliary instrument pod at top centre, the middle one being the turbo boost gauge.

have looked similar to that of the Sierra Cosworth 4 × 4, but had advanced in various ways, notably by using a hybrid TO3/T04B Garrett AiResearch turbocharger (it was really too big for road cars, but Motorsport needed a unit that big so that the engine would be useful for full-house Group A tuning).

This time round, the camshaft covers (of what were now coded YBT engines) were painted blue instead of the Sierra Cosworth 4 × 4's green, essentially to differentiate them from the Sierra units that remained in produc-

tion at Wellingborough during 1992. According to Paul Fricker:

> You may ask why? Well, we needed yet another different colour, and we thought it looked quite nice. Once again, we didn't consult Ford design until it was really too late to get into an artistic argument!

If you find an Escort RS Cosworth engine painted in red today, it may mean that it has been modified by one of the various tuning houses.

'First time out, First', is how Ford advertised the success of the Escort RS Cosworth rally car prototype, which won the Spanish Talavera rally in September 1990. This was the new model's sensational first appearance.

Motor sport rally development carried on, in the UK and in Spain, before the Escort RS Cosworth even went on sale. This was Malcolm Wilson in one of the early sessions in 1991.

With 227bhp at 6,250rpm (and with a limited duration overboost feature for overtaking), this Cosworth-described YBT engine was an extremely flexible power unit. Naturally it ran on unleaded fuel and an exhaust catalyst was standard. The days of raucous, exhaust spitting sports saloon engines was long gone – but the modern problem was in packaging the catalytic converters under the floor pan.

There was much more to the styling changes than might at first be apparent, and almost every change was made to manage the air flow round, under, over or through the engine bay. To embrace the massive eight inch

wheel rims and 225/45ZR-16in tyres, the front and rear wings had to be reshaped and flared, the front bumper moulding had to take account of optimized air flow into the engine bay, provision had to be made for exhausting hot air from the engine bay and the front brakes, a new high-tech instrument panel had to be laid out, and the entire package had to be made 'feasible' – capable, in other words, of manufacture in numbers.

Although this was always meant to be a supremely versatile road car – it had to pass all of Ford's ultra-demanding endurance tests (as an owner, I often had cause to bless this, for my

All ready to go on sale, this was the right-hand-drive version of the original Escort RS Cosworth of 1992. Note the four catalytic converters in the exhaust system, which somehow had to be squeezed under the floor pan.

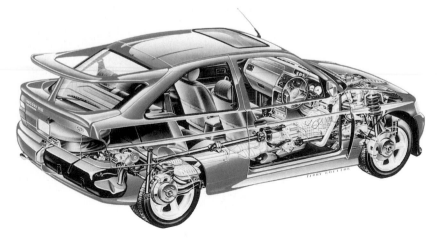

own cars never overheated in heavy traffic jams, or failed to start on icy mornings), the Recaro seats not only looked welcoming but were superbly comfortable, while electric window lifts were engineered into the doors – it also looked as sexy as a Ford car ever could. Those five-spoke alloy wheels, 16in diameter with eight inch rims, looked so sensational that they were instantly copied by wheel makers all over the world. Wider, and even more purposeful, rims would be used on rally cars in the mid-1990s.

Along the way, not only was this a car that developed positive aerodynamic downforce at all cruising and higher speeds (Ford claimed this was the first mass-production car of which they were aware to have that feature), but it was 11.2in (285mm) shorter than the Sierra Cosworth 4 × 4, with a 2.2in (56mm) shorter wheelbase. Even so, it was no lighter, for a lot of work had gone into making this an extremely rigid hatchback: not that the drivers ever noticed, for power-assisted steering and properly power-assisted brakes were both standard.

For a time SVE had to make do with the Escort RS Turbo-based 'mule', but eventually their first true prototype car was completed in February 1990. That car ('SV701' according to SVE's records) was by no means visually finalized, for it ran on old-style eight-spoke alloys, had no cooling louvres in the bonnet and was without a rear spoiler or Ford badging on the nose: there would not be a completely representative machine until 'SV710' was completed much later, and even then the correct road wheels were not yet ready.

In recent years I have been privileged to see a Test and Development schedule for the ACE 14/Escort RS Cosworth, which logs the work done, or due to be done, between late 1989 (when serious SVE development work began – programme approval came in January 1990, which meant that SVE had a flying start) and early 1992, when the very first 'production' cars began to roll off the track at Karmann. 'Strictly Confidential' at the time, this schedule listed the compressed career of nineteen prototypes, one of which was a clay model used to settle the style/design, and more than one of which were eventually subjected to the obligatory 30mph (48.25km/h) head-on crash test. In addition to those machines, there were six other body shells, which were allocated to other specialized tasks.

This was not the only project SVE was tackling at the time, and it is fascinating to see how slowly the on-the-road programme built up (it took time for authentic body shells to be completed), but how intense it then became in 1991. The original 'mule' was used until mid-

Unmistakable from any angle – this was the original Escort RS Cosworth road car all ready for sale in 1992, complete with the massive rear aerofoil, which was standard on UK-market models but could be deleted by special request.

see Chapter 10). By the time that the mainstream Escort/CE14 model was unveiled to the world's media at Blenheim Palace in August 1990, when the flame-blue liveried Escort RS Cosworth rally car also made its startling début, four Phase II Escort RS Cosworths were beginning to start work, and eight more Phase III cars were due to start testing before the end of that year.

The 'mule' had a very busy life, but was eventually crushed. One Ford insider tells me that SVE kept it for so long that when it was three years old it had to be sent to a nearby MoT station for a test:

> The local people just couldn't work out what we were giving them!

Intriguingly, even at that stage coy little references to two-wheel-drive versions were already being made in the progress/testing charts, though that was a derivative that had no significance to the market-place. Some tests, it seemed, needed to be done with the front-wheel-drive part of the transmission disconnected. Much later in the project there would, in fact, be an attempt to evolve a rear-drive only car based on the Escort RS Cosworth, but only one such prototype would ever be constructed (*see* Chapter 9).

By mid-1991 the testing programme was going ahead full blast. Since the rally cars had already put in appearances in British and Spanish rallies, there was no longer any need to fit disguises. Every single production part (except, as we now know, the Vecta alarm/immobilizer system) had been released by March 1991, and many try-out pieces were flooding into Rheine for approval.

With pilot production beginning early in 1992, and with series build due to start within three months, the Escort RS Cosworth was now ready to meet its customers.

Just to prove that the Escort RS Cosworth aero pack could be deleted for some markets, Ford-Germany issued this study showing cars of both types. Note that when the rear aerofoil was deleted, so was the front-end 'splitter'.

1990 (cold climate testing and intercooler development being among its more important tasks), and kept on the strength for some time after that, while work began on building the first prototype rally car in summer 1990 (for the Escort RS Cosworth's motor sport career,

Although the Escort RS Cosworth suspension was supple, it was difficult to get one to roll any more than this.

9 Escort RS Cosworth on Sale

During this development period there was another huge stroke of luck for Ford, whose resourceful planners surely deserved one. In 1991 FISA announced a reduction in the production numbers needed for manufacturers to achieve Group A homologation, from 5,000 to a mere 2,500 cars. By pushing Karmann to concentrate on Escort RS Cosworth assembly at Rheine, in Germany, during 1992, Ford would in any case have easily achieved its 5,000 target during the first year (the limit, in fact, was on the number of engines that Cosworth could manufacture at Wellingborough, and given notice they could just about have coped), but having to build only half that number made the project all the more comfortable to achieve.

The big breakthrough, in any case, had already come when Karmann of Germany won the prestigious job of becoming Ford's major partner in the ACE 14 project. Not only would they take on the task of building all the prototype cars, but they also made the tools and assembly jigs for the new structure, and set up a dedicated assembly line for building the production cars.

In 1989, when the deal was agreed, Ford had not yet built a single Escort RS Cosworth prototype apart from the legendary 'mule'. As ever a great deal of analysis went into the planning of the new car, primarily to work out where it should be manufactured in numbers. Ford's business, after all, was to build cars, so in-house manufacture was seriously considered, although

Even though the Escort RS Cosworth was based on the upper shell of a front-wheel-drive Escort, it looked so much more menacing in the flesh — especially when rushing up close to the next car, ready to overtake.

it was eventually rejected as too disruptive as far as 'mainstream' models were concerned.

Karmann, with modern and efficient facilities at Osnabrück and Rheine (50km west of Osnabrück), both in north-western Germany, was already building body shells, or complete motor cars, for companies as diverse as Ford, VW, Porsche and BMW, and was soon seen as an ideal home for the new car – not only to build prototypes, but also to look after body shell manufacture and final assembly. In any case, there was already a significant Ford connection at Karmann.

Since 1984 Karmann had been assembling the USA-market Merkur XR4Ti (a modified Sierra with a turbocharged Ford-USA engine), but they were also scheduled to assemble the new CE14-type Escort Cabriolet when it came on-stream in 1991/92. No other independent company, therefore, knew as much about the two principal elements of ACE 14 – the platform of the Sierra, and the superstructure of the Escort – or was as resourceful in producing special cars (coupés, convertibles, saloons, hatchbacks, or even its own-brand caravans) in the plants.

It was pure happenstance that the last of the Merkur (Sierra) XR4Tis was to be built in 1989, so certain Escort RS Cosworth preparations could be carried out using some of the redundant XR4Ti body framing and welding facilities. Even so, it was not as simple as that, as John Bull of SVE confirms:

I very quickly became responsible for building all the prototypes. Karmann actually went ahead and built a new prototype-build workshop at Rheine, and very soon they then built a new dedicated assembly line at Rheine to manufacture Escort RS Cosworths.

In fact I quickly became 'Our Man at Karmann', effectively what the industry calls the Resident Engineer on the project. I soon dropped into a routine. I kept a Sierra Cosworth 4 × 4 parked at Cologne airport. I would fly out on Monday morning, from Stansted, in the Ford plane, drive up to Karmann [it was about 100 miles, or one

autobahn hour's dash away], then, provided I wasn't due to work over the weekend, I would do the reverse journey on the Friday afternoon, have a weekend at home, then get ready to go out again on the following Monday. I did that for about 18 months, I guess.

As far as Karmann was concerned, the XR4Ti most conveniently hung around until the Escort RS Cosworth project was well under way, and once the team began assembling road cars early in 1992 the production rate built up rapidly. As already noted, in 1989 Karmann was told to face up to producing the first 5,000 cars in 1992 alone, but after the rules were relaxed Ford was happy to settle for 3,448 machines instead.

Production

In the first year the rush was not only to build a lot of cars, but to make many of them suitable for use in motor sport. Although there was only

Superficially, at least, the Escort RS Cosworth engine bay looked much like that of the last Sierra Cosworth 4 × 4, though the blue-painted YBT camshaft cover gives the game away. All in all, this was a snug-fitting ensemble, which gave great credit to John Wheeler's original concept.

one mechanical/chassis package – each and every car in the first 2,500 examples had the front splitter/high rear aerofoil package, because that was what Boreham needed for sporting homologation purposes – Ford's product planners then rather overcomplicated matters by specifying three different trim/equipment levels for sale throughout Europe, starting with the 'Standard' (intended for motor sport) car, and topping out with the 'Luxury' version.

During development, of course, SVE had allowed for all this, not only by testing cars in left-hand or right-hand drive, but with and without sunshine-roof fittings, with and without air-conditioning – and even with or without the rear aerofoil, which would become a 'delete option' at a later date. Once the car went into production, six colours – three 'solid' and three metallic – were listed. All cars were originally listed with cloth trim, but leather was optional on Luxury models.

Incidentally, how often have you seen an Escort Cosworth without its huge rear spoiler, and without the adjustable 'splitter' under the front spoiler? Perhaps not in the UK at all, but after the first 2,500 cars were built in 1992 (to satisfy the homologation authorities about 'identical specifications'), in other European territories the car was certainly made available with the less extrovert option of only a single, more modest, spoiler shape in the profile of the rear edge of the hatchback panel. The same 'delete aero pack' was mentioned in UK-market brochures, but customers wanting such cars found it amazingly difficult to get their own way!

For motor sport use, in any case, the car was only homologated with the complete twin-spoiler equipment in place, this being a very functional piece of kit that provided positive aerodynamic downforce at higher road speeds. This was most marked if the adjustable front-end splitter was placed as far forward as possible. It might have looked a bit strange, but it certainly worked.

'Standard' cars lacked some of the gizmos that many customers clearly wanted (such cars did not have tilt-and-slide sunshine roofs, electric window lifts, radio-cassette equipment, electrically heated front window, genuine Recaro front seats, nor low-mounted fog lamps in the front apron), since Ford reasoned that these items were not only heavy, but would be thrown out immediately when motorsport preparation began. Even so, the price reduction was well worth considering: in the UK a 'Standard' undercut the 'Luxury' model by £2,115.

All UK-market cars, make no mistake, had excellent anti-theft precautions, including Ford's first mainstream use of an engine immobilizer, although fitment of the Vecta system was only finalized at a late stage. As John Bull told me:

To his great joy, in the early 1990s the author ran two Escort RS Cosworths in succession as daily-drivers. This is the second car, painted in Mallard Green, in its usual travel-stained condition!

From 1993 Ford-UK was happy to supply Escort RS Cosworths without the 'aero' kit, like this example, but there were very few takers.

I can remember us rushing through the security system. That was a last-minute thing that came through the Marketing people, who said that if we didn't put an Alarm/Immobilizing system, in simple terms, they might find it difficult to sell the car.

It was a very simple installation, where you had to put a special key into the slot on the centre console before the car would fire up. We rushed that through in the last few weeks before Job One – with the Vecta people actually coming out to Karmann-Rheine, where we set them up in a department all of their own, and they took all cars off the line, and fitted them out in an 'after-market' sense.

Even so, the nation's low-life took some time to discover that it was never going to be easy to steal an Escort RS Cosworth – an entirely different proposition from the Sierra RS Cosworth, thank goodness. From personal experience, once, when my first car was parked overnight outside a Birmingham hotel, thieves managed to butcher the door lock and got into the cabin, before discovering that the Vecta immobilizer had totally defeated them. I was happy about that, although the door looked messy for the next few days! Purely out of spite, I guess, the same crooks levered off the 'Cosworth' badge on the tail gate and damaged the rear paintwork at the same time.

Another controversial fitting, which had no practical use, required the first 2,500 cars to be equipped with a simple 'water injection' kit. Rallying competitors, Lancia originally, had discovered that the injection of water into the inlet passage meant that the mixture would be cooled down and become more dense, which gave the promise of more power.

Engineering a rival system was easy enough (and, in any case, this could be enhanced for motor sport use), but the rules required this to feature in all cars counted for homologation purposes. In the case of the Escort RS Cosworth, this system involved nothing more 'high-tech' than a windscreen washer bag with some piping. Because 2,600 cars were fitted out, but because not all of these were in the first batch, something of an homologation rumpus brewed up, although in the end Ford got away with this stratagem. How many road cars ever had an operating water injection system? Very few, if you ask me.

In the UK, therefore, there were two prices: £21,380 for the 'Standard' and £23,495 for the 'Luxury' model (with an extra £481 charged for leather upholstery on the 'Luxury' version). A surprising number of lower-price 'stripped out' versions were actually delivered, which irritated Ford for a time as there was

Escort RS Cosworth (1992–96)

Layout
Unit construction steel body/chassis structure. Two-door plus hatchback, front engine/four-wheel drive, sold as four-seater sports hatchback.

Engine
Type	Ford-Cosworth YB Series
Block material	Cast iron
Head material	Cast aluminium
Cylinders	4 in-line
Cooling	Water
Bore and stroke	90.82 × 76.95mm
Capacity	1993cc
Main bearings	5
Valves	4 per cylinder, operated by twin overhead camshafts, via inverted bucket-type tappets, with the camshafts driven by cogged belt from the crankshaft
Compression ratio	8.0:1 (nominal)
Fuel supply	Weber-Marelli fuel injection, with Garrett AiResearch TO3/TO4B turbocharger
Max. power	227bhp @ 6,250rpm
Max. torque	224lb ft @ 3,500rpm

Transmission
Five-speed manual gearbox, all-synchromesh, and four-wheel drive incorporating 34%/66% front/rear torque split.

Clutch	Single plate, diaphragm spring

Overall gearbox ratios
Top	3.005:1
4th	3.62:1
3rd	4.923:1
2nd	7.530:1
1st	13.068:1
Reverse	11.801:1
Final drive ratios	3.62:1

22.28mph (35.85km/h)/1,000rpm in top gear

Suspension and steering
Front	Independent, by coil springs, MacPherson struts, track control arms, telescopic dampers and anti-roll bar
Rear	Independent, by coil springs, semi-trailing arms, anti-roll bar and telescopic dampers
Steering	Rack-and-pinion (with power assistance)
Tyres	225/45ZR-16in, radial-ply
Wheels	Cast alloy disc, bolt-on fixing
Rim width	8.0in

Brakes
Type	Disc brakes at front, discs at rear, hydraulically operated, with hydraulic ABS anti-lock control
Size	10.9in front discs, 10.8in rear discs

Dimensions (in/mm)
Track	
Front	57.2/1,453
Rear	58.0/1,472
Wheelbase	100.4/2,551
Overall length	165.8/4,211
Overall width	68.3/1,734
Overall height	56.1/1,425
Unladen weight	2,811lb/1,275kg

UK retail price
(at launch in 1992)
Road Standard	£21,380
Road Luxury	£23,495

Development changes
From spring 1994, the following specification changes were made:

Engine
Fuel supply	Ford EEC IV engine management system, with T25 turbocharger
Max. power	224bhp @ 5,750rpm
Max. torque	220lb ft @ 2,500rpm

Dimensions
Unladen weight	2,882lb/1,307kg

UK retail price
(at launch in May 1994)
Road Standard	£22,535
Road Luxury	£25,825

Every aspect of the Escort RS Cosworth − engine, transmission, suspension and aerodynamic equipment − was designed to make the car invincible in motor sport, the result being an incredibly purposeful machine. More than 7,000 were sold in less than four years.

more profit for them in the better-equipped types. Air conditioning, an optional extra, came on stream from late 1992.

The new car broke new ground: it was the first four-wheel-drive Escort (later there would be a few RS2000 4 × 4s with an entirely different type of engine/transmission installation) and it was the first to have the name 'Cosworth' attached to it. For a short time there was actually a waiting list, since Ford had pitched its prices very astutely. Well before the end of 1992, however, the rush was already over. In Britain the insurance industry was doing its very best to kill off the car's appeal, and theft or sheer bloody-minded vandalization had become a depressing feature.

Ford's reputation was not helped by Britain's most outspoken TV motoring presenter, Jeremy Clarkson, who ran an Escort RS Cosworth for a time while living in southwest London. It was his off-the-cuff remarks, on air, about the insane premium demands by his own insurers (were they really serious when they quoted him £20,000 for compre-

hensive coverage?) that did the most high-profile damage. Mind you, his other on-air remarks helped to give the car a broad-shouldered reputation. If I recall his words correctly, they were:

> In the end I had to get rid of the Cosworth. It was such an aggressive car. At the end of a gruelling day's filming at Pebble Mill, I would be exhausted, come out to the car park, and find my Escort lurking under the trees, looking for a fight.

Sanity eventually prevailed in the insurance industry, premiums fell (though not dramatically), and the vast majority of road cars survived into the next decade as much-loved classic cars.

Although both Ford and Karmann were proud of the way that assembly built up, they did not release detailed production figures at the time, but we now know that nearly 3,500 were built between February 1992 (when the first Geneva Show cars, and the first series-production cars were assembled) and the end of the year. True series production began on 27 April 1992, and the 'on-sale' date in the UK was 22 May 1992. At peak, but only in the summer/autumn of 1992, this meant that close to 100 new Escort RS Cosworths were being completed every working week at Rheine in Germany.

Market forces then took over, demand dropped right back in 1993, and by 1994 Karmann was building little more than 1,100 cars a year (that equates to 22–25 cars every week); the only way this could be done in any quasi-economic way was to close down the assembly lines for more than half of the working week.

Nevertheless, the new car received rave reviews wherever it was tested. Along with thousands of others, I was fortunate enough to run not one, but two (in succession) of the original spec. cars in 1993 and 1994, both of them being painted in the colour, unique to the Escort RS Cosworth, known officially by Ford as Mallard Green (although SVE, I hear, always referred to it as 'British Racing Duck'!).

Problems? Mechanically I had none at all − except I discovered that the soft-com-

Escort RS Cosworth 'Acropolis' – have you ever seen one? Probably not, because this was a 'limited edition' project that never went ahead.

pound 245/45ZR-16 Pirelli P Zero tyres wore out even quicker than I (or Ford) had ever expected. So much so that on my second car, on one sad occasion, I miscalculated the wear rate, had a worn rear tyre literally explode on a motorway and had to tackle a wheel change on the hard shoulder, in the rain, in the dark. Then I had to limp slowly home on the narrow-section, 'not over 50mph', space-saver spare tyre.

Even so, it was worth it, for the overall grip of a healthy car was matchless, and the ride was remarkable. As *Autocar & Motor* commented when comparing the new car with its deadly rival, the Lancia Delta Integrale:

> If you accept its fundamental firmness, the Ford's way with bumps is impressive. Edges are rounded, ruts and holes softened, and bumps smothered. No harshness, no jarring. Control and damping are simply brilliant.

Not that too many owners seemed content to leave the car as it had basked in the showroom. As with the Escort RS1600 and RS1800 types before it, hundreds of standard Escort RS Cosworths were turned into competition cars, many for rallying but a large number for racing and rallycross, which reduced the stock of road cars. Many owners, too, knew just what sort of reserves had been engineered into this engine by Cosworth, and spent thousands of pounds having the engines boosted to previously unimaginable heights.

We now know that true experts like Mountune could produce well over 350bhp, even while nominally retaining many standard components and matching the engine to Group A regulations. Where the only limit was an owner's bank balance, it was possible to add in various Sierra RS500 features (a large turbocharger, eight fuel injectors and a bigger intercooler) and to liberate more than 500bhp. Quite a number of private owners' cars received that treatment, to the awesome admiration of their friends.

No, I never actually drove such an Escort RS Cosworth, but all I can say is that my two standard-specification cars, both 'big turbo' cars with 'only' 227bhp, were exciting road cars, so a fully modified machine must have been mind-blowing.

Mid-life Changes

When my second car, another 'Luxury' model, was delivered early in 1994 I noted that, like all Fords of this period, the steering wheel had

Later-model Escort RS Cosworths had lightly modified facia/instrument displays, an air bag-equipped steering wheel, a different type of seat covering style, and (just out of shot) a container on the screen rail for the electric sunshine roof motor.

acquired an airbag, which fortunately I never had to assess, while the sunroof was now electrically operated. The performance, the ride and the general ambience, on the other hand, were still as superlative as ever. Other changes, however, were already on the way. These finally broke cover in June 1994 after series production had begun in May. Way back at launch time in 1992, Ford had already hinted that the original technical and visual package – big turbo, Weber-Marelli injection, 'whale tail' aerodynamics and a very basic 'Standard' specification – might be modified for 1993. Then in the spring of 1993 it was suggested that changes would follow in mid-year. In the event none of these changes were made for another year.

SVE's original intention had been to develop a more user-friendly version of the road car, to be available soon after the original 'homologation' run had been completed. In the end, this changeover was slightly delayed. With sporting homologation finally settled, the 'Mark 2' Escort RS Cosworth finally appeared in preview cars in May 1994, being slightly less extrovert, even better developed than before, and yet more driveable.

This version of the car, which in the event would actually be rarer than the original, featured changes to the engine, to the general ambience of the interior and (optionally) to the styling. The engine was the long-promised and more flexible development, the YBP. Although, internally, there were few changes, and the maximum sustained boost was still limited to 0.8 Bar, it now came complete with a smaller (T25) turbocharger, which had 60 per cent less rotating inertia than before, corporate-style Ford EEC 1V electronics instead of the original Weber-Marelli, a revised throttle body, exhaust manifold, new HT coil arrangements and new-style/new-shape camshaft and drive belt covers.

Ford's strategy had been to maintain the same level of peak power (the quoted figure, in fact, was three bhp less, but at 5,750rpm instead of the original 6,250rpm, while peak torque was developed at 2,500rpm instead of 3,500rpm) but with better driveability.

Those of us who had owned original-spec. cars had been used to feeling the boost come in with a rush at about 3,000rpm, but here was

Original Escort RS Cosworths had an engine bay that resembled that of late-model Sierra RS Cosworths, but with a blue-painted cylinder head. From 1994, however, this small-turbo version, with a different (black and silver) cam cover style, took over instead.

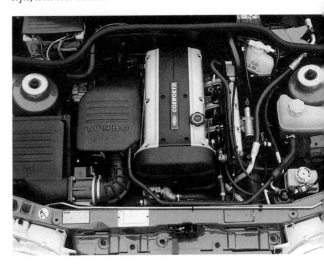

If one drove an Escort RS Cosworth fast, there often wasn't much time to look at the instruments. So now … note the air bag in the steering wheel on this 1994 model (there is a matching air bag hidden away in front of the front passenger), the 260km/h speedometer (this is a German-market car), and the fittings for the anti-theft immobilizer system mounted on the centre console to the right of the gear lever. The boost gauge (top centre, small dial) reads up to 1.3 Bar.

an engine that pushed seamlessly from only 2,000rpm instead. Those who were used to changing gear at high revs would notice little difference, but those whose driving was a bit more relaxed immediately saw the point. Paradoxically it seemed to make the revised Escort RS Cosworth livelier than ever in heavy traffic. Not only that but, if you insisted, in the UK it was now possible to order one without the big rear spoiler and its sturdy central pillar (and have a reasonable chance of getting such a car delivered!), although few real Escort RS Cosworth lovers in the UK ever seemed to do that.

Since 1992 (when the Sierra Cosworth 4 × 4 price was slashed by £6,000) the general level of Ford prices seemed to see-saw all over the place, but for the T25-turboed car there were still to be two versions, priced at £22,535 for the 'Standard' and £25,825 for the 'Luxury'. On top of this, leather seat trim cost £1,050, and air conditioning another £920. These, in fact, were the prices that already applied to late-model 'Mk I' Escort RS Cosworths.

Although the latest version was a fine car with a great sporting reputation – well over 5,000 original-type Escort RS Cosworths had already been built, and Ford Motorsport's fine record in World Championship rallies had

made all the effort worthwhile – it arrived at an awkward time for the Blue Oval.

The Escort RS Cosworth's biggest problem was that, because the entire Sierra range had been superseded by the Mondeo in 1993 (a car built on a totally different, transverse-engine, front-wheel-drive platform), its own platform was no longer shared with any other Ford. As a result unit prices rose rapidly, since the Escort RS Cosworth was being built in limited numbers, and whenever Ford's all-powerful finance staff see those trends they tend to reach for a plug to pull.

There was more. Car sales across Europe were still under pressure, responding to the after-effects of an early 1990s trade recession, while the vicious (and, in my opinion, quite unjustified) attack on all such high-performance cars by the insurance companies had an effect.

Not only that, but Ford had very definitely lost heart, lost faith even, in its 'RS' enterprise. It wasn't long before rumours began to spread about the imminent demise of the Escort RS Cosworth.

In 1994/95 Ford launched a special-edition car in the hope of boosting the car's appeal, although this seems to have made little impact on overall sales. It retained standard running gear, the improvements being purely cosmetic. To celebrate François Delecour's amazing victory in the 1994 Monte Carlo rally, Ford put the Escort RS Cosworth 'Monte' on sale, this being painted in a choice of three colour schemes – a subtle dark maroon (Jewel Violet), Mallard Green or Black – with OZ-style road wheels (just like those used on the Boreham rally cars), and with cloth trim picked out with 'Monte Carlo' embroidered into the front seat squab. The 'delete aero option' was available, which meant that some cars did not have the large rear spoiler. Just 200 such cars were produced, some with the large turbo, but some with the later T25 turbo.

Another proposed limited-edition model, this time painted in a vivid yellow, was the 'Acropolis' version (intended to celebrate Ford's success in the 1993 World Championship rally). As far as I can see, only one such car, which retained the standard wheels, was ever produced and the proposed 200-off run was aborted.

Also spotted in a picture in *Autocar* on 30 March 1994 was a single normally aspirated 16-valve RS2000-engined/rear-wheel-drive car, but nothing came of that either.

Ford-watchers in the mid-1990s experienced momentary hope, and then confusion, when the existence of another SVE-developed prototype became clear. This was based on the Escort RS Cosworth chassis, but with rear-wheel drive, and was powered by the torquey 2.9-litre twin-cam-per-bank Scorpio 24-valve power unit, which is fully described in Chapter 11. Nothing became of this car, which was never intended for motor sport use, and naturally it was not seen in public until its development had been cancelled. As John Bull says:

That was an attempt to overcome the poor sales. It was obvious that we weren't selling as many Escort RS Cosworths as we had hoped, but we had contractual obligations to both major partners – Karmann and Cosworth.

One or two of us – and people at Karmann – started to think: 'What can we do?' Eventually we came up with the marriage of the Cosworth 24-valve FB engine to the rear-wheel-drive MT75 gearbox, but only in rear-wheel-drive form.

The engine was a bit big, and it was difficult getting it in. I remember cutting and carving the radiator and engine bay panels to make it fit. We had a special fan built up too. But it was really only a one-off toy, very much an under-the-table pro-

In 1994 Ford sold the Escort RS Cosworth 'Monte' as a 200-off limited edition. It was mechanically standard, but fitted with these authentic OZ alloys, an alloy gear lever knob and special cloth trim. This particular car had the 'delete aero option' – and, yes, that really is the actual 1994 Monte Carlo Rally-winning car in the background. (Courtesy: John Bull)

ject, we certainly didn't spend much money on it. The engine was quite a bit heavier than the YB, but as we were deleting the front prop shaft, the front diff and the front drive shafts that would almost have balanced it out.

It was built up at Karmann, in a corner of the prototype/development workshops there, not at SVE in the UK. It really was a very nice car, it was subdued, and it didn't need the big spoilers, so it just had the neat single spoiler at the back.

We built it at about the time VW was introducing their own VR6 (V6)-engined Golf, and it would have been an obvious competitor for that. I remember writing a product paper, detailing what it consisted of, and spelling out just how many we needed to sell to make it a viable programme. Really, it was only hundreds of cars, not thousands – because we weren't proposing to spend a lot of investment money on engines and transmissions – but even so we couldn't get any of the marketing territories (not one, if I remember rightly) to sign up for it.

And that really was the last significant engineering initiative that went into the Escort RS Cosworth programme. Well before the end of 1995, Ford had taken the major decision that the existing 'RS' era should come to an end and the legendary badge put back into the 'pending' cupboard. The announcement came in September 1995: the Escort RS Cosworth was to be killed off in January 1996 and the front-wheel-drive RS2000 would follow later in the year. Production, in fact, could easily have been stopped in 1995, but by advertising a '1996' cut-off date this would allow Ford Motorsport to keep on using the car, and its planned derivative, the Escort WRC, for a further season at top level. Boreham's specialists, it seemed, had lost none of their guile.

The official reasons given were that the car could no longer meet the new exhaust emission laws or the latest 'drive-by' noise tests. Some suggested that this was spurious reasoning, and that poor sales had really brought on this cancellation, while others accepted the inevitable. If sales had been healthier, Ford's

engineers could certainly have redeveloped the existing car to meet the new challenges, but if that expense had to be spread over a disappointingly small number of cars then it was never going to be justified economically.

Richard Parry-Jones, then Ford's vice-president of the small/medium vehicle technical centre, commented:

> It's a sad day for hot-hatch fans. For a period at least, there will be no more high-performance Fords.

But the dream was over. After the final car (VIN No. SP93313, registered as N912 FVX)

The Escort family of 1995 was led, of course, by the Escort RS Cosworth along with (left to right in the background) Cabriolet, Ghia and RS2000 models. Although mainstream Escorts received a new slitty-grille nose (this one) for 1995, the style of the Escort RS Cosworth was unchanged throughout its four-year career.

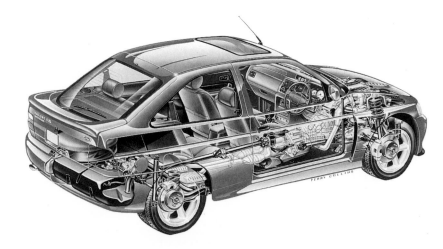

No, this is not an exact repeat of the cutaway shown on page 129, for artist Terry Collins has managed to incorporate the small turbo engine, and the air bag steering wheel.

had rolled off the line in Germany, the assembly track was speedily converted to other use. More than 7,100 road cars had been built – and now there would be no more.

Unofficially, I have been told that there was one further, rather sad, moment at Ford during 1996. Soon after that final car had been completed (it carried 'The Last Car' stamped on its chassis plate), it was retained by Ford and eventually used to take a staff member to an appointment at Donington Park. When he returned to where it had been parked it was no longer there, and has never been seen again. Stolen, for sure. Cloned, probably. Stripped so that the component parts could be sold on? Maybe – unless you know better …

There was still more to come, however. As far as motor sport usage was concerned, however, Boreham had one final hand to play.

Escort World Rally Car – The Last Cosworth-engined Escort

Although the last Escort RS Cosworth road cars were produced in early 1996, this was not quite the end of the story. In 1997 and 1998 a very limited number of made-for-rallying Escorts were produced, called Escort World Rally Car types.

Since it did not carry the 'Cosworth' name as part of its title, should this car even be

included in this book? On the one hand, it was not a true, series-production road car (there was never any such model as an Escort World Rally Car model in the price lists), but on the other hand it was an obvious, close relative to the Escort RS Cosworth. Technically, it was a fascinating final statement of the Sierra/Escort four-wheel-drive theme, and it shows just how versatile the Cosworth YB engine actually was.

The Escort World Rally Car was conceived by Ford Motorsport, at Boreham, in a real hurry. Because there was no need to get involved with legislation, marketing requirements or cost accountants, there was no question of calling in the main design/engineering base at Dunton.

For 1997, Ford Motorsport knew that it needed a new model to remain competitive in World rallying. Not only was the Escort RS Cosworth now matched by its rivals, but soon there would be new regulations in force. Instead of Group A, a new category for World Rally Cars was on the way.

To make it easier for manufacturers to break into World rallying, and not to have to build special four-wheel-drive models – at least 2,500 of them – to gain homologation, companies such as Citroën and Peugeot started lobbying heavily for a new category to be introduced.

After discussions had occupied most of 1994 and 1995, the result was the launch in

Now here's a chilling thought – the police using Escort RS Cosworths as chase cars in the mid-1990s. Some did, for sure, but found them too small to carry all the safety gear that a modern police vehicle needs.

1996 of what became known as the World Rally Car category. Only such machines would have to be built in one season (none of them for use as road cars, all of them for World rallies), and they had to be based on models of which at least 25,000 cars (such as front-wheel-drive Escorts) were being made in a year.

Almost every other modification of the basic design was allowed, including conversion from front-wheel-drive to four-wheel-drive, with turbocharged engines to be of 2-litre capacity. The cars themselves had to be at least 157in (4.00m) in length and have an unladen weight of at least 2,712lb (1,230kg).

For Ford, this might have seemed like an opportunity to update the Escort RS Cosworth. Even so, there was a major problem. One of the cornerstones of the new rules was that WRCs had to be based on a 25,000 per year model that was already in production.

Not only had the Escort RS Cosworth never sold like that, but by this time it was already out of production.

Yet there was no other obvious Ford model that immediately qualified. The existing Fiesta was thought to be too small, and the replacement for the existing 1990s-style Escort, to be badged 'Focus', was not due to be launched until 1998, or ready until 1999.

It was time for the FIA's bluff to be called: Ford hoped that some compromise could be reached. Ford therefore consulted the FIA, explained their problem and suggested an interim solution. If they would allow Ford's first-generation WRC to be based on the old Escort RS Cosworth (which was, itself, based on the Escort), then 'works' Fords could be on the starting line for the Monte Carlo rally in January 1997. If not – well, they would simply be obliged to withdraw from rallying until 1999.

Although the FIA finally agreed to this, there was then a big rush to get a competitive and viable Escort WRC ready. Concept work started as late as June 1996 and the first prototype (only two were ever built) was completed on 13 October. The first tests were com-

146

pleted a week later, the car was unveiled on 3 November (immediately before the Catalunya rally), and homologation inspection of the twenty necessary kits of parts was completed on 19 December! Even in such a high-pressure sport, it never gets much quicker than that. With no road car development, no legislation and homologation pressures to worry about, the Escort WRC went from 'Good Idea' to WRC homologation in six months! It had to be so, for if Ford was to stay in World rallying in 1997, the twenty sets of parts had to be ready before the end of 1996. To satisfy FIA inspectors, promises of production were not enough: the pieces would have to be there, on the floor, to be counted.

As Engineering Manager Philip Dunabin commented at the time of launch:

> Our request to the FIA to base the World Rally Car on the existing Escort 4 × 4 has allowed us to build a long-term plan on the existing and future Escort models ... the decision to base the World Rally Car on the current Escort was never really questioned.

What did all this cost? Ford has never released a figure, but by most previous standards it must have been very little indeed. Time, not money, was the enemy in 1996, for there was one inescapable target that could not be missed: as far as Ford was concerned, two 'works' cars had to be on the start line of the Monte Carlo rally in January 1997.

Although the Escort WRC was not a true road car (the only road motoring any of the cars did was during the rallies themselves), it was such a logical, and lineal, descendant of the Escort RS Cosworth that it deserves analysis here.

To evolve the Escort WRC, Ford Motorsport looked at their state-of-the-art Escort RS Cosworth rally car (not the road car, of course) to search for improvements, and these can be summarized as follows:

Engine: New (smaller, to suit a 34mm restrictor) IHI turbocharger, different exhaust mani- fold, and fuel injection changes (with eight instead of four active injectors). This, we now know, resulted in a peak power output of 310bhp at 5,500rpm, with a meaty and very solid torque curve. This work was done in conjunction with Mountune (Cosworth was not directly involved), and as far as is known there was no separate 'YB...' code for the type.

Engine bay cooling: There was enhanced airflow through larger front apertures, with relocated intercooler and water radiators.

Rear suspension: By the mid-1990s the semi-trailing arm system that had evolved over the life of the Sierra and Escort RS Cosworth ranges had shown up many detail failings (John Taylor once commented that 'when it moved up and down, there was a war going on among the bushes'). For the WRC it was ditched, a lighter and stronger sub-frame was fabricated, and there were new-style MacPherson struts.

Aerodynamics: There was a new front bumper, and a smaller/reshaped rear aerofoil to generate more downforce with less drag. The front-end and its air intake were modified to suit the new radiator and intercooler installations.

Weight distribution: This was improved, with an 80-litre fuel tank, spare wheel, and a 40-litre water reservoir (to provide cooling sprays of intercooler and brakes) centrally positioned in the rear compartment.

The aerodynamic improvements had been honed in Ford's wind-tunnel at Merkenich, in Germany, following initial suggestions by Nigel Stroud of Reynard. These resulted in improved front and rear downforce. In any case, the new aerofoil was needed to meet the new regulations, for the old Escort RS Cosworth style of spoiler was too large to pass through the regulatory 'template'.

At the front, these changes were needed to help package a 33 per cent larger water radiator, and a 50 per cent larger turbo intercooler positioned ahead, rather than on top of, that radiator.

Although the two 1997 Monte cars were partly built at Boreham before the World Rally

Escort World Rally Car (1997–98)

Layout

Unit construction steel body/chassis structure. Two-door plus hatchback, front engine/four-wheel drive, sold as two-seater sports hatchback, purely for rallying.

Engine

Type	Ford-Cosworth YB Series
Block material	Cast iron
Head material	Cast aluminium
Cylinders	4 in-line
Cooling	Water
Bore and stroke	90.82 × 76.95mm
Capacity	1993cc
Main bearings	5
Valves	4 per cylinder, operated by twin overhead camshafts, via inverted bucket-type tappets, with the camshafts driven by cogged belt from the crankshaft
Compression ratio	9.6:1 (nominal)
Fuel supply	Ford Pectel fuel injection, with IHI turbocharger
Max. power	(official) 300bhp @ 5,500rpm
Max. torque	434lb ft @ 4,000rpm

Transmission

Six-speed manual gearbox, non-synchromesh, and four-wheel drive incorporating variable front/rear torque split and 'active' differentials

Clutch	Diaphragm spring

Suspension and steering

Front	Independent, by coil springs, MacPherson struts, telescopic dampers, track control arms, and anti-roll bar
Rear	Independent, by coil springs, MacPherson struts, telescopic dampers, track control arms and anti-roll bar
Steering	Rack-and-pinion (with power assistance)
Tyres	Various – 16in, 17in, 18in radial-ply
Wheels	Cast alloy disc, bolt-on fixing
Rim width	Various

Brakes

Type	Disc brakes at front, discs at rear, hydraulically operated, with no ABS anti-lock control
Size	(Typically) Tarmac: 14.9in front discs, 12.3in rear discs. Gravel: 12.4in front discs, 12.4in rear discs

Dimensions (in/mm)

Track	
Front	60.2/1,530
Rear	60.2/1,530
Wheelbase	100.4/2,551
Overall length	165.8/4,211
Overall width	69.7/1,770
Overall height	56.1/1,425
Unladen weight	2,712lb/1,230kg

UK retail price

Special order, depending on specification and extra parts ordered

Escort RS Cosworth production

To meet Group A regulations for homologation into motor sport, Ford needed to build only 2,500 Escort RS Cosworths. Even though series production did not begin until April 1992, this was achieved before the end of 1992.

Production then continued at a lower, but essentially stable, rate for three more years, though at an average rate of less than 30 cars every week. This was a gross under-use of Karmann's facilities, since these cars could all have been built in one working day. Although one reason given for the Escort RS Cosworth's demise was that it would not meet new European noise legislation, the over-riding reason must have been that production at such a low rate was no longer viable.

These are the official year-on-year figures:

1992	3,448
1993	1,143
1994	1,180
1995	1,306
1996	68

This makes a grand total of 7,145 road cars. Many more competition cars were created around Karmann-built body shells, which were sold through Ford Motorsport, so we may never know exactly how many Escort RS Cosworths eventually took to the road.

What might have been – SVE built a one-off rear-wheel-drive prototype, powered by the Scorpio 24V V6 engine, and with different wheels. Though the engine was a tight fit into the engine bay, the result was a very capable, fuss-free, machine. Look closely and you can see the '24V' badge on the hatchback lid. SVE wanted to see this car in production, but the analysts could never make the 'business case' to justify it. (Courtesy: John Bull)

contract was awarded to Malcolm Wilson's M-Sport team in Cumbria, later cars were all built by M-Sport, or from kits of parts provided by M-Sport to a remote location.

By mid-year the construction of those new cars at Dovenby Hall was almost a batch production business. By the end of the season no fewer than twenty-nine Escort WRCs had been completed, ten of them actually being converted Group A machines of 1995 or 1996 vintage.

There was still one more season of World Rallying to be tackled by the Escort WRCs, so no fewer than nineteen Escort WRCs appeared in the 1998 World Championship series, fifteen of them being brand new. When a number of privately financed conversions are added in to the 'works' M-Sport total, this brings the number of Escort WRCs built in two years to well over fifty. Not bad for a stop gap design.

10 Escort RS Cosworth in Rallying

As I have already noted (in Chapter 8) the Escort RS Cosworth's rallying career began well before the new model went on sale. Not only did it win the Talavera rally, which was so crucial to its future, but in the next two seasons a great deal of development, if not actually much sport, took place.

During 1991 (this was still well in advance of the production car going on sale) Escort RS Cosworth development continued, both at Boreham and in Malcolm Wilson's and Mike Taylor's workshops, where prototypes were

Malcolm Wilson spent much time in 1991 and 1992 developing the Escort RS Cosworth rally car. Here he is, well-sideways, in the Centurion rally of 1992.

based. In both cases, the cars had to tackle events where there was a category for non-homologated machinery. Occasional rally appearances were made in British events (where cars driven by Malcolm Wilson showed the promise of enormous pace and agility), and in Spain, where Mia Bardolet won several events in the Spanish Gravel series.

It was the same story in 1992, for although the road car went on sale in the spring there was no hope (or plan) for gaining sporting homologation until 1 January 1993. These cars used the very best of everything that had already been 'blooded' in the 'works' Sierra Cosworth 4 × 4s (and which was always being further improved), including the 300bhp-plus YB engines.

This was the period in which FISA (the international sporting body that governed rallying) clamped down further and further on the output of turbocharged engines. Although teams publicly clung to the fiction that a Group A turbocharged 2-litre produced 'only' 300bhp, the fact was that considerably more than that was already being developed.

For 1990 (the year in which the Sierra Cosworth 4 × 4 had been launched) the first 40mm diameter restrictors (mounted upstream of the turbocharger inlet) had become compulsory. These restricted flow through the turbocharger itself, especially above certain revs when a sonic shockwave pattern built up in the manifolding.

Experience showed that 40mm was really too large (some said that the 'real' figure being achieved was at least 360bhp and more), so it was reduced to 38mm for 1992 (the last year of the Sierra Cosworth 4 × 4 and also the start of Escort RS Cosworth rallying). Even that didn't do the trick, so there would be a further reduction, to 34mm, for 1995 and beyond, which finally reduced the real-world peak figure to 300bhp or thereabouts: that limitation still existed on World Rally Cars as the sport entered the twenty-first century.

Further developments of the Group A Sierra Cosworth 4 × 4 drive line were also adapted – including the latest iteration of the seven-speed non-synchromesh gearboxes from FF, along with the larger (and, unhappily, heavier) front and rear axles, which featured a 9in diameter crown wheel at the rear, and an 8.5in diameter crown wheel at the front: the latter item was finally fitted to Sierras from 1992. Viscous Coupling limited-slip devices were used in all three differentials.

Magnesium wheels (of 16in, 17in and eventually even 18in diameter) were designed, while huge brake discs (up to 14in diameter at the front), massive disc brake calipers, Bilstein struts and dampers, different front cross-members, different square-section rear cross-members, safety bag fuel tanks, and much more, were all finalized. In the 1990s, more than ever

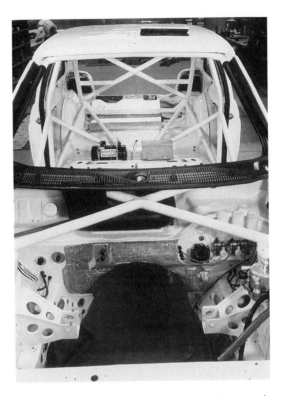

Boreham's sophisticated roll cage added much to the structural rigidity of the Escort RS Cosworth rally car. This was the original, 1992/93, version.

before, well-specified Group A rally cars could be very special indeed.

In 1993 the only Escort RS Cosworth rally car item still shared with the road cars was the basic body shell, and even then it was advisable for serious competitors to purchase a special assembly complete with welded-in multi-point roll cage and thin-gauge skin panels. Such assemblies (without sunroof apertures, and painted in white, so that sponsors' colour schemes could be laid over them) were already available from Boreham even before the first complete road cars reached the showrooms.

But there was more, much more, than this. By this time the 'works' team and its associates had built up so much experience with the new car that they evolved two completely different 'packages' – a specialized one for its own 1993 'works' team, and a less ambitious, and afford-

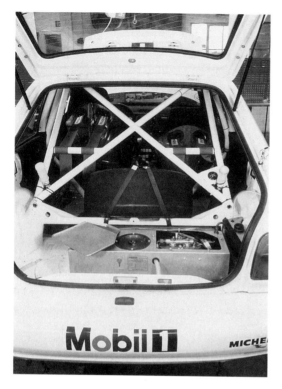

For 1993 Ford's original 'works' Escort RS Cosworth rally cars featured a rock-solid roll cage, with the Premier fuel bag and pump installation behind the line of the rear axle.

Original-spec. Boreham 'works' Escort RS Cosworths were always left-hand-drive, and had their exhaust pipes exiting under the passenger door.

able, one for the scores of private owners. The difference between the chassis types was profound: new 'works' cars would be just that – new, while private owner cars could be conversions.

For the private owners, who would be in a hurry to get their cars out into motor sport, and might want to create a new Escort RS Cosworth rally car by buying one of those new body shells from Boreham, and then use almost all the running gear from their existing Sierra Cosworth 4 × 4 competition cars, most of the chassis pieces were easily interchangeable (or developed) from those of the 1990–92 'works' Sierras.

In 1993 not one or two, but scores of 'new' Escort RS Cosworth race and rally cars were created in that manner. This, perhaps, explains why Patrick Snyers's Bastos-sponsored car took second place in the Boucles de Spa just five weeks after homologation had been achieved, and why Sebastian Lindholm's car won the Hanki rally in Finland on 28 February. There was strength in depth, too: of the ten European Championship rounds held in June 1993, six were won by privately financed Escort RS Cosworths.

For the 'works' team, though, John Wheeler and Philip Dunabin's test teams, along with the Malcolm Wilson and Mike Taylor teams, had

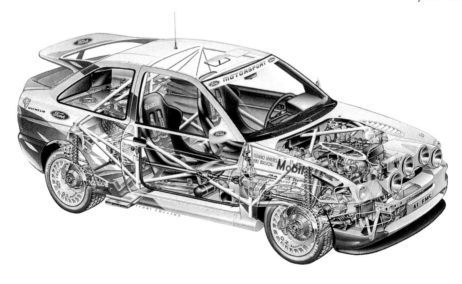

established during 1991 and 1992 that, compared with the Sierra Cosworth 4 × 4, there was a need for more suspension wheel movement to improve the traction. Accordingly, for 'works' use only at first, a new and integrated 'wide-track' package was developed, with different springs, struts, dampers, track control and wishbone arms, anti-roll bar kits, magnesium semi-trailing arms, drive shafts and steering gear. It wasn't possible to 'cherry-pick' one or two items from this little lot: to make everything work, all of it had to be purchased, at considerable cost and after long delays – as the less well-financed private owners soon discovered!

Well before the end of 1992 FISA inspectors counted the number of Escort RS Cosworth road cars already built at Karmann's factory in Germany and, having seen that well over 2,500 (the magic minimum number) had already been completed, granted sporting homologation to take effect on 1 January 1993.

For that season, the same 'works' drivers were retained – this being a really cosmopolitan line-up, with François Delecour of France and Miki Biasion of Italy as regulars, with Malcolm Wilson joining in at times, and regularly running in the British series.

Delecour had been the Sierra driving star since 1991, while ex-double-World-Champion Biasion had moved across from Lancia in 1992, already itching to get his hands on the smaller, lighter and definitely more agile new Escort RS Cosworth.

As it happened, and to the surprise of almost everyone outside Boreham (though seemingly not to deep thinkers like team manager John Taylor), the mercurial Delecour was always the more fiery, and the more effective, for Miki Biasion never seemed to show as much aggression in these cars as had been hoped – although his contract ran to the end of 1994, it was almost as if he had decided to coast towards a well-paid retirement.

In preparing for the Escort RS Cosworth programme, there was a bigger emphasis on testing and development: to match this the Boreham facility itself was quite transformed. The workshops (originally built in 1963, don't forget) were renovated and rejigged, almost F1 style, so that cars were prepared in individual bays. Other workshops nearby, which had once been used by Ford's truck development department, were absorbed and put into service, while the design, purchasing and administrative offices were all relocated to larger and more modern (ex-truck development) buildings.

Not only that, but within a few years Ford would sell the rights to the extraction of the millions of tons of gravel known to be hidden under the surface. Boreham airfield itself began to look very different – and the Essex police even housed a traffic surveillance/rapid response helicopter in the middle of the complex!

First Blood

Because sporting homologation was achieved on 1 January 1993 (more than 3,000 Escort RS Cosworth road cars had already been produced – and were increasingly seen on the roads of Europe), World and European rallying began at once. For the moment, the 'works' Motorsport facility at Boreham turned its attention from test and practice machines to two brand-new cars. Registered K746 GOO and K748 GOO, these were earmarked for the Monte Carlo rally.

By this time Ford's contracted rally-car engine builders, Mountune of Maldon, had spent years working on improvements to the YB engine. Although Escort RS Cosworths were now obliged to run with a 38mm restrictor, for 1993 they had a turbocharger that was better matched to the 2-litre engine itself, and were able to run with a reliable 360bhp at 6,500rm. (Ford never officially admitted to this peak, but when the figure was first 'leaked' in mid-1993 there was much consternation, on the grounds that FISA still naïvely believed that all 'works' Group A cars were running

The Escort RS Cosworth's first World Championship rally win came in Portugal in March 1993, when François Delecour dominated the event. It was the first of many successes.

with 'about 300bhp'. High hopes, or innocence? In later years we learnt that both Lancia and Toyota had even more power than Ford!)

Once again aided by backing from Mobil (oils) and Michelin (tyres), Boreham planned an ambitious ten-event assault on the World Championship in 1993, while private owners' cars were soon ready for European and national series all over the world. Those were the days when World Rallying was at its most expansive – and most expensive. To back a two-car 'works' team of Escort RS Cosworths, Boreham regularly fielded no fewer than fifteen service vans and two big trucks (stuffed full of heavy spares, sub-assemblies, wheels and tyres),

together with a communications aircraft and more than 100 people. By Ford's standards, this was huge spending, although even that was dwarfed by the effort displayed by teams such as Toyota.

Ford might very well have won the Monte in 1993, for until the final day, with just five stages still to take place, François Delecour's car led Auriol's Toyota by a fairly comfortable 71 seconds: it was only then that the disbelieving Delecour was passed by an astonishingly fast Toyota on those stages. How? No-one ever found out, but there were rumours of illegal 'rocket fuel' being used, and in later years the same team was thrown out of the World series for a full year, when it was found to be cheating in other ways.

Victories soon followed, however. The first ground-breaking success came in Portugal, where Delecour and Biasion beat everyone, setting twenty-seven fastest times over the thirty-seven stages, to give Ford its first World

Boreham built them tough in 1993 – this being Miki Biasion's hard-working Escort RS Cosworth on its way to winning the Acropolis rally.

Championship rally victory since 1988 (Corsica, in the three-door Sierra RS Cosworth). Boreham, it has to be said, was greatly relieved – for the Escort RS Cosworth had already been under development for four years, and had been in rallying (un-homologated, of course) since 1990.

Happily for all Ford fans, there was more to come. Eight weeks after the Portuguese success the 'works' team did it again, this time

Escort RS Cosworths were competitive on gravel, on tarmac and, especially, in super-tough conditions. This was Miki Biasion's winning car, in Greece, in 1993.

It was only dusty conditions like this, which cut the driver's visibility, that foiled Miki Biasion of victory in Argentina in 1993: in the end, he had to settle for second place.

on the tight mountain roads of Corsica, which witnessed a Delecour benefit, driving one of a pair of 'tarmac lightweights' that annihiliated everyone else, including Toyota (how satisfying …).

Four weeks later there was a third outright success, this time for Miki Biasion, who battled through the dust, the rocks and the searing heat of Greece to win the Acropolis rally. Once again this was sweet success, for Ford's last

Acropolis victory had been way back in 1981, when Ari Vatanen had been driving a Rothmans Escort.

The rest of the season, in fairness, could not quite be expected to unfold like that. Miki Biasion (using an old test car that had been hastily refurbished and air-freighted to South America) was second in Argentina, Delecour took second place in New Zealand and was third in Australia.

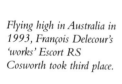
Flying high in Australia in 1993, François Delecour's 'works' Escort RS Cosworth took third place.

The most famous Cosworth-powered victory of all? François Delecour won the 1994 Monte Carlo rally in this Escort RS Cosworth – Ford's first Monte win since 1953!

Then came more success in San Remo, all the more pleasing because it was not by a 'works' driver, but by an Italian private owner, Franco Cunico. On this 27-stage event Ford now had strength (and talent) in depth – Delecour led from the start before going off in foggy conditions, Biasion then took over until his engine let go, after which Franco Cunico (in a Rome-registered machine) serenely took command.

Only three weeks after that, Boreham provided François Delecour with yet another brand-new lightweight 'tarmac' Escort RS Cosworth for the Catalunya (Spanish) rally, where he set no fewer than fifteen fastest times (of the total of twenty-nine), easily beating major opposition from Toyota and Lancia.

Five World Championship victories in their first season! Ford had not notched up so many wins since their World Championship-winning year of 1979 and it had a marvellous effect on the team's morale. All this helped Ford and Delecour take second place in their respective Championships – a performance backed up by eighteen privateer victories in European Championship events. This was a wonderful

After they had won the 1994 Monte Carlo rally, François Delecour (right) and Daniel Grataloup celebrated with champagne spray in the usual way.

The Escort RS Cosworth's fifth World Championship victory of 1993 came in the Catalunya (Spain) rally, with François Delecour at the wheel.

achievement for the first season by a new model, especially as private owners also gave Ford victory in the Group N World Rally Championship category.

This, though, was an immediate high point that Ford would struggle to match in the future. In the following years there would be good times and bad. Sometimes the Escorts seemed to be the world's best rally cars, but sometimes they seemed to be struggling. Sometimes management was lacking, sometimes there was a shortage of funds and commitment – and sometimes there was a great deal of bad luck. Most of the big successes gained in 1993 were lost by 1995; it was only the determined bullying of Carlos Sainz that turned things round in 1996.

There were further improvements to the RS Cosworth's specification during the 1994

season, including wider track suspension, anti-lag fuel injection systems and regular updates to the integral roll cage layout. Mountune, the team's engine builders, worked hard on the engine: much development went into transmission differential settings, while a sequential gearchange system was tried (but later rejected). A six-speed main gearbox was tested, but was not fully adopted until 1995.

The 1994 season started well, with François Delecour winning the Monte Carlo rally with an emphatic performance (Miki Biasion was fourth overall). Demonstrably fastest in all conditions, Delecour finally made up for the heartbreaks of 1991 (when his Sierra Cosworth 4 × 4 broke down on the last stage) and 1993 (when Didier Auriol's Toyota achieved a very questionable victory).

From that point, however, the season went downhill. The worst blow of all was François Delecour's accident, which kept him out of the team from April to August: badly knocked about in a non-rallying crash (in a friend's

Franco Cunico drove this privately prepared Escort RS Cosworth to win his 'home' event, the San Remo rally, in October 1993.

Ferrari F40!), he suffered broken ankles and never seemed to recover his full performance after that.

As a result of Delecour's accident a whole series of substitute drivers, some more successful than others, had to be drafted in. These included Malcolm Wilson, Ari Vatanen, Tommi Makinen, Franco Cunico and Stig Blomqvist. It wasn't enough, for Miki Biasion,

de facto team leader from April 1994, faded gradually away. Bruno Thiry was faster in Corsica, 'guest' drivers often matched his pace, and it was soon clear that he was on the way out.

Tommi Makinen's victory in Finland in the 1000 Lakes, on his only 'works' drive in an Escort, inspired the troops (he went on to become World Rally Champion four times

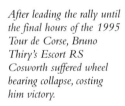

After leading the rally until the final hours of the 1995 Tour de Corse, Bruno Thiry's Escort RS Cosworth suffered wheel bearing collapse, costing him victory.

after that – but in Mitsubishis). This was something to cheer, but after nine events the team boasted only two victories and four third places, with no other minor podium positions.

At the end of the year, in the RAC rally, there was one other bright spot. Driving a front-wheel-drive Escort RS2000, which had been prepared by Gordon Spooner Engineering, but with a great deal of support from Boreham, Gwyndaf Evans won the new front-wheel-drive 'Formula 2' category.

From mid-1994, in any case, Boreham had been in turmoil. In July Colin Dobinson announced that the 'works' team would close down at the end of the year, and that he envisaged Boreham as an R & D centre for future

Three important personalities in Ford's 'works' Escort RS Cosworth rally team of 1996: left to right, John Taylor (operations manager), Stig Blomqvist and Carlos Sainz (star driver).

motor sport products. This meant that Ford needed to find other contractors to take over the running of cars in the World Rally Championship. RAS of Belgium and Schmidt of Germany made bids for this contract, and had to commit at least £200,000 per event.

Before this could be finalized Dobinson took early retirement, eased out to make way for 56-year-old Peter Gillitzer from Ford-Australia, who faced up to Boreham's problems. These included a severe lack of funds for the 1995 season. Not only was the 'works' team being sentenced to death, but the successful British Touring Car Championship programme (Mondeos, run by Andy Rouse Engineering) was also in danger.

Somehow or other Gillitzer – a blunt, straight talker and a master of 'corridors of power' tactics – saved the day. Not only did he rejig the Escort's rallying future in a novel way, but he also saved the BTCC/Mondeo.

For 1995, Boreham remained, and many

Carlos Sainz returned to the 'works' rally team for 1996, driving Repsol-sponsored Escort RS Cosworths. Here he is, on the way to second place in the Swedish rally.

'works' Escort RS Cosworths were developed and prepared: RAS Sport sometimes prepared Bruno Thiry's car. At Boreham, that very important personality John Taylor became Operations Manager, though RAS Sport ran the cars on events. There was no more Mobil sponsorship, and most support came from Belgium. At this time John Wheeler moved out, to become Chief Engineer on the Aston Martin DB7 project.

Although this all sounded promising, the result was disappointment. In a year when the Escort RS Cosworth should have been reaching its peak the team often struggled, for pace and credibility. RAS-Ford personalities clashed repeatedly with Boreham, and the driving team was not consistent: enthusiasm was sometimes lacking.

Out in Europe, though, it wasn't all bad news. In 1994 Malcolm Wilson's Escort RS Cosworth dominated the British Rally Championship, and Escorts won no fewer than twenty-nine European Championship rallies. Johnny Milner's Shell-backed RS Cosworth won the Group N category of the RAC rally, with

Gwyndaf Evans using a GSE-prepared front-wheel-drive RS2000 to win the F2 category.

Although the record shows that Ford finished third in the Makes Championship, the Escorts never won an event. François Delecour did not seem to be as fast, or as flamboyant, as in 1993. Second driver Bruno Thiry (nominated by RAS-Ford) was often not as fast, and certainly not as lucky.

There was one stunning performance. The Escort might have won in Corsica, but Thiry's car failed at the last moment: after setting twelve fastest stage times the car's wheel bearing broke up, far from service, and he had to retire. Although Delecour took a storming second place in the Monte, and another fine second place (beaten by just 15 seconds) in Corsica, that was the height of it. The further the season progressed, the less capable the team looked, and by the end of the year a complete

For 1997 and 1998 Ford developed the strictly motor sport-only Escort World Rally Car. Compared with the Escort RS Cosworth it had a modified engine and aerodynamics, plus a totally new type of rear suspension.

divorce between Boreham and RAS Sport was brewing.

Technically the main innovations in 1995 concerned the transmission. Sequential gearchange work was abandoned, and from Corsica the team adopted a six-speed derivative of the original seven-speed gearbox. Traction control and 'active' centre differentials were both adopted.

Like all other teams, Ford was now using a turbo anti-lag strategy, and a compulsory (smaller) 34mm turbocharger restrictor. Engineer Philip Dunabin later admitted that for 1995 the Escort's peak horsepower was therefore reduced by 50–60bhp. Since he confirmed that 1995 engines gave about 300bhp, it meant that the 1993/94 cars must have been good for at least 350bhp!

Once again, at European level, Escort RS

Cosworths won no fewer than twenty-seven events (more than half of all those in the Championship), while in the RAC rally Gwyndaf Evans once again won the increasingly important F2 category in an Escort RS2000.

Even so, at the end of the year the Escort rally programme seemed to be in complete disarray, the links with RAS-Ford had been dissolved, and no drivers had been rehired for 1996. The formidable John Taylor, more of a Ford stalwart than anyone else most people know, then moved swiftly to sign up Carlos Sainz, which was a real coup:

> I told Peter Gillitzer that we needed a front-line personality like Carlos to regain credibility. He agreed that I should fly out to Spain, and the rest you know.

Although Sainz had already agreed to drive for Toyota, that organization was then banned from World rallying after being found cheating. When the ban was enacted on 3 November 1995 Sainz found that Toyota could no longer offer him a seat, and he was effectively out of work. Taylor, who had managed Sainz's earlier efforts in Sierra RS Cosworths, swooped at once, flew to Spain and spent much time persuading the double World Champion that he ought to sign for Ford.

Taylor later admitted how hard he had to try to convince Carlos, but it worked: Carlos returned to Ford with a two-season deal, bringing with him a valuable sponsorship deal with the Spanish oil company Repsol. For 1996 this was a new beginning, with 'works' cars run from Boreham by John Taylor. François Delecour soon left the team and Bruno Thiry eventually became a regular team member, with an unsettling turnover of guest and one-off drivers.

Incidentally, even though there were no factory Fords in the Monte Carlo rally in January, RAS Sport built an Escort RS Cosworth, Patrick Bernadini drove it, and the result was an emphatic victory!

Sainz, in the meantime, began to transform 'his' team. Although he won only one event during the season (Indonesia), he took three second places and two third places. There were only two failures and the brightly liveried Repsol Escorts always looked likely to win. At the end of the year Carlos took third place in the Drivers' Championship.

Although there were no major technical innovations, Philip Dunabin's design team refined the car in many ways – with more responsive engines, active differentials at front and in the centre, stronger suspension components, new-type Dynamic shock absorbers and relocated fuel tanks.

For Sainz the whole season was a personal battle against Mitsubishi, and Tommi Maki-

The Escort World Rally Car was competitive to the very end – this being Juha Kankkunen celebrating second place in the 1998 Network Q RAC Rally.

Under the skin, the Escort World Rally Car was very different from the Escort RS Cosworth, although the basic body shell was little changed.

nen. Second to Tommi in Sweden by only 23 seconds, he then won in Indonesia in spite of suffering two crashes and a broken gearbox. Third in Greece and second in Argentina – both rough and tough events – showed that the Escort might be a touch heavy, but it was still very strong , while third in Australia was achieved in spite of the car drowning out for some time in a deep watersplash in mid-stage! Although Carlos set more fastest stage times than Colin McRae on the San Remo, he was still defeated by just 22 seconds.

In Britain and in Europe, there was much success to celebrate. In the British Championship Gwyndaf Evans's F2 Escort RS2000s won the Series at a canter, while in the European Rally Championship, twenty-four of the fifty-three qualifying events were won by privately entered Escort RS Cosworths.

Despite these successes, however, Ford recognized that the Escort RS Cosworth's glory days were over, and that they needed a new model.

All Change for 1997

By mid-1996 there were major changes in Ford Motorsport. After two years Peter Gillitzer left his post, his place being taken by Martin Whitaker. Martin was a smooth talker with much 'previous' at Ford. Amazingly, he also seemed to know where the money was buried –money that had not previously been available to Ford Motorsport – so the prospects for a resurgence were bright.

And there was more. Ford Motorsport, although somewhat short of investment funds, needed a new model to go rallying. The Escort RS Cosworth was now being matched by its rivals, but soon there would be new World Rally Cars regulations. As already described in Chapter 9, the result was that Motorsport conceived the Escort World Rally

The very last appearance by a 'works' Escort World Rally Car came in February 1999, when Petter Solberg took eleventh place in the Swedish Rally.

Car as a final evolution of the Escort RS Cosworth, and persuaded the FIA that it should be allowed to use that machine on an interim basis until an all-new WRC (the Focus) should come along.

Then came the really big gamble, for Motorsport Director Martin Whitaker also elected to 'farm out' the running of the team. For the very first time, Ford's 'works' cars would be run by an outside agency. Boreham closed its doors on top-level World Championship motor sport, and Malcolm Wilson's M-Sport team, based near Cockermouth, in Cumbria, took over. Although Boreham completed the design and development of the Escort WRC, and the hurried manufacture of the first twenty sets of components, it was Malcolm Wilson's team that would always run the cars.

There were driver changes too. Carlos Sainz led the team, and for the first part of 1997 he was joined by the German driver Armin Schwarz. Unhappily, Schwarz's promised financial sponsorship never arrived, so from

mid-season he was dropped in favour of the Finnish four-times World Rally Champion Juha Kankkunen.

As far as the new car was concerned, the only real drawback was that the Escort WRC showed a distressing tendency to shed its massive front bumper/spoiler in deep watersplashes. Not only was this embarrassing (and exposing the radiator/intercooler installation to further damage) but costly, as these huge mouldings were made from a carbon fibre-based material.

Somehow, and in a frantic rush, M-Sport put two brand-new cars on to the start line in Monte Carlo. The rest of the season, Malcolm Wilson admitted, was always a race against time, but it was completed by using only nine separate cars during the year. Technical advances during the year included changes to

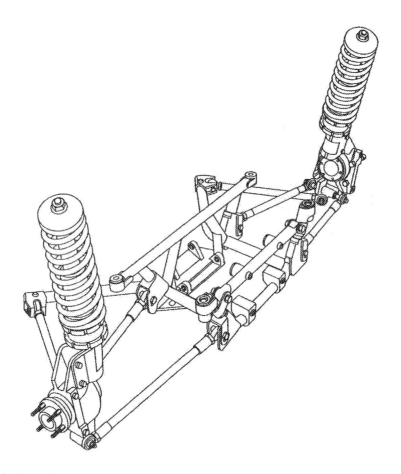

Compared with the Escort RS Cosworth, the strictly motor sport-only Escort World Rally Car had an entirely different, strut-type, rear suspension. It was the only car in this long-running family not to use semi-trailing arms.

the differentials, with an Xtrac sequential gear change, and with Hi-Tech dampers replacing Dynamic types from mid-season.

In 1997 Ford came very close to glory, for the team finished second in the Makes Championship, while Carlos Sainz took third place in the Drivers' series. Carlos won in the Acropolis and in Indonesia, and backed this up with second places in Monte Carlo, Sweden, the Tour de Corse and New Zealand. Not only that, but in Corsica he was foiled by a mere eight seconds, in New Zealand by 13 seconds and in Sweden by 16 seconds. Armin Schwarz notched up a third and two fourth places, but

his replacement, Juha Kankkunen, was immediately on the pace. By the end of 1997 he had recorded no fewer than four second places, two of them immediately behind Carlos Sainz.

Privately owned WRCs were also successful, with Patrick Snyers's Bastos-backed Belgian car winning European Championship rounds in Belgium and Poland. There was also a magnificent performance in the Middle East, where Mohammed Ben Sulayem dominated the Championship in Escort RS Cosworth and, later, Escort WRC cars.

For 1998 the entire world of rallying, it seemed, knew that the Escort WRC would be made obsolete at the end of the year. There were few funds available to improve the old Escort WRC. In fact, the team started the new season with a different turbocharger housing, which helped liberate more power. Most cars now had to carry ballast, and electronic 'launch control' of the engines was used to give even more effective stage starts.

Because Carlos Sainz left the team at the end of 1997 (and Repsol, his sponsors, left with him), Juha Kankkunen became team leader and was joined by Bruno Thiry, who had driven 'works' Escort RS Cosworths in earlier years.

In their final full 'works' season, the Escorts finished fourth in the World Rally Championship, with no outright victories but any number of fine performances and podium positions. Juha Kankkunen took fourth in the Drivers Championship, with three second places (in the year's most high-profile events – Monte Carlo, the Safari and RAC Rally of Great Britain), and was third four times more.

It was fitting but, above all, sad that the 'works' Escort team should start its last event on home ground in the Rally of Great Britain. This was almost, but not quite, like old times, for in a consistent display Juha and Bruno finished second and third overall.

There were six outright Escort WRC victories in European Championship rounds, Escort RS Cosworths won seven times in European events too, and once again Ben Sulayem won the Middle Eastern series in his Escort WRC.

Immediately before the 1998 Rally of Great Britain, Ford celebrated the 'works' Escorts' long career by hosting a glittering celebratory dinner for every important Ford personality who could be persuaded to attend. The all-new Focus WRC would take over for 1999 and Ford wanted to celebrate the Escort's retirement in some style.

Six World Rally Champions attended: Bjorn Waldegard, Ari Vatanen, Hannu Mikkola, Juha Kankkunen, Carlos Sainz and Tommi Makinen. Timo Makinen (a triple Escort rally winner), Ove Andersson, David Richards, Malcolm Wilson and Andrew Cowan were also there. Walter Hayes, Stuart Turner, Martin Whitaker, Bill Barnett and many others joined them – only Peter Ashcroft, who by this time had retired to live in the United States, could not be present. It was an unforgettable evening.

Even then, the Escort WRC's career was not finally over, since in February 1999 the 'works' team's new recruit, Petter Solberg, finished eleventh overall in Sweden in an M-Sport car. But that was finally that. Ford's future lay with the Focus: only two weeks later Colin McRae took the Focus WRC to its first victory, in the Safari.

The proud rallying career of Cosworth-engined Ford production Fords had come to a close. The first Cosworth-engined Escorts had started winning in 1970, and the first Cosworth-badged victory had followed in 1988. Even so, this was not the end of the Ford and Cosworth rally connection, for the Ford-owned Cosworth Racing continued to design, develop and build the 'works' Focus WRC engines well into the early 2000s. It was an illustrious link that few, it seemed, wanted to break.

11 Scorpio 24V – 'Cosworth' Under the Bonnet

Did you ever get a chance to drive a Scorpio 24V? If not, you missed a treat. Not only was the Scorpio a big, comfortable and capable machine, but that '24V' acronym signalled a powerful V6 engine, which quite transformed the car's character. And how do I know all this? Because I ran a new Scorpio 24V for more than 20,000 miles in the early 1990s: in my garage it followed a brace of Sierra Cosworth 4 × 4s, and preceded two Escort RS Cosworths.

Apart from the Sierra and Escort RS Cosworths, which I have covered in great detail, the Scorpio 24V was the only Ford road car to carry 'Cosworth' badges. In this case that identification did not appear on the outside of the car, but under the bonnet, applied to the plenum chamber of the engine itself.

So, how did it evolve and why? As happens so often with the development of a new Ford high-performance model, this was not a simple story. When the third-generation Granada/Scorpio range was launched in the mid-1980s, there was no thought of a truly high-performance version, and Ford certainly had no on-going contract with Cosworth on the V6 engine at that time.

Yet in December 1990, with sales due to begin during 1991, the company announced the Scorpio 24V, complete with its Cosworth-developed 2.9-litre engine. At a stroke, the company had a 195bhp flagship instead of the previous top-of-the-range 150bhp machine, which allowed the Scorpio's top speed to go up from 123mph (198km/h) to 136mph (219km/h).

V6s from Cologne

Way back in the early 1960s, Ford of Germany laid down a new family of V4 and V6 engines, simple units with a 60-degree vee angle, cast-iron cylinder blocks, cast-iron heads, two valves per cylinder, and pushrod overhead-valve operation. These engines, colloquially known as 'Cologne' units, were completely different from the British 'Essex' engines of the same period.

Originally meant for use in the Taunus 20M of the period, and later used in cars like the German-built Capri coupés, big-engined Sierras and the earlier-series Granadas, these heavy and rather arthritic V6 lumps gradually grew up from 1998cc to 2293cc, 2551cc, 2637cc and finally to 2792cc. All of them had heads with siamesed exhaust ports, the only sporting versions being the fuel-injected types used in Capri RS2600s and Capri 2.8-litre Injections, plus Granada/Scorpios of the late 1970s and 1980s.

For the new-generation Granada/Scorpio of 1985, these engines were originally built in 2294cc and 2792cc, still with their poorly breathing cylinder heads. Two years later, from early 1987, they were substantially revised. Not only did they finally get new cylinder heads, with individual inlet and exhaust ports, but their sizes were pushed out to 2393cc and 2933cc. Within the limitations of the existing (and age-old) cylinder block casting, little further enlargement was possible: the stroke was already at its limit.

By the early 1990s assembly of these old-style pushrod engines would be transferred from Germany to Cosworth's production factories at Wellingborough (Northants), but the twin-cam derivatives outlived that move. Although the 24-valve twin-cam FB carried on until 1998, the very last of these pushrod power units was produced in 1996.

Why? We now know that Ford was finding its European big-car sales under pressure, for it had the least powerful engine in its class, and the least performance. Not only were the Rover 827 (which had a 177bhp/2.7-litre V6 engine) and the top-of-the-range Opel Senator (177bhp/3-litre engine) both beefier, but Uncle Henry also wanted to have a crack at cars like the BMW 530i (188bhp) and the Mercedes-Benz 300E (180bhp). To match and, preferably, beat such cars, Ford programme manager Bill Camplisson's aim was not only to have a 200bhp Scorpio, but one that would confront this sort of opposition in all respects. Bill, though, was not only an enthusiast (he owned an RS200 for some years) but also a pragmatist, and realized that, although it was one thing to develop a 200bhp engine, it was quite another to ensure that it was refined and reliable too.

It was a coincidence, but an ominous one, that at the end of 1988 Ford's engineering consultant, ex-World F1 Champion Jackie Stewart, sampled the very first 250bhp/4.0-litre V8-engined Lexus LS400 in Japan and advised any top Ford man who would listen that this was going to be real competition for any other car maker!

Even so, there was no way that the existing V6 engine could be persuaded to give that sort of horsepower. For a time Ford was stuck with those ancient-style engines, the only ones they already had. In their origins the Scorpio's V6s dated back more than twenty years, and pushrod overhead-valve units had reached their development limit.

Autocar's comments, in a back-to-back comparison with the Rover 827, tell their own story:

Turn the Rover's key and you are hardly aware that the Honda-sourced V6 is running … Heave up the Granada's bonnet and the all-iron 2.9-litre pushrod V6 looks crude by comparison. It's neither pretty, nor technically advanced and, when idling, a slight vibration can be felt throughout the shell. The Ford's engine lacks the immediate response of

the Rover … It is unfortunate that far too much mechanical noise and coarseness creep in as the rev-counter rises towards the red sector. It's clear from driving the two cars together that the Rover easily outpaces the Ford.

That, in itself, was damning enough, but the final verdict emphasised that even more:

The Granada looks frumpy and drives like it. Alongside the Rover it's too soft, under-damped, under-powered and unrefined.

If *Autocar* could only have known it, however, help was on the way for Ford.

Hart Engineering

In the meantime the hyperactive Brian Hart, finding himself with a few slack weeks in the middle of a frenzied 1980s programme, had turned his attention to the 'Cologne' V6. In the same way that Cosworth had decided to investigate the marketing of twin-cam conversions of the Pinto, so Hart looked at the possibilities of 'doing a twin-cam' on the V6. This was done with the active encouragement of Ford Motorsport at Boreham.

Hart, the one-time Cosworth engine builder who had designed the original aluminium-block for the BDA, then built hundreds of engines for use in 'works' Escorts, designed his own ultra-successful Hart 420R series of 4-cylinder race engines, after which he saw that engine enlarged and turbocharged for use in F1.

Next, from 1985, Ford asked Brian to develop the ultimate BD-based engine for use in the RS200 'Evolution' car. To quote Stuart Turner:

After much research, he concluded that the engine ought to be expanded from 1.8 litres to 2.1 litres … but to do this he would have to design and develop a new version with more space between the cylinder bores. We agreed this, and Brian (not Cosworth) produced the 2.1-litre BDT-E, which

Brian Hart's makeover converted the ageing Ford pushrod engine (left) into a smart and purposeful 24-valve twin-cam engine. This studio shot dates from 1986.

delivered well over 600bhp in 1987 rallycross form.

That was the good news. The bad news was that the day after Group B was cancelled the BDT-E found itself without a future: Brian had planned to make a lot of BDT-Es later in 1986 and 1987 and, although financially compensated for this hiatus, was now faced with an empty workshop and idle staff.

A pessimist would have found this to be a complete disaster but, nudged along by helpful hints from Ford, Brian and his small team immediately settled down to work on a comprehensive updating of the Cologne V6 power unit. Over months, in 1986, Brian Hart Limited (BHL) evolved the very first twin-overhead-camshaft conversion that had ever been carried out on the old Ford-Germany engine. In Ford's Photographic Archive there is pictorial evidence showing that the first engine was completed by December of that year.

Brian's original idea had been to build such engines in limited quantities at his factory at Harlow New Town in Essex (as a private ven-

In 1986 Brian Hart's neat conversion of Ford's Cologne V6 featured 4-valve heads and twin overhead camshafts. Much would change – visually or in engineering detail – before the engine was launched in 1991.

Brian Hart's 24-valve twin-cam conversion of the 2.9-litre Ford-Cologne V6 engine featured new aluminium cylinder heads, with camshaft covers carrying the logo '24V DOHC' – this would not survive the prototype stage.

ture, certainly not in thousands for supply to Ford in Cologne), but although the very first engine was completed before the end of that

Introduced in 1991, Cosworth's definitive 2.9-litre 24-valve V6 engine was coded FB, and was more obviously 'styled' than the original Brian Hart effort had been. The name 'Cosworth' was proudly emblazoned on the inlet plenum casting.

year, financial manoeuvrings then changed everything. Even before the 24V Scorpio project went public (hence the secrecy), Brian told me:

> We were then approached directly by Keith Duckworth in November 1986, wanting to take us over. At the time Cosworth had more work on racing car engines than it could foreseeably cope with. We, on the other hand, had designed a very promising twin-cam conversion of an established road car engine, but we were not capable or interested in putting it into production.
>
> Since we had already said to the client [which was Ford, but this was not spelt out at the time], 'Look, we're only small, we can only build prototypes, you'd better go to Cosworth for production engines, there's no-one else in Europe who has that sort of facility', I suppose the solution was obvious.

The formal takeover, in which Brian Hart retained 25 per cent of his business, was formalized in February 1987.

Politics

The story, though, was not altogether simple, as Cosworth's John Dickens, who was the company's contracts manager, and Dave Lee, who became project manager, spelt out. Impressed by Cosworth's 'can-do' skills in engineering, developing and manufacturing the YB four-cylinder engine, Ford next set another challenge. Using only the bare bones of the Brian Hart engine, Cosworth was asked to evolve a 24-valve twin-cam-per-bank road car engine, silky-smooth and able to meet all known and pending noise and exhaust emissions regulations, which would turn the Scorpio into a high-performance luxury model. It would be sold throughout Europe, but never in North America (although the pushrod-engined Scorpio was sold there, but badged as a 'Merkur'). Only one specification was proposed, the 'standard' FB engine, married to Ford four-speed automatic transmission. Manual transmission was never officially available.

Motor sport applications were not, repeat not, ever considered. In 1987, therefore, the FB project was born. And why FB? In the usual Cosworth way a new project needed a two-letter acronym, so that drawings, documents and computer-aided schemes could readily be identified. Way back in 1967 there had been the FA (later FVA) project, so as this was also a Ford-sponsored design the next example – FB – was chosen.

As John Dickens told me:

Although Ford was impressed with what we had done on the YB, this was another major project, and we needed a new engineering team to tackle the FB. In any case, our contact at Ford was to be different. Whereas Ford's SVE people had always been our link with the YB, with the new FB we talked to Bill Camplisson in marketing, and to the 'mainstream' engine engineers at Ford-Cologne. Our main engineering contact was Dave Mundy.

The first thing we did was to get hold of an engine from Brian Hart – he had made maybe three or four, that was all – put one into a car to enable some car work to be done, but that was about it.

Dave Lee, who had already been involved on the manufacturing and quality assurance side of the YB programme, was then called in by Richard Bulman, then Cosworth's managing director, and asked to become Project Manager. Wary of such a task, Dave held off until both Mike Costin and Keith Duckworth urged him to take over:

Which I did. Another key thing was that Geoff Goddard and Tony Hart set about productionizing the 'Hart V6' – at that time, incidentally, Brian Hart's design was wholly on paper, not on CAD (Computer Aided design) programmes.

There were six months before Geoff handed over to John Hancock, who had been purely involved in racing up to then. John became chief designer on the FB.

Like Dickens and Lee, John Hancock already had a considerable track record at Cosworth,

---

Brian Hart and the FB

Although Cosworth would like everyone to believe that they were totally responsible for the FB V6 engine that powered the Scorpio 24V range, the original inspiration came from a twin-cam conversion that stemmed from Brian Hart's resourceful little business at Harlow New Town, Essex. Only three engineers had a hand in drawing up the twin-cam conversion – Brian, his brother Tony and John Lievesley – but they had taken it only up to the prototype stage before Cosworth purchased 75 per cent of Brian Hart Ltd in February 1987.

When the takeover took place, the agreement was that Hart would completely hand over the V6 engine design to Cosworth and take no further part in it, in exchange for build and development work on existing Cosworth DFV F1 engines. But it didn't work out happily, as Brian Hart told me:

In a word, we didn't get the work in exchange that we had been promised. When Keith [Duckworth] stepped down from the chairmanship of Cosworth,

managing director Richard Bulman ... made it clear he thought we were something of a corporate irritation.

It was only after Mike Costin took over as Chairman that he agreed that Brian Hart should buy back the 75 per cent of his own business, to 'go private' once again. By the 1990s Hart was once again on his own, though in the meantime the twin-cam V6 power unit had evolved into a production engine and became an important part of the Ford Scorpio range.

Brian Hart then settled down to design a new series of normally aspirated F1 engines, including V8 and V10s for constructors such as Jordan, Minardi and Arrows. His business was taken over by Tom Walkinshaw's TWR concern in the late 1990s, shortly after which he retired and went to live overseas. It wasn't long before the collapse of Walkinshaw's Arrows F1 effort meant that the ex-Hart-Power operation had to close down, too.

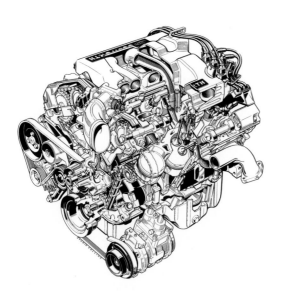

Although cutaway drawings often make an engine look impossibly complicated, the Ford-Cosworth 24-valve FB power unit was neat, compact and as simple as possible. In initial form it developed 195bhp.

for he not only designed the crankshaft of the YB, but (along with Geoff Goddard) had helped produced the 3.5-litre DFZ F1 engine in double quick time, and was also involved in engineering the new, lightweight HB F1 V8.

Anyone who has ever tried to race-tune an FB engine will know that it has certain obvious limitations. Neither Cosworth nor Ford make any excuses for this, since all concerned make it clear that this was always to be a road car engine, and never one intended for motor sport usage. Not only would the cast crankshaft and the standard connecting rods have needed to be discarded, but the cylinder heads themselves did not have the right sort of inlet and exhaust port sizes or profiles. Although Cosworth could certainly have provided appropriate pistons and camshaft profiles – this was the sort of expertise that any experienced Cosworth engineers could dial up among themselves at coffee-break time – the key restraint on the FB was the bottom end of the cast iron cylinder block itself.

Experience showed that as more and more power was demanded of this engine, the block casting would tend to crack around the main bearings. Changes were requested from Ford before production could begin. These included adding extra webs to support the main bearings, and the deletion of holes that had previously surrounded the valve pushrods. Not that this experience was new to certain areas of Ford. At Boreham, for instance, ace rally engineer/mechanic Mick Jones once described V6 blocks as being made out of 'f★★★★g Weetabix', which, being politely translated, meant that he was not very impressed.

Even so, the top end of the engine had recognizable links with Cosworth's famous racing heritage. Inlet valves were 34mm (1.34in) in diameter, and exhaust valves 30mm (1.18in), the angle between the line of valves being 31.5 degrees. The compression ratio was 9.7:1, and the engine easily met the latest demanding exhaust emission regulations.

Although this was always a speedy programme, there were no compelling motor sport deadlines to be met. Even so, work began in 1987, definite engines were available in 1988/89, and the first Cosworth assembly-line produced power units followed before the end of 1990. In the end, when Ford launched the car, they advertised 195bhp, although Cosworth never had much difficulty in exceeding that figure:

> But don't forget we had to use the standard iron crankshaft and standard main bearings, though at least the connecting rods were steel.

Design centred around the need to use the standard block, the crankcase and as many other details as possible – and it was always clear that space inside the Scorpio's engine bay was at a premium. Both the overall length and height of the FB engine would be constricted by the existing Scorpio sheet metal, and there was never any question of that being changed to allow more volume. The new engine was

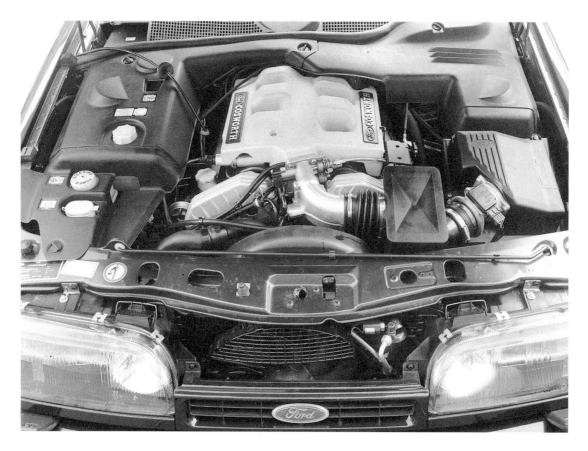

Although Ford's planners did not think that the word 'Cosworth' should appear on the exterior badging of the Scorpio 24V, when the bonnet was raised they were happy that the origins of the engine should be apparent.

somewhat taller than the pushrod original, and the only way to install the original primary 'light-off' catalytic converters was to bolt them directly to the exhaust manifolds, one on each side of the engine, with larger, flat converters mounted under the floor towards the back of the platform.

Other technical details included the use of Ford's modern EEC IV engine management system and, as with the YB engine, hydraulic tappets were a 'given'. In fairness, much of the original Hart Engineering detail had to be discarded or modified in idealizing the engine for use in a smooth, high-priced road car. The camshaft drive was by chain (unlike the YB, which used a cogged belt), but Cosworth also thought that chains would last much longer than cogged belts as they were currently developed. As Dave Lee recalls:

> Even so, space behind the radiator was so limited that we couldn't use separate duplex chains to each cylinder head – so the first engines had one very long chain.

There was never much trouble in reaching the 200bhp target figure. Although the original road car was officially rated at 195bhp, that was a typical, ultra-cautious, Cosworth figure and the team spent much time on exhaust emissions and NVH (Noise-Vibration-Harshness) reduction. Ford's engineers in Cologne apparently wanted to do all such work themselves and were very demanding customers, but

Scorpio 24V (1991–98)
[Revisions from October 1994, where applicable, in brackets]

Layout
Unit construction steel body/chassis structure. Four-door notchback saloon, five-door hatchback, or five-door estate: front engine/rear-wheel drive.

Engine
Type	Ford-Cosworth FB Series
Block material	Cast iron
Head material	Cast aluminium
Cylinders	6 in 60-degree vee
Cooling	Water
Bore and stroke	93 × 72mm
Capacity	2935cc
Main bearings	4
Valves	4 per cylinder in each head, operated by twin overhead camshafts, via inverted bucket-type tappets, with the camshafts driven by chain from the crankshaft
Compression ratio	9.7:1
Fuel supply	Ford EEC IV fuel injection and engine management system [Ford EEC V]
Max. power	195bhp @ 5,750rpm [204bhp @ 6,000rpm]
Max. torque	203lb ft @ 4,500rpm [207lb ft @ 4,200rpm]

Transmission
Four-speed automatic transmission

Overall gearbox ratios
Top	2.73:1
3rd	3.64:1
2nd	5.365:1
1st	9.00:1
Reverse	7.68:1
Final drive ratio	3.64:1

25.5mph (41.03km/h)/1,000rpm in top gear

Suspension and steering
Front	Independent, by coil springs, MacPherson struts, telescopic dampers, track control arms, and anti-roll bar
Rear	Independent, by coil springs, semi-trailing arms, anti-roll bar and telescopic dampers
Steering	Rack-and-pinion (with power assistance)
Tyres	205/50ZR-16in radial-ply [205/65R15in, 205/50VR16in or 225/45VR17in]
Wheels	Cast alloy disc, bolt-on fixing.
Rim width	6.5in

Brakes
Type	Disc brakes at front, discs at rear, hydraulically operated, with hydraulic ABS anti-lock control
Size	10.9in front discs, 10.7in rear discs

Dimensions (in/mm)
Track	
Front	58.0/1,477
Rear	59.0/1,500
Wheelbase	109.0/2,761
Overall length	(Hatchback) 184.0/4,670
	(Saloon/estate) 186.8/4,745 [190.0in/4825]
Overall width	70.0/1,766
Overall height	57.0/1,450
Unladen weight	3,282lb/1,490kg

UK retail price
(at launch in 1991)	£27,383
(at relaunch/face-lift in late 1994)	£23,230

eventually came to respect what had been achieved at Northampton.

One of the first meaningful 'discussions' with Ford (for 'discussion' read 'argument', of which there were plenty in this programme) concerned where, and why, should the name Cosworth appear on the Scorpio. In the end it was concluded that, though it was inappropriate to put a Cosworth badge on the outside of the car, it was fitting that the engine itself should carry logos reminding the customer where the new engine came from.

Right from the start, too, Ford made it clear that their production facility in Cologne was quite incapable of building between 7,000 and 10,000 such specialized engines in a year, and

Three body styles of Scorpio 24V would eventually be available, two of them being the four-door notchback saloon (foreground) and the five-door hatchback; an estate car type was also on offer.

that Cosworth would have to manufacture the FB engines. For that reason, Cosworth's second brand-new plant in Wellingborough (logically known as 'Wellingborough Two') was built to house the machine tools, assembly line and test-bed facilities needed. Cosworth made provision for building only 2.9-litre engines, failing to take into account the enlarged capacity units that were eventually conceived.

Ford would supply the standard cylinder block, ready machined, the standard crankshaft and connecting rods, while Cosworth would cast and machine the heads and camshafts, buy

in pistons and many other details, but look after total assembly and sign-off:

> We had difficulty in out-sourcing the plenum chamber, because it was a complex casting … in the end we dashed around Europe, and ended up at a supplier in Austria.

Ford started running prototype cars (actually Merkur-badged machines) before the definitive FB was ready. One car, briefly, was fitted with the Brian Hart engine, while others had pushrod engines with twin-turbocharging conversions by Turbo Technics:

> But after the second one burnt out, Ford decided that wasn't a very good idea.

Another early car had a 4-cylinder tur-

176

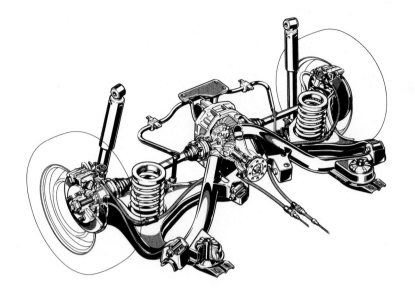

The Scorpio 24V featured semi-trailing link independent rear suspension of the same generic type as the Sierra RS Cosworth that preceded it.

bocharged YB engine installed: this couldn't give the same feel, or refinement, or correct torque curve, but gave similar straight line performance.

Scorpio 24V on Sale

Although Ford's initial request was that Cosworth should build up to 9,000 units a year, this figure was not quite reached (although the equivalent monthly rate – upwards of 700 engines – was met on several occasions), since sales settled at around 5,000–6,000 units a years. There are still people at Cosworth who comment, wistfully, that if only Ford-USA had decided to fit the 4-litre version (coded FBD) to the Explorer SUV vehicle, Cosworth could have built an even larger factory.

Originally previewed in December 1990,

Squashy, well-equipped and comprehensive – the facia/driving position of the Scorpio 24V, as launched in 1991.

The original hatchback version of the Scorpio 24V of 1991 has wider-rimmed cast alloy wheels, but otherwise almost hides the fact that there is a high-performance twin-cam V6 engine up front.

the new Scorpio was labelled simply '24V', and was marketed either as a four-door (notch-back) saloon or a five-door hatchback, both of these types being built on the same platform. Ford made it clear that they foresaw the new Scorpio as a businessman's 'express', not a sporty car, although the specification was very complete.

Although four-speed automatic transmission was standard (manual transmission was not, and never would be, available), a Sierra Cosworth-type viscous coupling limited-slip differential was standard equipment. The all-independent suspension had been especially

retuned, with front damper settings uprated by 15 per cent: at the rear there was an anti-roll bar as standard, 23 per cent stiffer coil springs, and dampers that had been firmed up by no less than 75 per cent. Alloy wheels of 16in diameter had wider (6.5in) rims, and 205/50ZR16 Pirelli P700z tyres, while the four disc-brake installation was lifted straight from the Sierra Cosworth.

At the time, *Autocar*'s description was head-lined 'Scorpio gets the grunt it needs', which was no overstatement, as by this time there was a 3.5-litre-engined BMW 535i with 211bhp, a Mercedes-Benz 300E-24 with 220bhp, and an Opel Senator 3.0i-24V with 204bhp. Bill Camplisson's forecasts about the opposition, made in 1987, had come true in no uncertain manner.

Right from the start Ford made clear their intentions about the 24V, when Ford-UK's

Above *Four-door notchback saloon versions of the Scorpio 24V had the same performance and accommodation as the hatchback type – but some customers wanted a separate, lockable boot compartment.*

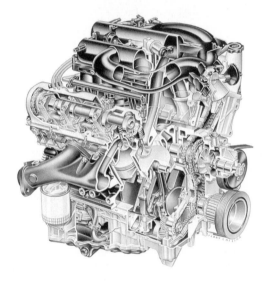

Left *Although Ford has never advertised the fact, Cosworth was originally involved in the layout of a single-overhead camshaft engine update of the Cologne V6. Only tenuously related to the Scorpio 24V (Mike Hall's office finalized both engines, the single cam being known as the JB, in the same time period), it was later abandoned in favour of this German-inspired unit. Enlarged to 4.0 litres, and with two separate camshaft chain drives – one at the front, one at the rear end of the cylinder block – it evolved with the aid of the German tuning shop Schrick, and with the engineering consultants Ricardo. For this reason it is sometimes cynically known as the 'Schricardo' V6. It became an important engine in cars like the Ford-USA Explorer, and the third-generation Land Rover Discovery.*

managing director, Derek Barron, commented that this car was:

> rather different from any of our previous Cosworth programmes.

In any case, this was a car that came loaded up with air conditioning, automatic transmission, electrically adjustable front and rear seats, electric windows, mirrors and sun-roof actuation, remote door locking, cruise control and a trip computer, plus a CD player, and a choice of cloth or leather upholstery (cloth was £511 cheaper).

'Might-have-been' projects

Look carefully at the definitive list of Cosworth-badged Ford road car engine projects on page 188, and you will see several FB-based engines that never made it into road cars on sale. Secret for years, these have now come into the public domain.

FBB: From 1985 to 1991 there was a four-wheel-drive version of the conventional pushrod-engined Granada/Scorpio range, this sharing its FF-derived transmission installation with the Sierra XR4 × 4 of the period, although that car was only sold with a manual gearbox.

The FF system not only included a transfer gearbox amidships, and a front propeller shaft that threaded its way forward alongside the engine sump, but had its front differential bolted to the right side of a cast alloy engine sump, with a drive shaft threading its way through that sump to the left-side front wheel.

In the late 1980s, when Cosworth was finalizing the 195bhp FB twin-cam V6 engine, it was asked to consider a second version for a proposed Scorpio 24V 4 _ 4, which would have included a beefed-up version of that transmission bolted to a special sump under the V6 engine. Although the majority of this engine, coded FBB, was identical to the FBA, there were sufficient differences below the line of the crankshaft to justify a new project code.

One or two 24V 4 × 4 prototypes were built and successfully tested, but these had manual gearboxes, whereas the calibration and the engine detailing had been completed for automatic transmission.

In the meantime Ford's marketing policy changed. Four-wheel-drive Sierras apparently sold well, but four-wheel-drive Granada/Scorpios did not, one reason being that they were never available with automatic transmission. Because of this disappointment, Ford therefore abandoned the Scorpio 4 × 4 models from 1991: since this was also when Scorpio 24V sales began, no FBB/4 × 4 version ever went on to the market.

FBC 3.4-litre: Early in the 1990s Ford-USA decided to give the ageing Cologne V6 engine a new, long-term lease of life. Not only were ways found of increasing the engine capacity (first to 3.4 litre, then to 4.0 litres), but Cosworth was also proposing for that V6 power unit the layout of a new single-overhead-camshaft/2-valves per cylinder/aluminium cylinder head engine, with twin cogged-belt camshaft drives. A handful of such engines, coded JB, were produced.

What Cosworth did not know was that Ford-Germany themselves, along with Dr Schrick's German business, and Ricardo, also evolved their own variety of single-cam layout: the result was that series production of that unit, comprehensively redesigned for mass production, was taken up by Ford-Germany and built in Cologne. By 2005 this SOHC engine, which Cosworth once colloquially nicknamed the 'Schricardo' V6 (work it out for yourselves!), was in use in the latest Ford Mustang, the Ford Explorer SUV and (for USA-market types) the latest Land Rover Discovery.

The 2.9-litre engine had a bore of 93mm and a stroke of 72mm. Due to the use of a much-modified cylinder block with deeper banks, the definitive 4.0-litre had a bore of 100mm and a stroke of 84.3mm. There was also an interim 3.4-litre size, never publicized, which presumably combined the larger 100mm bore with the original 72mm stroke, or the 93mm cylinder bore with the 4-litre's longer stroke. Both would have given an approximate 3.4-litre capacity!

At Ford's request, Cosworth developed another version of the Scorpio 24V engine, coded FBC 3.4-litre, which combined the entire top end of the FBA/FBC 2.9-litre engines – cylinder heads, modified manifolding and Ford engine management system – with the interim 3.4-litre cylinder block and bore.

FBD: Moving on one stage further from the FBC 3.4-litre, the FBD was a full 4.0-litre version of the FBA, which, of course, had started out as a 2.9-litre engine. As far as is known, this was never intended for fitment to a European Ford (indeed, no European Ford ever had 3.4-litre or 4.0-litre V6s of any type), but was briefly considered for high-performance Ford-USA models. Although about half a dozen such prototype engines were built, there were engine bay packaging problems (even in the Explorer, which was and is a sizeable machine!) so nothing came of this project.

FBF: This was an uprated version of the FBD, in the same way that the 2.9-litre FBC was an uprated version of the FBA. Once again, it was a full 4.0-litre engine, with twin overhead camshafts, but with updated electronics and engine management systems. As Dave Lee told me, with a grin:

This was installed in a Scorpio, but it was basically quite unviable, as the automatic transmission wouldn't take it, so that car then got a manual transmission, but it was *soooo* fast ... We also put one of those in a Ford Bronco, too.

continued from page 176

FBG: Although Ford-USA could never quite bring itself to fit full-house twin-overhead-camshaft Cosworth V6 engines to any of its production cars, it dabbled with the idea on several occasions. This FBG derivative, therefore, was a carefully redeveloped version of the FBF (itself a derivative of the FBD), specifically intended for fitment to the Explorer SUV.

Originally launched in 1990 and similar in overall size to, say, the Land Rover Discovery of the period, the Explorer was a five-door SUV (Sport Utility Vehicle) that went on to sell in enormous numbers. In the mid-1990s it was powered only by the pushrod overhead-valve version of the Ford-Cologne-V6 4.0-litre engine, so the FBG (derived from that basic layout) would clearly have fitted comfortably under the bonnet.

Prototypes were built, and tested, but cost considerations eventually saw the project killed off.

Priced at no less than £27,383, the 24V was much the most expensive of all the Granada/Scorpio types, and cost within a few pounds of the contemporary Sierra Cosworth 4 × 4, but there were plenty of customers who seemed happy to buy one as a fast, refined and completely effortless machine.

In its independent test remarks, *Autocar* noted:

> Cosworth had the unenviable task of making a silk purse out of a sow's ear, but it succeeded beyond most critics' expectations … The Cosworth treatment is aimed as much at improving refinement and reducing emissions as at achieving higher power and torque.
>
> So, Cosworth has worked its magic again. The Scorpio 24V engine makes the 12-valve V6 appear hopelessly under-powered … but what comes as a shock is the manner in which Cosworth has succeeded in smoothing off all the rough edges. Gone is the thrummy vibration at high revs. No longer is there a lumpy tickover. At idle, the engine note is strictly background material, and high revs don't set your teeth on edge.

Not that Ford's own upgrading efforts were ignored:

> With its new-found poise and reduced body roll, the Scorpio is a far more pleasing car to drive briskly and much better balanced than before, particularly through medium-speed corners …
>
> There's no doubt that the Cosworth treatment has transformed the Ford V6 almost beyond recognition. From being the worst feature of the car in 12-valve form, the 24-valve engine is now its best feature. Not only does it deliver at the test track and in general road performance, but the Cosworth V6 makes huge strides in terms of refinement and noise suppression. With it come chassis improvements that lift the Scorpio clear of mediocrity.

And, make no mistake, this was a fast car. Not as fast as the Sierra Cosworth 4 × 4, of course, and not as grippy as Ford's latest four-wheel-drive cars either. But no-one was likely to complain about a top speed of 136mph (219 km/h), 0–60mph acceleration in 8.5 seconds, or even a day-in-day-out fuel economy figure of about 23mpg (12.3ltr/100km). This was a car that the author used for daily transport, covering about 20,000 miles in 1992. Coming to the Scorpio 24V from a Sierra Cosworth 4 × 4, initially I was prepared to be disappointed, but that never happened. I can't remember completing such stressfree 400-mile (640km) driving days in any other Ford. If I hadn't been salivating at the idea of running an Escort RS Cosworth to replace it, when the time came for it to go, I might have produced some impressive temper tantrums.

Here was a car, at the top of Ford's price bracket, that helped provide the Granada/Scorpio range with a real 'halo effect', and it sold steadily for the next three years. A third derivative of the chassis, the five-door estate car, was added in the autumn of 1993. Unhappily, because this car was not seen

Above *Look very carefully and you will see a tiny '24V' badge on the bottom left of the hatchback lid. Apart from the wider-rim wheels this is the only exterior sign of extra power in the 1991 Scorpio's design.*

Below *Would you rather have had a Scorpio 24V in saloon (here) or hatchback guise? Both were available from 1991 to 1994.*

From late 1994 the Scorpio range received a controversial restyle, complete with this smoothed-out nose. The 24V got a power boost to 210bhp, though.

as an ultra-sporting machine, unlike the Sierra and Escort RS Cosworth models, its used-car values plummeted during the 1990s until ten-year-old models could eventually be picked up for what almost seemed like petty cash.

The face-lifted model that followed in 1994 added further controversy to its reputation.

Mid-life Face-lift

I must be brutal about this. When the Scorpio range received a so-called face-lift in September 1994 (deliveries actually began in early 1995), it was not well received in the media. Work on the chassis, the interior and the engine of the 24V model was carefully and competently carried out – but it was the overall visual style that caused so much controversy.

Working to a brief that the Granada name was to be ditched, the hatchback version was to be dropped completely, and that they should only work on four-door notchback saloon and five-door estate car types, the stylists were told

that they must leave the platform, cabin and basic structure alone, although they could change the front and rear ends.

The result was that for 1995 the Scorpio became more rounded, with strangely contoured headlamps (Ford called them poly-ellipsoid!) and a more curvaceous tail than before. Front and rear wings, bumpers, bonnet, boot-lid and rear quarter windows were all new and differently shaped. Frankly, many thought this was not a success, even though the interior inherited a Mondeo-like facia/instrument display and the seats were undoubtedly plushier than before. Although the chassis was much improved, the car's popularity plummeted because it looked so, well, er … strange.

Technically, in fact, there had been a carve up, for there was a new line-up of petrol engines, the MacPherson strut front suspen-

From late 1994 to 1998 the final style of Scorpio 24V had this much rounded-out body style. Great chassis, sparkling performance – but not many people liked the looks.

sion was much changed, the rear suspension mountings and sub-frame had been made a lot more rigid, and the body structure itself had been beefed up in several areas to make the car run rather more quietly than before.

To some of us there seemed to be confusion over the wheel and tyre specification, reflecting the fact that Scorpios were being sold all over Europe where – say – a British customer's preferences might differ from those of a German, or of an Italian, or of a Frenchman, for example.

When the revised car was launched, the engineers said that in the interests of refinement the 24V model would henceforth run on 205/65-15in tyres (smaller than before), and that was indeed the specification of UK-market road test cars, but before long the European-wide specification listed 225/50-16in or even 225/45-17in sizes as alternatives: take your pick!

In this application, Cosworth's FB engine progressed from FBA/195bhp to an even more healthy FBC/204bhp (Cosworth always listed it, internally, as 210bhp, by the way). These improvements were achieved by a combination of a different throttle body, variable-length intake passages, new camshaft profiles and valve springs, and two separate chain drives to the twin overhead camshaft heads, along with Ford's latest EEC V engine management module, which had a much enhanced memory over the outgoing EEC IV.

Mechnically, the important update was to the camshaft chain drive. On the original FBA one enormously long chain had been used to run around all four camshafts and the central jack shaft. Although the average customer might never have noticed (I certainly did not, on my own car), some Ford engineers complained about a whine from the chain-drive area at about 1,200 rpm in neutral.

Cosworth therefore redesigned the drive, in detail, so that henceforth there were to be two separate chain drives (both still very long – though not as long as before!), plus two chain

These two shots, taken by Cosworth themselves while developing the FBC (right) from the original FBA, show how the entire chain drive/tensioners/front cover detail was changed to eliminate a Ford complaint about a whine. It was only later that Ford discovered that the noise actually came from their own automatic transmission!

tensioners instead of one, and some new machining detail. Incidentally, only later did Ford discover that the errant whine had been pinned down to the transmission torque converter instead!

Once again, this was a Cosworth-engined model meant to deliver high performance in great comfort, rather than with great excitement, and it certainly did all of that. This time round, *Autocar's* testers recorded a top speed of 138mph (222km/h), not quite into the Sierra Cosworth 4 × 4 league, but all done in great comfort, if in questionable style. The Scorpio 24V, after all, came with traction control, automatic transmission, ABS brakes, air conditioning and cruise control. And at £23,740 (or £26,275 for the Ultima variety) it was a whole lot cheaper – nearly £5,000, actually – than the original 24V of 1991.

It was no wonder, therefore, that their test summary began with the words:

> If you can live with the looks, the Scorpio will please Granada drivers and convert owners of rival models too.

Ford, in fact, soldiered on with these cars for four more years. The last of the pushrod-engined 2.9-litre V6 Scorpios was built in 1996, but the nicely specified 24V carried on until the summer of 1998. In that time, the company had rung the changes with different trim packs and titles: Executive, Ghia, Ghia X

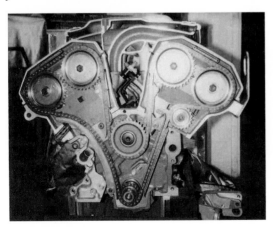 

Engine applications

Although only two basic Cosworth engine designs – YB and FB – powered all the cars surveyed in this book, Cosworth produced or proposed an astonishing number of derivatives.

With grateful thanks to Cosworth Technology for permission to use information from their archive, here is the official list of every type.

Year Cosworth Title   **Description**

YB (4-cyl/16-valve) family

Year	Cosworth Title	Description
1984	YAA	Prototype 16-valve normally aspirated conversion of Ford T88 (Pinto) engine, 2-litre
	YAB	Prototype turbocharged version of YAA
	YBA	Updated version of YAB, with approx. 180bhp
1985	YBB	Ford Sierra RS Cosworth road car engine, 204bhp
	YBC	Race version of YBB, for kits and further development
1986	YBD	Ford Sierra RS500 Cosworth road car engine, 224bhp
1987	YBE1A	Version of YBB, for use in Panther Solo road car
	YBF	Race version of YBD, for kits, and further development
1989	YBE2A	Version of YBD, for use in Panther Solo
	YBG	'Green' version of YBB, meeting 83US emissions, 220bhp
	YBG (AIR)	Modified YBG, with air-conditioning pumps/installation
	YBJ	'Green' version of YBB, meeting 15.04 emissions, 220bhp
	YBJ (AIR)	Modified YBJ, with air-conditioning pumps/installation
	YBM	Race version of YBG/YBJ, for kits, and further development
1990	YBP	Evolution of YBG/YBJ, for use in Escort RS Cosworth, with EEC IV engine management

	YBR	Ford rally engine, for use in Sierra Cosworth 4 × 4
	YBS	Ford rally engine, Group A rally kit, parallel to YBR
	YBT	Rally version of YBG/YBP, for use in Escort RS Cosworth
	YBT (AIR)	Modified YBP/YBT, with air-conditioning pumps/installation
	YAC	Naturally aspirated derivative of (1989) YBG, for kit cars, with carburettors instead of fuel injection
1992	YBG Group N	Race version of YBG
	YBV	2.3-litre methanol-burning version of YBM, by Cosinc (USA)
1994	YBT Group N	Green race version of YBT

FB (V6/24-valve) family

1990	FBA	24-valve/DOHC engine, based on 2.9-litre Ford 'Cologne' V6 engine, for use in Ford Scorpio, 195bhp
	FBB	4 × 4 version (different sump, front axle attached, etc) of FBA, also for use in Ford Scorpio.
	FBC 2.9-litre	Modified road car version of FBA, 210bhp. In production from late 1994
	FBC 3.4-litre	Modified road car version of FBA, but based on 4-litre cylinder block
	FBD	4-litre road car version of FBA
1991	FBE	Racing version of 2.9-litre FBA, with 300bhp
1993	FBF	Road car version of FBC, with full 4.0-litre capacity
	FBG	FBF-based 4-litre engine, for use in Ford-USA Explorer

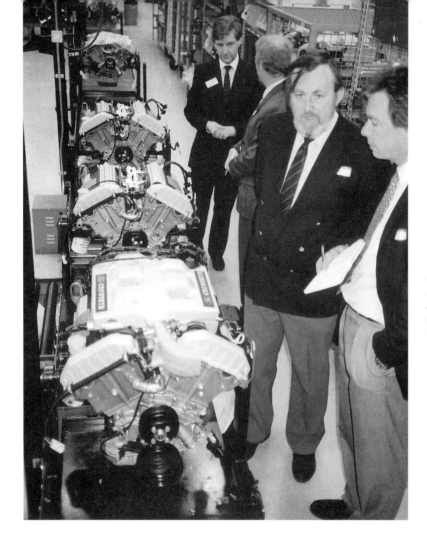

Soon after the Scorpio 24V model was announced, Cosworth arranged for the press to have a look at engines being assembled at Wellingborough.

and Ultima saloons and estate cars, eight derivatives in all.

From late 1997 there was one further visual change, intended to defuse comment about the styling, when careful redecoration of the car's nose saw some of the very Transatlantic-type decoration (the 'jewellery', as some cynical insiders used to call it) abandoned, the front grille and headlamp surrounds slimmed down, and the bumpers reprofiled.

By this time the Scorpio range was almost a forgotten car, so it really came as no surprise when Ford announced in March 1998 that it was to fade away quietly in mid-summer. Clearly this would leave a void in Cologne, and also at Cosworth's factory in Wellingborough, but the end came with a whimper and no further ceremony. As a badge, or Ford-only insignia, the 'Cosworth' name was then finally laid to rest.

In the years that followed the more excitable motoring magazines talked frequently about the rumoured development of new Fiesta-Cosworths and Focus-Cosworths, but none of these cars ever made it beyond the 'look-see' or prototype stage. Once Ford had absorbed the racing side of Cosworth in the autumn of 1998 – logically, it was soon titled Cosworth Racing – work was certainly carried out on a variety of Ford-based projects, but Ford's interest eventually cooled.

The real end, it seems, came in 2004, when Ford sold off Cosworth Racing to Kevin Kalkhoven and Gerald Forsythe, two USA-based entrepreneurs, who apparently did not carry forward any road car links with Ford. After more than forty years, therefore, the marriage was finally over.

Index